To: Dave Blue

Save Our System

Remember
- Knowledge is our weapon
- Ballots are our bullets

Regards,

Lynn Cleland

L. Lynn Cleland, PhD

SAVE OUR SYSTEM

Why and How "We The People"

Must Reclaim Our Liberties Now

Two Harbors Press

Two Harbors Press
212 3rd Avenue North, Suite 290
Minneapolis, MN 55401
612.455.2293
www.TwoHarborsPress.com

ISBN-13: 978-1-936401-38-3
LCCN: 2011921138

Distributed by Itasca Books

Book Design by Nate Meyers
Cover Photo © 2010. All rights reserved - used with permission.

Printed in the United States of America

Contents

Introduction

American history shows us that there has always been a struggle among citizens regarding the best direction for our nation. This struggle, however, has become more intense in recent decades, resulting in divergent, if not diametrically opposite, approaches to addressing our most pressing issues. It is my belief, as an informed and concerned citizen, and a systems analyst and researcher, that it is time we reclaim control of our country. While the career politicians continue to serve their own interests, our governmental systems and policies perpetually fail. This detrimental chain of events will not stop unless we American citizens act decisively as a united political body. By exploring career politicians' psychological and financial tactical tricks, along with our current deficient and failing systems, we will be best equipped to act and vote intelligently.

Many of us are increasingly frustrated with our political system's career politicians and political parties whose bickering and divisiveness impede their ability to address our problems. Over the past few decades our politicians have redesigned our political system to benefit career politicians and their political parties. Maintaining their careers and gaining power has been the focus of this redesign. Career politicians have gradually stopped civil debates and begun waging wars between the political parties - wars to defend the interests of their party, rather than their constituents.

Politicians use numerous tactical tricks to scare, mislead, and seduce citizens into becoming recruits and foot solders in these wars. Politicians use these same tricks to convince us to re-elect them over and over again. Unveiling and understanding these tricks can protect citizens from being inadvertently drawn into the wars between the political parties. In this book we'll explore fifteen of these most commonly used tricks.

Many systems important to our nation's future (e.g., social, financial, political, educational, etc.) do not serve us well. Most of these failing systems have evolved slowly, making their negative effects less evident. Too often the governmental system owners and overseers have adopted short-term and oftentimes selfish strategies. We must take a longer-term view, focusing on the likely future global theater in which the United States will have fewer leading roles. We need to improve our failing and deficient systems, and establish a new set of priorities.

System problems can best - and frequently only - be solved by eliminating each problem's causes. Understanding key problem sets, their causes, how they evolve, and their solutions are critical steps we must take for each of us to make informed decisions. In this book we will analyze and provide solutions for six key government systems that are near catastrophic failure (including our political system), as well as five systems that have significant deficiencies.

Our choices for the future are limited. We can proceed on the destructive path we are on now, or we can initiate our own war to reclaim our liberties. Certainly we wouldn't hesitate a moment to declare war on a foreign country if they attempted to impose a centralized government of elitist leaders (most of whom spend a lifetime in office), and to move us towards becoming a socialist nation while taking away tens of trillions of dollars from our present citizens and unborn future generations. This is where we are today. It is time we fight to win back our liberties before it is too late. Since some of our failing systems have reach "tipping points" - meaning they could soon fail catastrophically - time is of the essence.

As in wars of our country's past, we must be prepared to make the sacrifices necessary to fulfill our mission. So, what is *our* war's mission, exactly? We need to restore balance by returning our country to the underlying principles on which our nation was founded, most specifically, the major principle stated by our Founding Fathers: a proper balance of power.

There are several of these balances that must be maintained:

✪ Balance of powers between the federal government, state government, local entities, and individuals
✪ Balance between personal self-interest and helping others
✪ Balance between individual freedoms and the greater good of the nation
✪ Balance between what we might want and what we can afford

We must decide what we are entitled to by our governmental systems - what we all innately deserve as U.S. citizens - and what some of us have access to without explicitly earning it. Obviously those who cannot work and develop their skills should obtain assistance from the rest of society. The rest of us are not entitled to free food, housing, jobs of our choice, TV sets, transportation, or anything else, without at least attempting to earn them. Otherwise, where does it stop, and who pays? Expecting future generations to pay the bills is not the answer. Each of us must be responsible and accountable *now* and we must do the same as a nation.

Our Founding Founders understood the need for these balances and developed principles and *The Constitution* to assure such essential balances would remain. We became a great nation and international power based upon these principles of balance. Deviating from them, as we are seeing now, results in a loss of our present world status, a reduction of the spirit, drive, and will of our citizens, and, ultimately, a significant decline in our standard of living. If these balances are not maintained we can easily damage capitalism and become an insignificant player in the world of the future.

Only if we educate ourselves and act now can we reverse the adverse impact of many of the problems our career politicians, often with our unwitting support, have created. Fortunately, our war does not require the deadly weapons used in most wars. Greater knowledge of how our politicians and governmental systems work is enough for us to *fight and win*. Politicians' financial and psychological tricks to scare, mislead, and seduce us, the general public, are some of our politicians' major weapons. Our weapons are well-informed citizens; our bullets are ballots.

*****

My motivation for studying and writing about our political problems, their causes, and possible solutions, stems from sixty-plus years of observing a changing nation. As I have watched our nation move away from its roots over the past few decades, I have begun asking myself questions: Is the present direction good for our nation in the long term? What has happened to cause the direction change? What are likely future outcomes if our nation continues down this path? Can the direction be changed? If so, how should it be changed? These and many more questions led me - a researcher and conceptual thinker - to analyze some key national problems. As a systems engineer and problem solver, I sought solutions. This book presents my thoughts on the changing direction of our nation, the causes for these changes, and what we citizens can to do to preserve our great nation. Like all Americans I care about our nation but I am particularly concerned about what we are leaving for our future generations to inherit.

Many of the examples and quotes I use to aid in understanding the current national situation refers to the party in power: the Democrats and President Obama. This should not be construed to mean that they are worse than the Republicans. Other examples from a more distant past could easily be substituted with names from the Republican Party. Similar, but perhaps different, examples would have been used if Republicans were currently in power, because they were not fiscally responsible, either. My goal is not to implicate any political party or specific politicians. The underlying concepts apply to all career politicians and political parties. I am equally critical of several professional groups. I will welcome any adverse responses to the conclusions I present as positive since it is my hope that this book inspires dialogue among citizens.

As you read this book you may wonder who I am professionally and politically. Professionally, I have managed many people with all kinds of backgrounds and experiences in the physical sciences. This list includes paleontologists, environmentalists, virtually every type of professional engineer, as well as most scientists (physicists, chemists, computer scientists, geologists, physicians, etc.). From an operations management perspective, I have managed construction projects, maintenance and related crafts workers, policemen, firemen, medical personnel, and groups of strategic and tactical planners. Not counting contractors, I simultaneously managed over 1,600 people with annual budgets over $185 million (in 1997 dollars). I have interacted with hundreds of federal, state, and local agencies and entities, as well as the general public. I have had to manage many crises. Undoubtedly, my professional experiences have provided an analytical approach and lens employed in this book.

Politically, I was born to Democratic parents. I have four siblings and half are Democrats and half are Republicans. Affiliation with a party was required to vote in primary elections when I came to California. Then, as now, I believed a balance between the two parties is important, so I chose to register with the minority Republican Party. I voted as an Independent for many years. During the last two decades, as I have become increasingly concerned about the direction in which our nation is headed, I have become a *fiscal* conservative. "Conservatism" is diametrically opposite to what is often, in history, called "progressivism." I am not a hard-core or radical right-wing ideologue. I also agree with some tenants of progressivism.

Progressivism is a "feel good" system that might be great in an ideal world under the control of one government. It supports some of "liberalism's" issues (e.g., labor unions, progressive taxation to help the poor, and universal health care), but it tends to be skeptical of big government and advocates government reforms. I, too, support some labor unions for private sector employees, but *not* for public sector employees. I believe in progressive taxes as long as they are fair and are balanced against significant adverse impacts on our capitalistic system. I am skeptical of big government and a proponent for government reform.

The major problem with progressivism and liberalism is that our nation does not rule the world and does not have unbounded resources. The world has many diverse governments. We in the United States have an ever-decreasing control of - and increasing dependency on - foreign governments. We cannot afford to become a totally progressive or liberal society and hope to survive in the world of the future. If we are to survive as a nation, we must maintain a balance between what we might want and what we can afford. Unfortunately, we cannot afford what we have now, as is indicated by our high and rapidly increasing national debt and continuing annual spending deficits. Our only way out is to become more like our Founding Fathers intended, which is to return to a more balanced position. Yes, back to the future.

It is time to learn more about career politicians' tactical tricks, political party strategies, and our inadequate governmental systems they've created. Let's grab some "knowledge weapons," load our ballots, and begin firing at those career politicians that are serving themselves rather than "we the people". It's time we once again become the masters and our politicians our servants. We must act now before it is too late for our children, grandchildren, future generations, and ourselves. Our first major battles took place in 2010, but we must continue the fight to 2012, 2014, and well beyond.

It is the duty of every citizen according to his best capacities to give validity to his convictions in political affairs.[1] — **Albert Einstein**

PART I: SETTING THE BATTLEFIELD STAGE

Before we start defining the tactics and issues we are up against, let's review two sets of information and two processes that will set the foundation for analyzing our current systems' effectiveness, and developing our war's strategy.

Our capitalistic economic system greatly impacts our future chances of creating jobs, accumulating wealth, and ensuring a favorable future for our nation. Our deviations from capitalism, and from the traits and principles of our Founding Fathers are at the heart of our problems. We'll briefly explore information for both of these topics.

Congress commonly uses a process for shaping policies that allows politicians to exploit their tactical tricks to scare, mislead, and seduce us. This process focuses on problem symptoms and political solutions. A better process is to assess problem causes then establish solutions by fixing the causes. The first symptom-based process has lead our nation to its present state and the second cause-based process is the one used to derive the solutions presented throughout this book.

Chapter 1: Economic Systems Overview

Chapter 2: Traits and Principles of Our Founding Fathers

Chapter 3: Problem Solving Processes

Chapter 1:
Economic Systems Overview

The country's economic system greatly affects its people. Often the system is dominated by the socio-economic philosophy and policies of the county's government. In the U.S., the economic system has a dominant impact on our present and future chances to create jobs, accumulate wealth, and ensure a favorable future for our nation.

Capitalistic Economics

There is a general agreement that capitalism encourages economic growth, typically measured in a country's Gross Domestic Product (GDP). Economic growth refers only to the quantity of goods and services produced - not how they are produced. When an economy grows faster than its population, wealth (money, resources, or other valuable possessions) is created. The possibility of increasing one's own wealth is why our nation is often considered to be "the land of opportunity" by immigrants. Thus, capitalism is the primary mechanism that attracts people from around the world to the United States. If those immigrants are reasonably intelligent and work hard they can increase their wealth. This is not the case in true socialist or communist societies due to their continuous wealth redistribution.

Two Key Capitalistic Facts

First, it is important to recognize that jobs are a result of economic and wealth growth. It takes wealth to pay someone who is hired, and additional wealth to buy the material the person will use. Most economists put emphasis on the market mechanism, i.e., the degree of government control over markets, and property rights. Some politicians and a few economists emphasize private property, power relations, wage labor, and class.

Second, it is equally important to recognize that government spending creates no wealth. Ignoring this plain fact, politicians claim to be able to do all sorts of miraculous things that are simply impossible. Without creating wealth, governments can only create jobs by taking wealth from others, whether by taxation, the sale of bonds, or imposed mandates that result in job or efficiency losses in the private sector. However it is done, transferring wealth is not creating wealth. When a government uses transferred wealth to hire people, it is essentially transferring jobs from the private sector to the public sector, not adding to the net number of jobs in the economy.

History shows job and wealth increases are best achieved through capitalism. For example, the Roosevelt Administration created huge numbers of government-sponsored jobs during the 1930s, but unemployment remained in double digits throughout his first two terms. Government spending may create jobs temporarily, but these jobs are generally not optimum or self-sustaining. If the government pays your neighbor $100 to dig and fill a hole and pays you to do the same, the economy has created two jobs and the GDP has been raised by $200. However the benefits of digging the holes are not of much utility to anyone. People earn money by providing things other people want or need and spend their money buying things they want or need, but the same cannot always be said of the government. Government stimulus packages can increase economic wellbeing providing that a rigorous cost-benefit analysis of each government project is conducted. These analyses are hard to do quickly, and the economic downturn may be over before the stimulus funding arrives.

Federal stimulus spending for "shovel ready" infrastructure projects is a good example of government job creation that is not quick enough to have much immediate effect on unemployment. "Shovel ready" sounds good to a layperson since the name implies the projects are ready to immediately start hiring workers and most laypersons recognize the need for infrastructure improvement. In truth there is always a long delay until actual construction work begins. There are environmental reports, development of plans and prioritizations, materials pricing and availability, bid packages, the bid processes, engineering tests, federal, state, and local approvals, and many other items all of which take time as many of these items are done sequentially. Large projects take longer than small ones, but even small ones may take many months before a large labor contingent starts to work. So why did the Obama Administration pursue funding for tens of billions of dollars for these projects? Certainly they knew of the delays. One theory is that "shovel ready" sounds good and the bulk of the jobs created will still exist in 2012 for the next big election.[1]

Christina D. Romer, President Obama's first Chairwoman of the Council of Economic Advisers, and her husband, David, show the benefits of capitalism in a recent publication. The publication shows a tax of one percent of the GDP *reduces* output [GDP] over the next three years by about three percent. They also show that tax increases have a large negative impact on investments (and, therefore, jobs).[2] In another recent publication, Christopher J. Nekarda, a member of the Federal Reserve Board of Governors, and Valerie A. Ramey, University of California, San Diego, indicate that increases in government demand [spending] raise output [GDP] and hours, but lower real product wages and productivity.[3] These results are consistent with the neoclassical and Chicago

5

School models of government spending, but they are not consistent with the effects of government spending as indicated by the New Keynesian model many politicians prefer.

Neoclassical economics argues capitalism is made up of individuals, enterprises, markets, and government in which individuals engage in a capitalist economy as consumers, laborers, and investors. Individuals decide which jobs to prepare for, and in which markets to look for work. Investors decide how much of their income to save and invest. Investments provide the money businesses need to grow. Growth is what creates jobs and wealth. The capitalism argument is that market economies are inherently stable if left to themselves.[4] Keynesian economics argues that private sector decisions sometimes lead to inefficient outcomes and therefore advocates active policy responses by the public sector to stabilize output over the business cycle.[5] The former minimizes government control over individuals and entities, whereas the latter requires considerable government control over individuals and entities.

Given the problems of conducting cost-benefit analyses, different economic preferences, and a seeming need to give away money to solve every problem, many politicians fund and promote their "pet projects" independent of the overall economic cost benefit. What matters to career politicians is being re-elected, even if their policies needlessly prolong a recession or depression. Unfortunately, since the Great Depression, government spending and taxes have continued to increase much faster than the GDP or the population. Unless actions are initiated soon, spending, taxes, and debts will become more problematic as baby boomers retire and start collecting their promised benefits. Although these problems should give Congress pause as it considers whether to increase spending to stimulate the economy, we, as citizens, shouldn't expect such qualms to stop them. The prevailing doctrine among the nation's political elite holds that increased government spending is always the right medicine for what ails the economy.

Business Taxes and Capitalism

Despite contrary statements by some politicians, *people* pay taxes; businesses do not. An old book by Ferdinand Lundberg, *The Rich and the Super-Rich (New York: Bantam Books, 1969)*, points out that business taxes were first suggested by the super-rich owners of businesses in the 19th and early 20th centuries as a means of making the masses believe they were being spared paying taxes thanks to the high taxes paid by businesses. These super-rich people understood a fundamental requirement of capitalism.

This requirement is that the owners of privately or publicly owned businesses must make a profit from the commodities or services they provide or they cannot stay in business. The profit expectations of the owners determine if they will continue to support the business (buy stocks or reinvest in the business). Suppose business owners (investors) require an actual profit of eight percent (growth in value or dividend) to maintain their investment in the business and a (new) tax is imposed on the profits, which absorbs twenty-five percent of this profit (in other words, it reduces the overall profit to six percent). Then the business must take actions to re-establish the eight percent or the owners will invest elsewhere (such as in other businesses in the United States or in a foreign country). The business has two basic options:

Option one: Raise the prices of the commodities or services provided so that after the twenty-five percent tax is added the effective profit will still be eight percent. This requires an equivalent profit before the new tax of about ten percent. In the 19th and early 20th centuries when most commodities or services were provided by U.S. businesses to our citizens and foreign competition was minimal, this was an easy way for businesses to accommodate a new tax. The tax was simply passed down to the business's customers (mostly U.S. citizens). This worked well for the super-wealthy business owners at that time. Now, in the era of a global economy and labor force, this action

7

would give foreign competitors an advantage that might start a spiral of declining sales for U.S. businesses resulting in lower tax payments and fewer U.S. jobs.

Option two: Reduce costs or improve efficiencies by cutting labor, supplier or other costs to improve productivity. A company always has competition, so it is constantly striving to improve productivity. One way to further reduce costs is to revert to lower-cost sources of labor and materials from foreign sources. This also results in fewer U.S. jobs.

The bottom line is that Option two is the "lower business risk" option to address tax increases. What would you do if you owned the business?

Governments do not pay taxes, either. Even government employees who may pay taxes do not pay enough to cover their benefits, much less their wages. We certainly need some government employees and most are hard-working and valued, however, any governmental functions that can be eliminated or carried out by the more efficient private sector employees frees funds for expanding private sector jobs and wealth growth.

Income Taxes and Capitalism

In general, the art of government consists of taking as much money as possible from one party of the citizens to give to the other.[6] — **Voltaire**

Some level of progressive income taxes is reasonable. Here are some key questions we should be asking when it comes to progressive taxes: What amount of progressive taxation stifles economic growth? What is fair? To what extent should those who pay nothing (and, thus, have no investment,) have a say in how tax money is spent?

Every dollar not paid in taxes goes into some type of economic investment. This investment may range from buying food for a family, to buying a new house, or to making a business investment. While a family's food is more important than a business investment, each are still investments. Each creates jobs and hope for others: farmers, construction workers, and business owners and their employees. Jobs and hope will only be possible so long as enough people have enough money to invest in the private sector to create them. Too much taxation stifles growth and hope. Again, balance is the key.

The bottom line is that progressive taxes are reasonable so long as they do not tip the scale to the point where we can no longer compete in the world. I believe we, in the United States, are at a tipping point. The problem is that those who decide how progressive taxes are spent are now mostly those who do not pay them and who vote for politicians who are not responsible or accountable, either. How might this be changed? We could require income tax payments from *all* citizens - even those who receive what I refer to as free money[7] - and all citizens' taxes should rise with any rise in spending. This would improve free money accountability, since it would drive home the fact there is no free money for politicians to dole out without impacting *every* citizen.

Capitalistic Economics Summary Bullets

✪ Capitalism encourages economic growth, typically measured in a country's Gross Domestic Product (GDP).

✪ History shows job and wealth increases are best achieved through capitalism.

✪ Government spending creates no jobs or wealth since governments can only create jobs by taking wealth from others.

✪ Taxation is the primary way governments obtain money. Selling national resources is another source.

✪ Research has shown that for each dollar spent the private sector is much more efficient and effective than a government in creating jobs and wealth.

- Businesses must sustain a profit or a growth rate acceptable to their investors in order to retain their investors and remain in business.
- Only people pay taxes. Businesses pass their tax costs on to their customers in order to maintain their profit margin or growth rate.
- Some taxes are reasonable, including progressive taxes, so long as they do not interfere with a nation's ability to compete in the world.

Chapter 2:
Traits and Principles of Our Founding Fathers

Our wise Founding Fathers did an excellent job of establishing a government that was balanced and appropriately bounded. In our recent history, we have drifted away from this balance and have pushed, or exceeded, many boundaries. While some changes were appropriate to reflect the times, the basic principles need to be protected. It is good to be reminded of what our Founding Fathers had in mind. Below is a summary of our Founding Fathers' traits and the principles used to develop *The Constitution*.

Traits

Our Founding Fathers' traits (values) seem to be waning in some of our country's citizens today. Their traits included generosity, service, courage, resilience, hard work, and personal responsibility. These traits, described below, support both *The Constitution's* guiding principles and our capitalistic economic process.

Generosity has always been a reputable American trait, but generosity can be abused—especially when it leads to dependency and a lack of self-worth or, worse yet, it becomes viewed as a right or entitlement on the part of the recipient.

Service takes on many forms such as in the forms of businesses, or in those who protect us, and our leaders. The Founding Fathers believed strongly that our political leaders should serve the people and the country and not their personal self-interests.

Courage is exemplified in our *Declaration of Independence,* our soldiers, and others who protect and have died for us, including the handful of citizen passengers who fought to retake control of Flight 93. Now it seems self-preservation trumps courage for our political leaders since focusing on long-term problems and root causes might upset their big money donors and some of their electorate.

Resilience of the nation is exemplified by our demonstrated ability to recover from many past wars, and crises of all kinds.

Hard work and our capitalistic structure are the keys to greater personal and family rewards. "Free money" (in essence robbing Peter to pay Paul) is not a substitute for hard work.

Personal responsibility includes both being responsible for obeying our laws and doing what is perceived as "the right thing to do". It is easy to blame others for our own failings, or to let someone else be considered responsible. The Founding Fathers expected citizens to take personal responsibility for their actions when they were creating the original blueprint documents that would form our nation's government.

Constitutional Principles

Our Founding Fathers had broad knowledge and experience with national structures and the nature of human beings. They used this knowledge to develop an outstanding strategic document: *The U.S. Constitution*. They started with seven principles that are briefly described below:

1. Popular Sovereignty — the belief that the legitimacy of the nation is created by the will or consent of its people, who are the source of all political power. Benjamin Franklin expressed this concept when he wrote: *"In free governments the rulers are the servants and the people their superiors and sovereigns."*[1]

2. Republicanism — the leaders are appointed by means other than heredity (in the United States, this means by elections). The Founding Fathers also realized that a republican form of government would only work with common cultures and faiths, and a well-developed set of civic values. Thus, the Founding Fathers developed the ingenious concepts of items three through six, below.

3. Federalism — a system in which the power to govern is shared between national and state governments. The federal government has certain *express powers* (also called *enumerated powers*) which are powers spelled out in *The Constitution* and the "Necessary and Proper" clause gives the federal government the *implied power* to pass any law "necessary and proper" for the execution of its express powers. Powers *The Constitution* does not delegate to the federal government or forbid to the states — the *reserved powers* — are reserved to the people or the states.

4. Separation of Powers — a political doctrine under which the executive, legislative, and judicial branches of government are kept distinct to prevent abuse of power. In the United States, this form of separation of powers is associated with a system of checks and balances.

5. Checks and Balances — a concept set up in *The U.S. Constitution* whereby the various powers of any government are divided into three separate branches (executive, legislative, judicial). None of the three branches is able to be so powerful it becomes a virtual monarchy. All three must work together in relative harmony since each needs the others to perform its obligations properly.

6. Limited Government — a legal doctrine that states the government cannot intervene beyond the minimum in personal liberty and economic issues. *The Constitutional Convention* developed the system of federalism to maintain a limited national government since government is the only institution in a society that holds the legal monopoly on the use of force. This makes the government the most dangerous institution in any society— the institution that must be most closely watched and limited. *The Bill of Rights* and the first ten amendments to *The Constitution* contain the bulk of these limits. For example, they spell out the belief that the federal government is the servant of the states, not their master. This limitation of government's powers and control over the individual citizen is *the* central issue underlying our Founding Fathers' political philosophy.

7. Individual Rights — refer to the rights of individuals, in contrast with group rights. An individual right is the sanction of independent action. Of course, individual liberty does not mean the freedom to do anything one pleases. Freedom is not the same as anarchy. Freedom recognizes bounds placed on human conduct by common morality. Under *The Constitution*, law-abiding citizens can live according to their own choices rather than those of someone else. For example, there are no significant restrictions on whether or not you may obtain an education, what you can read, or where you may travel. If you want to start a business, no one will stop you. Your business

may make you rich, and no one should plunder your wealth or tell you how you must spend it.

Founding Fathers Summary Bullets

✪ Traits or values include generosity, service, courage, resilience, hard work, and personal responsibility.
✪ *The Constitution* is based on seven key principles aimed at assuring the people have individual rights and control of the government.
✪ Checks and balances were put in place to ensure limited government power.

Chapter 3:
Problem Solving Processes

For now, let's discuss two topics that will be used herein. The first topic is a common mode of operation (or process) used by our politicians, particularly Congress and the administration, to shape citizens' thinking on political issues that lead to our policies and laws. Observations of some problem's symptoms generally initiate this process. Our thinking is greatly influenced by numerous tricks politicians use to scare, mislead, and seduce us into supporting positions the politicians develop. This process helps them gain more power, which also increases their likelihood of re-election. The key tricks are discussed in the next three chapters.

The second topic is a tool used in the private and public sectors to determine key causes of problems. You will see that a better process for determining problems' causes is needed because the solutions selected by leaders are frequently symptom-based and inadequate.

These topics are demonstrated by using the 2010 health care and 2009 financial system (housing) crisis debates as examples.

Observed Political Mode of Operation

"...[I]n politics nothing is accidental. If something happens be assured it was planned this way.[1] — **Franklin D. Roosevelt**

I have observed a common political process or mode of operation used by Congress for problem solving that has a consistent and disturbing pattern. Unfortunately, this problem solving process is politically based and generally focuses on problems' symptoms rather than problems' underlying causes. Let's take a closer look.

Once a politician, group of politicians, or political party decides some action is needed, that person or group establishes a strategy and initiates a set of process steps (or tactics) to achieve their objectives. What they think is necessary is based on their own values, experiences, greed, hunger for power, and belief of what they might be able to enact into law. What might be in the best long-term interest of the nation is often not a prime focus for these politicians. These steps rarely consider results from a rational root cause or other logical non-political analysis. The intent of our Founding Fathers has been replaced by many career politicians' need to be re-elected, thus replacing productive civil debates with fruitless wars between the political parties. The steps involved in this mode of operation are indicated below. A few health care-related comments are provided (*in italics*) to show an example for each step.

Step One: Analyze the problem based on a political party's and/or some politicians' values - and personal benefits and experiences - but frame it as being in the best interest of the nation. This analysis is usually done "behind closed doors." *Health care is costing too much; costs are rising too fast; it is not covering everyone and is impacting the economy. The financial "sky is falling." We (politicians) must act now. We can no longer delay.*

Step Two: Develop a political solution consistent with political party power politics, but do not yet divulge any solution to the public. The proposed solution should include tactics for Steps Three and Four (below). This is also done "behind closed doors." *Provide health care coverage for everyone. The government will run and/ or control health care. More people will pay something, but the "rich" will cover most costs. Devise ways to add new taxes such as taxing employer contributions and health care equipment. Determine take-a-ways such as Medicare reductions and/or fewer profits for insurance companies and the medical profession. Collect taxes immediately but delay implementing the costly parts in order to claim a savings over ten years. Present a political bottom line: "We will save you; others will pay the costs!"*

Step Three: Publicly blame anyone but themselves for the problems. Amplify the blame (demonize) and drive wedges between groups of people, large entities, the opposite political party, the wealthy, or some combination of these, using public hearings and the media. *Say that the insurance industry is making too much money, is not responsive, and does not cover pre-existing conditions. Say that doctors and hospitals are not efficient and the wealthy can afford to pay more.*

Step Four: Find and use "Isn't it awful?" examples and parade these examples before the public using propaganda machines, such as public hearings and the press - who know sad stories boost ratings - while emphasizing those who are to "blame". Imply that the examples showcased are typical (even though they generally are not). *Point out that the demons in the case of health care reform are the insurance companies that have mistreated those being paraded before the public. Carefully avoid the fact that Congress has failed to require insurance companies to cover these individuals in the past. President Obama used this exact tactic in the final push for the Health Care Reform Bill by presenting a rate increase by one insurance company as being representative of them all: a perfect "Isn't it awful?" example.*

Step Five: Draft legislation using the solution derived in Step Two while continuing to use the tactics adopted in the other steps. Use scare tactics, distortion, and financial and psychological tricks to fool citizens, or otherwise confuse the facts to sway citizens. *Create legislation so that funds collection starts in 2010, but the actual costliest parts of the program will start after the 2012 Presidential election. Immediately start taxing employer contributions for employee insurance as ordinary income, meaning higher taxes for everyone whose employer has a health care program suggesting employer paid health care is provided to the "rich."*

Step Six: Use political tricks that can be applied to "market" their solution. *Throw the elderly a bone in the form of the $250 donation to the Medicare drug "donut hole," while reducing Medicare by $500 billion over ten years. Provide subsidies to many, implying it is free money that will be somehow extracted from the "rich."*

Step Seven: If necessary, buy votes by promising voters "free money" and/or buy off fellow politicians by providing funding in the legislation for unrelated things. *Promise the underinsured they will have free money made available to them by taxing the "rich" and health industries to pay for their subsidies. Promise money to certain Senate and House members for their votes by including an estimated $3.5 billion of pork barrel items.*

Politics is the art of looking for trouble, finding it whether it exists or not, diagnosing it incorrectly, and applying the wrong remedy.[2] — **Ernest Benn**

The health care factors listed above show how politicians used many tricks to scare, mislead, seduce, and confuse the majority of citizens with the intent of recruiting us for their causes. This mode of operation by congressional and White House administrations has been used for years, but with modern communications it has become a more systemic political problem. Now more than ever, we citizens need to be more conscious of these tricks.

Some politicians have argued they cannot use logic that might result in doing the right thing because they have to craft bills that will get the votes needed to pass. Thus, they work the problems backwards, and then employ political tricks to convince us their solutions are good solutions. While this meets their needs, it seldom meets ours. I believe we citizens can and will understand and support doing the right thing if we are given *all* the facts. If they choose to do so, our politicians (including President Obama) have the oral skills to present an honest, complete detailing of the solution's true costs, its short and long-term impacts, and why any proposed solution is a good solution.

Democracy must be something more than two wolves and a sheep voting on what to have for dinner.[3] — **James Bovard**

Root Cause Analysis

Many organizations try to fix system failures or problems quickly by merely addressing the immediate obvious symptoms without ever finding what caused them in the first place. This frequently results in the same or new (sometimes worse) problems appearing. In some areas of both the private and public sectors, established tools are being used to assess system failures and weaknesses so that they can be avoided and the system can be improved. One of these tools is *root cause analysis*. Root cause analysis is a process for finding and correcting problems by determining their causes. This is done because only when the root causes are identified and eliminated can the problems they cause truly be solved. There are many less-structured problem identification methods;[4] however, in order to develop a logical and repeatable approach, the process of root cause analysis uses more formal techniques. These techniques are used throughout this book.

There is usually more than one root cause for any given problem. Of course, complete prevention of recurrence by a single intervention is not always possible; thus, root cause analysis is often used as an iterative process tool for continuous improvement. Root cause analysis can be used as a reactive method to solve detected problems, or as a proactive method to improve systems by being able to forecast the possibility of an event or problem even before it occurs.

There are numerous options for conducting a root cause analysis. The process is best done by a group of knowledgeable individuals, such as government employees and any affected citizens, or management and workers. In general the process includes:

✪ Defining the problem or goals for the best solution
✪ Gathering data and evidence
✪ Asking "Why?" as often as necessary to get to the cause and identify the causal relationships associated within the defined problem
✪ Identifying which causes - if removed or changed - will prevent recurrence
✪ Identifying effective solutions to prevent recurrence, which are controllable, meet the defined goals and objectives, and do not cause other problems
✪ Implementing the recommendations
✪ Observing the solutions over time to ensure effectiveness

A "tree" graphic or hierarchal table can be developed asking the question "Why?" (or "Who?") at each hierarchal level to determine likely causes. Asking "Why?" at up to five or more levels is common.

The one root cause that is uncovered from analysis most often (based on my and others' observations) is a failure of leadership (or management) to act or react as needed. This root cause is a significant one that crosses all of my observations and concerns in this book.

Financial System Example

The sudden near-collapse of the financial markets was a clear indication that the nation's financial system was at a tipping point. Congress and both the Bush and Obama Administrations initiated the "common mode of operation" to address the financial system's problems. Since time was of the essence, they quickly got to Step 3: Publicly blaming anyone but themselves. Congress played the blame game by pointing their fingers toward the "bad guys" in the private sector and, later, toward the outgoing Bush Administration. How the mode of operation played out is now history. Would the same history have happened if a root cause analysis had been conducted?

Let's look more closely at this near-catastrophic failure. Many cartoons show children whining "not me" following some minor disaster. The majority of us have been financially responsible, but now we must pay for the excesses of others and the failures of our leaders. Homeowners who are now in trouble should have known they could not afford their loans if asset values or interest rates changed. They may have been made to believe that their decisions were justified by encouragement from creative private lenders, but what motivated these lenders to provide these loans? They were motivated by the actions of the most disgusting of all the "not me" whiners: Congress. Here is why:

Under President Carter's administration, Congress passed the well-intended Community Reinvestment Act, to help meet the needs of borrowers, including those in low and moderate- income neighborhoods. Not satisfied with the progress of that program, the Clinton Administration put pressure on financial institutions such as Fannie Mae and Freddie Mac, banks, thrift institutions and mortgage companies to (creatively) expand mortgage loans among low and middle-income people, the so-called subprime borrowers.[5]

Most leaders from both parties should have seen the looming crisis coming, (after all, they created it), but only a few did. For example, in April 2001, (as part of the 2002 Budget Request) the Bush Administration briefed Congress asking for tighter regulatory authority over Fannie Mae and Freddie Mac (two so-called government-sponsored enterprises or GSEs) because if either one failed their size was a potential problem that could *"cause strong repercussions in financial markets."[6]* In 2003, the Bush Administration again raised a red flag saying the lack of regulatory oversight was *"a systemic risk that could affect more than the housing market."[6]* Treasury Secretary John Snow sought a new strong regulatory agency to supervise both Fannie and Freddie to ensure the safety and soundness of their activities. All of these efforts fell on deaf ears.

Congressman Barney Frank, then ranking member and later Democrat Chairman of the House Financial Services Committee, stated: *"Fannie Mae and Freddie Mac are not in a crisis...they are fundamentally sound and...the government should do more to encourage home purchases."* He called the threat an *"exaggeration"* among other things, and the legislation was blocked.[6]

In February 2005, Federal Reserve Chairman Alan Greenspan weighed in with testimony stating: *"...Enabling these institutions to increase in size – and they will once the crisis in their judgment passes – we are placing the total financial system of the future at a substantial risk."* At a later hearing he stated: *"If we fail to strengthen GSE regulation we increase the possibility of insolvency in crisis."[6]* All of these efforts by Greenspan and the Bush Administration also fell on deaf ears, and the Bush administration stopped pushing for change.

Senator Charles Schumer, at a Senate Banking Committee hearing in April 2006 stated: *"...I think Fannie and Freddie over the years have done an incredibly good job and are an intrinsic part of making America the best-housed people in the world...if you look over the past 20 years or whatever years, they've done a very, very good job."[6]*

In May 2006, Senator McCain jointly sponsored a bill to reform these large institutions. He stated: *"For years I have been concerned about the regulatory structure that governs…and the sheer magnitude of these companies and the role they play in the housing market…the GSE's need to be reformed without delay."*[6] The Committee split along party lines and the bill failed to go to the floor of the Senate.

Nothing is so admirable in politics as a short memory.[7] — **John Kenneth Galbraith**

Table 3-1 depicts a simple three-level root cause analysis that justifies failure conclusions. In the graphic, items in **black bold** type are **major causes**, those in black *regular italic* type are contributing, or secondary, causes. Minor or negligible causes have not been included.

Table 3-1: Root Cause Analysis of Financial Systems

1. **Failure of political leadership**
   a. **Failure of Congress (and/or States)**
      i. **Did not recognize potential problems**
      ii. **Did not act on or react to potential problems**
      iii. **Created conflicting policies (Low cost housing vs fiscal policies)**
      iv. **Chose politics (Power & Greed) over the greater good**
   b. **Failure of Administration**
      i. *Did not act forcefully enough after problems were recognized and Congress was given propose solutions*
      ii. *Chose politics (Power & Greed) over the greater good*

2. **Failure of corporate leadership**
   a. *Did not recognize potential problems*
   b. **Chose profit (Power & Greed) over the greater good**

3. **Failure of Individuals**
   a. *Did not recognize potential problems (e.g., home values cannot exceed inflation forever!)*
   b. **Were not concerned about accountability**
   c. *Put excessive reliance on political & corporate leaders*
   d. *Did not consider long term consequences; chose short term benefits*

Code: **Major Causes (bold)** — *Secondary Causes (italic)*

A root cause of the recent near-catastrophic failure of our financial system was really a failure of the government leaders in Congress and the executive branch. After they developed the systems they failed to oversee them or establish appropriate performance standards and regulations (bounds) to prevent a catastrophic failure. The private sector leaders failed in important ways, as well, which were pointed out by the politicians. A secondary, contributing, cause included the citizens who were caught up in the dream of owning a home without due consideration of potential risks.

What are the lessons learned from what happened? Our political leaders failed us and blamed others despite the fact that they had had clear indicators of problems. Corporate leaders took advantage of both lax government oversight and their clients' lack of understanding of the risks. Individuals eager for home ownership and assuming their property value would continue to rise over-extended their financial ability to pay as prices dropped. The tipping point occurred when the accumulated bad debts began to be recognized by investors, who went into a "panic mode." All of us no doubt noticed how quickly our politicians— the masters of deflection and deception— placed the blame on others and drafted solutions that served their own agendas.

Government is like a baby. An alimentary canal with a big appetite at one end and no sense of responsibility at the other.[8] — **Ronald Reagan**

Problem Solving Processes Summary Bullets

✪ Congress and administrations use a common problem solving process that is politically based and generally focuses on the problems' symptoms rather than the problems' underlying causes.

- ✪ Congress' process includes a sequence of planned steps that allow politicians to utilize many tactical tricks to convince their constituents to go along with their plans.
- ✪ Root cause analysis or other formal problem solving processes would lead to better solutions for our nation.
- ✪ There are significant root causes for most of our problems, but our leaders generally choose to ignore them!

PART II: OUR OPPONENTS' TACTICAL TRICKS

The old adage: "You cannot fool Mother Nature," does not apply to *human* nature, which is often fooled. Politicians and some business leaders are well-versed in how to fool the general public. Politicians have only two, four or six years to raise money and convince us they are taking good care of us. This short timeframe drives career politicians to use tactical tricks to scare, mislead, and seduce us into believing our country and its people are their top priorities, but the evidence suggests otherwise. As we will show re-election and political party power are really their top priorities. Tricking citizens is the mechanism they use to achieve their priorities.

Fifteen frequently used tricks used on us are presented next. None of these tricks were covered in my university Psychology 101 or Business and Industrial Psychology courses and I have not found them listed anywhere else. I am sure you will recognize some but not all of them. Unfortunately, we have come to expect their use by our career politicians as we become numb to our elected officials' tricky tactics. Some of the tricks are psychological in nature, and others are financial— where the numbers are misleading.

Chapter 4: Politicians' Recognizable Psychological Tricks

Chapter 5: Politicians' Subtle Psychological Tricks

Chapter 6: Politicians' Financial Tricks

Chapter 4:
Politicians' Recognizable Psychological Tricks

The financial and health care examples in Chapter 3 showed how quickly politicians lay blame - particularly when they are responsible for much of the problem. Blame is also used to form "us" versus "them" wedges. These and other psychological tricks are used to divide voters into groups that the politicians hope to control. All of these tricks and more are used by politicians (as well as business leaders, sales and marketing people, etc.) to recruit us into fighting for them and for their causes.

The Blame Game

Whenever something goes wrong, politicians quickly try to "lay blame" (also called "finger-pointing," "finding fault," or "demonizing"). It is a classic method to foster misdirection and uncertainty about an issue in the minds of voters. This is one of their most commonly used tricks. Politicians use this trick to remove themselves from any responsibility for a problem, and to vilify or demonize some other person or group. In "the blame game," accusations are exchanged among people who refuse to accept sole responsibility for some undesirable event. The blame game is initiated when Person X, let's call him Jim, feels guilty or uncomfortable about something, so Jim finds a rationale of why someone else, let's call her Jane, is to blame. Jim then proceeds to publicly blame Jane.

Jim gains several benefits from this. He is excused from what he (or others he is protecting) have done, allowing Jim to do it again. Jim can also play the "poor me" card. He can claim social capital, as Jane now owes him something in return for Jane's apparent failure. Jane may join in the game by passing the blame back to Jim or to someone else because she can also play "poor me" and claim social capital. Both of them can also play "it's *your* fault" in return. Players get to play the role of the persecutor, and get to enjoy the associated pleasant feelings of power. Blame games include:

✪ *Look what you made me do*: Jim blames his own failure on Jane's actions (or possibly on her mere presence).

✪ *If it wasn't for you*: Jim wants something, but also may not want it. Nevertheless, Jim does not get it and blames this on Jane's actions or inactions, instead of his own.

The financial system example in Chapter 3 indicated that Democrats were at least as responsible as Republicans for creating many of the country's financial problems, but that Democrats more successfully played the blame game. Because of this, most of us blame the Republicans, some of whom did try to preempt the problems. The blame game for this crisis is still ongoing.

In April 2010, the Congressional Financial Crisis Inquiry Commission was still trying to lay blame on anyone except themselves. For example, the panel chairman Phil Angelides accused Alan Greenspan, the Federal Reserve chairman for many years prior to the crisis, of a failure to regulate the lenders. This was said *after* Greenspan had pointed out that the Federal Reserve did not have the needed regulatory powers to do so. Nevertheless, Angelides got in some sound bites for the press, which, as usual, did not challenge his statement.

It is not surprising that the atmosphere in Washington, DC is so rancorous. Logically, determining what caused a problem should take place before determining blame, but that is not how it works for politicians. What should we do when politicians start playing the blame game? A good first assumption is that those playing the game are probably partly or completely responsible for the issue of concern to us. Thus, we should ignore what the "blamers" are saying, so that we do not to get sucked into their tricks. As indicated by the financial system example, we often get sucked into believing what is really not true. Second, we should seek out the actual causes of the issues of concern and study the proposed solutions, if there are any. Be alert to other tricks even while listening to proposed solutions. Are the solutions highly biased by party politics or social agendas rather than root causes? If all else fails, try a mental chant:[1]

Chant: Blame game; shame; shame! (pointing your finger) You, too, are to blame!

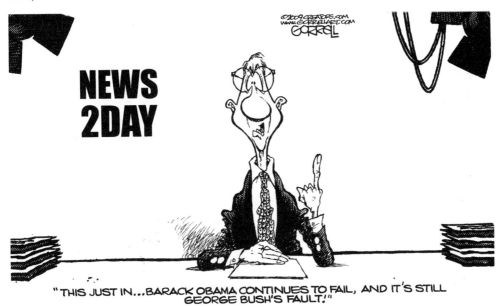

"THIS JUST IN...BARACK OBAMA CONTINUES TO FAIL, AND IT'S STILL GEORGE BUSH'S FAULT!"

Wedges (Divide to Conquer)

Politicians try to drive wedges between groups of voters in order to increase their likelihood of conquering one group for their cause (frequently by using other tricks). Thus, the more wedges the better for a politician when he wants to confuse or mislead voters. Politicians usually start by playing the blame game. Wedges are used individually or in combinations, but the overarching wedge is "us versus them." This is applied as needed. It may be "little guy or worker versus big business," or "Main Street versus Wall Street." The opposing groups can be big or small. In fact, leaders - to make a wedge happen - may use every trick mentioned in this book. Ideally, the politicians want to evoke outrage by using a wedge to anger one of the wedge groups. Politicians do this because this is what they have found works well to convince voters that they should want what the politicians want.

Sometimes one "us" group gangs up on several "thems" or vice-versa. For example, President Obama, in discussions of the financial meltdown, stressed the point that the "little guy" was being mistreated, mislead, etc., by big financial "businesses," greedy wealthy people, greedy managers, and previous administration government employees. While this process may be good for politics, it is bad for the nation. President Obama fired managers of private sector businesses and stiffened regulations. Certainly some of what was accomplished needed to be done, but were wedges necessary— or the best way to do it? Probably not, if the desired end result was to unify groups or seek their cooperation.

Another interesting example of wedge-driving has recently evolved. The Democrats have become concerned about the Tea Party movement, and feel the need to make them appear as dangerous radicals, or, alternately, simply stupid. The first volley in this wedge-driving was by former President Clinton, who without mentioning the Tea Party by name, cautioned that "radicals" must be careful of what they say because they might incite someone to become an Oklahoma City-like bomber. Rush Limbaugh countered with a similar direct caution to Clinton. Between these two wedge-like charges, President Obama, mentioning the Tea Party by name, essentially said it was funny that the Tea Parties were demonstrating for lower taxes since he had already lowered taxes. The implication was that these radicals did not know what was going on - that they were stupid. In actuality, taxes are only one of many concerns within the Tea Party movement.

On June 16, 1858, Abraham Lincoln gave a speech that included the famous quote, *"A house divided against itself cannot stand."*[2] Although he was talking about the U.S. government over 150 years ago, the quote is still relevant to our contemporary government and the workplace today. An "us versus them" mentality easily develops during times of change and pressure. The problem is, whatever the size and scope of the "us" and "them" groups, wedges cause undue tension and a lot of consternation. By definition, a wedge is a divider. Too often we hear politicians claim they want to work together and, in the same sentence, evoke a wedge. This battleground-like environment saps productivity and capacity to get things done. It distracts people and politicians from the big picture. It prevents them from serving the nation, various constituencies, and customers to the best of their abilities.

Whenever we hear a politician invoke a wedge, we should give him or her a "hitting below the belt" penalty. I find it particularly disheartening when a president does it since we need leaders who unite us, not wedge us apart.

Chant: Wedges divide to conquer. Unite, don't divide!

Isn't It Awful?

This is a commonly used trick by politicians, and is a key one for congressional hearings. Every congressional hearing is an opportunity to: (1) convince the public that some "bad" citizens caused our problems; and, (2) exploit the miseries of a few citizens to try to convince the rest of us these miseries are quite common.

When the politicians have a predetermined agenda, this trick allows them to gain leverage by demonizing a person or group of people, large entity, process, or some combination of these. Unfortunately, politicians always have a predetermined agenda.

Individuals or families who do testify at congressional hearings deserve our sympathies. While most of their stories are heart wrenching, they usually represent the rare, extreme case and not the norm. Also, this situation does not allow the demonized "bad guys" to respond, so they are automatically presumed guilty. The news media loves human interest stories and the more bizarre or terrible the story, the more desirable it is to the media. So, if a politician plays the game right, he is assured of news coverage to both demonize the bad guys and seek sympathy for his cause on national TV. Politicians' goals are to gain leverage, evoke outrage, and set the stage for the "wonderful way" they plan to fix the problem they are pointing out. In the case of the health care debate, "Isn't it awful?" was played out many times.

Only "politically correct" testimony is sought by whichever party is in power. For example, the following was apparently not important enough to make a real splash in the national news: This real-life account took place at a Florida hearing by Carol Plato Nicosia, Director of Corporate Business Health Systems at Martin Memorial Health Systems, Fort Pierce, Florida. She described several of the hospital's emergency room cases. One patient entered the emergency room in 2001 and was released in 2003. His hospital costs were $1.5 million. Since he was an illegal resident patient, he was released and sent to his home country of Guatemala. The hospital paid an additional $30,000 to transport him home. Relatives then sued the hospital because they thought it was inappropriate for the hospital to return this illegal patient to his home country. This cost the hospital additional legal fees. The hospital won in this particular case.

Ms. Nicosia described another case of an illegal patient from Mexico who had at that time been in the hospital for 760 days. His charges to date - for almost two years of care – amounted to $1.5 million. The hospital contacted the Mexican Consulate four times, and U.S. Immigration, and nobody would help the hospital return this patient to Mexico, even though the hospital was willing to pay for it. Nicosia also pointed out that the hospital was providing renal dialysis for six illegal patients three days per week, and that a high percentage of the hospital's newborns are from illegal parents.[3]

This "politically incorrect" example indicates two health care cost issues that are apparently too politically sensitive to be mentioned in the center of the health care debate. First of all, while it would be nice if we could take care of every person in the world who needs help, we cannot afford to do so. Second, legal fees add costs to health care - and many other goods and services - no matter how ridiculous the case. The bottom line is that the "Isn't it awful?" ploy is used very selectively and never tells the whole story.

Chant: Sympathy, yes; how many; who pays?

Tell Them What They Want To Hear

One of the first tricks every politician learns is "tell them (their audience) what they (the majority of the audience) want to hear." It is not the first thing presented in this chapter because this trick usually utilizes many other tricks in its implementation. Politicians *do* listen. They listen to the intended audience, select the items that audience will resonate with, and tell them only what they want to hear. It is almost never the whole story. What they tell their audience frequently is not anything they can even do or plan to do. Individuals who are part of a large group are so eager to hear what they want to hear, that they stop thinking for themselves.

When engaging in live political rhetoric, politicians look for positive reinforcements from the audience in the form of joy, applause, and head-nodding to indicate to them that their selected sentiments are aligned with what the audience hoped to hear. We, as audience members, have been suckered if not scammed by these tricks so often that we now expect it. Now, when someone tries to tell the whole truth, they are often labeled as being "too pessimistic!" Paul Harvey, a famous journalist, always talked about "the rest of the story." Every politician should be asked about the rest of the story whenever he or she speaks.

Key methods to identify when this trick is being used to transfer blame are to listen for the blame game (anyone but the politician is responsible for the problems), or the "Isn't it awful?" ploy with defined villains or other psychological tricks. Listen for offers of free money for some voters, claims the government is cheaper or better, and a recommendation to tax the rich, corporations, or other selected groups (e.g., smokers) to provide the needed money. These are tricks to help secure your vote. These politicians hope to invoke wedges to divide and conquer, and, possibly, outrage us.

We need to start listening and thinking before we shout and applaud the speaker! Below is a ninety-second excerpt from then-candidate Obama on one topic near and dear to many of us. Almost any other career politician's speech could have been used as an example.

Example: Obama as candidate ~1.5 minutes of a typical stump speech

I will make our government open and transparent so that anyone can ensure our business is the people's business. As Justice Louis Brandies once said: "Sunlight is the greatest disinfectant." As President, I am going to make it impossible for congressmen or lobbyists to slip pork barrel projects or corporate welfare into laws when no one is looking because, when I am President, meetings where laws are written will be more open to the public. No more secrecy. That is the commitment I make to you as President.

And, when there is a bill [that] ends up on my desk as President, you the public will have five days to look on line and find out what is in it before I sign it so you know what your government is doing.

When there are meetings between lobbyists and a government agency we will put as many of those meetings as possible on line for every American to watch.

When there is a tax bill being debated in Congress, you will know the names of corporations that would benefit and how much money they would get and we will put every corporate tax break and every pork barrel project on line for every American to see you will know who ask for them and you can decide whether your representative is actually representing you.[4]

Loud, enthusiastic shouting and applause followed each statement. Let's dissect this typical stump speech. The first paragraph is exactly what the audience wanted to hear, but is it something he plans to (or can) deliver? The answer is that he is either naive or misleading the audience since, for example, after a year in office he signed an omnibus bill containing at least 5,000 pork barrel projects totaling at least $3.8 billion and there have been the "usual" amounts of secrecy.[5] Another interesting point is embedded in that paragraph: he mentions those "villain" corporations getting "corporate welfare," but avoids others who also have lobbyists but are his supporters, such as unions and lawyers. The speech also does not address the big problem of free money! The second and third statements have not been implemented, but they, too, sounded good. The last statement follows the first one regarding "evil" corporations, but avoids others and - again - nothing is said about free money.

The bottom line is that when we listen to politicians and they tell us what we want to hear, we want to believe them. And, in the excitement of the moment and the group mentality, we do! Politicians know this, so when we should be outraged that they are treating us as stupid, we ignore rational thought. In this way, virtually every career politician can trick us. In our "gut" we know this, and perhaps this is why politicians are held in such low esteem.

Chant: Tell the whole story!

Mudslinging and Dirty Tricks

"Mudslinging," "dirty tricks," and "character assassinations" are all close relatives to the "blame game". These, too, are simply political methods used to foster misdirection and uncertainty about an individual or policy issue in the minds of voters. These tricks are most often used during campaigning. After campaigns, however, more subtle use is still common.

In general, "mudslinging" is trying to win an advantage by referring to negative aspects of an opponent or a policy rather than emphasizing one's own positive attributes or preferred policies. The goal of mudslinging is to destroy an opponent's character or policy.

"Dirty tricks" common in negative political campaigns generally involve a politician (or his staff) secretly leaking damaging information to the media, who gleefully accept the information.

This isolates a candidate from backlash and also does not cost any money. The material must be substantive enough to attract media interest, but if he is not careful it could backfire on the perpetrator and severely damage his or her campaign if the truth is discovered. Other dirty tricks include trying to feed an opponent's team false information in the hope that it will be used and they will embarrass themselves.

Negative campaigning has become the norm in most political races and several variations are used such as claiming an opponent is weak, inexperienced, voted a certain way on an issue, beats their spouse, or even "is running a negative campaign." If not immediately challenged, these dirty trick claims become ingrained in our minds as the truth when in fact they rarely are. There is some risk in employing these dirty tricks. Sometimes when the true facts come out, the trick backfires into the original perpetrator's face.

Negative campaigning can be effectively used by a relatively unknown candidate (or one running against an incumbent) when he or she is either outspent or has hard evidence of some wrongdoing. Research indicates negative ads are more memorable than positive ads when they reinforce a preexisting belief and are relevant to the central issues of a campaign. Researchers at the University of Georgia found the impact of negative ads increases over time, while positive ads used to counteract negative ads lack the power of negative ads.[6] Research also suggests negative campaigning introduces controversy and raises public awareness through additional news coverage.

What should we do when politicians start slinging mud and playing dirty tricks? These tactics are psychologically very hard to ignore, particularly when they are repeated frequently, but we should assume all claims are false, twisted, or "spun" information. Thus, for as long as possible, we should ignore them since these claims add little to the important issues. Instead, we should seek the candidate's actual positions on the issues of concern and how he or she intends to address them, if any.

Below are a few historical examples of these tricks, none of which were proven. Every time you hear mud slinging or a dirty trick remember one of these to help you forget what is being said.

- ✪ The Coffin Handbills used by supporters of John Quincy Adams against Andrew Jackson in the 1828 presidential campaign where Jackson's mother was called a prostitute, and his wife an adulteress.
- ✪ The Willie Horton ad used by George H. W. Bush in the 1988 presidential campaign against Michael Dukakis.
- ✪ The attacks against George W. Bush's military record in the 2004 presidential election, and attacks against John Kerry's Vietnam service record by some Navy Swift Boat veterans of the Vietnam War.
- ✪ Miller Brewing Co.'s and Anheuser Busch Brewing Co.'s 2005 advertisements attacking each other's products.
- ✪ Pepsi's advertisements attacking Coca-Cola, and vice-versa.
- ✪ The now-infamous *3:00a.m. Whitehouse Phone Call* commercial made by the campaign of democratic presidential hopeful Senator Hillary Clinton in her 2008 presidential campaign against democratic presidential candidate, Senator Barack Obama. The ad backfired when the young girl from the stock footage, Casey Knowles, came out as an Obama supporter.

Chant: Mud causes DRIPs (Don't Re-elect Incumbent Politicians)!

Broken Government Promises

There are two levels of "broken government promises." One is a major change to an older law that results in broken promises; and the other is a specific promise made by a politician or candidate which is later broken.

42

The government regularly breaks promises through changing laws that were passed based on earlier promises. The Social Security example (presented later in this text) is one promise that has had enormous impacts on almost all citizens. Almost every promise made at its inception has been broken. Most changes to past laws have resulted in increases in taxes or other forms of expanding government or free money to benefit politicians.

The breaking of specific candidate or politician individual promises is commonplace. Every politician makes promises he or she knows are not realistic. (The candidate Obama stump speech segment listed under "Tell them What They Want To Hear," above, is an example.) Yet we let them get away with these promises. Basically, Congress can pass bad laws, blame someone or something when a fault is identified, and change the law. The tricks work because we have short memories and the promises sound good at the time. All we can do is be alert to broken promises.

Chant: No more broken promises!

Politicians' Recognizable Psychological Tricks Summary Bullets

✪ Politicians employ many tactical tricks to scare, mislead, and seduce constituents into going along with their plans and to re-elect them.

✪ Easily recognized tricks include Blame Game, Wedges, Isn't It Awful, Tell Them What They Want To Hear, Mudslinging and Dirty Tricks, and Broken Government Promises

✪ "Tell Them What They Want To Hear" is the most commonly used trick but it is generally used in conjunction with many other tricks.

Chapter 5:
Politicians' Subtle Psychological Tricks

The recognizable psychological tactical tricks discussed in the previous chapter are augmented by more subtle psychological tricks such as "human perceptions of risk," "adversary truths," "religious twists" and others that are used to divide voters into groups these politicians hope to control. These tricks, and more, are used by politicians to recruit us into fighting for them and for their causes. You will see these "expert psychological tricks" really take it to the next level. Once we understand all of the psychological tactical tricks we will be less likely to be taken in by them.

Risk - Benefit, Aversion, and Outrage

Politicians tend to focus on benefits without fully assessing risks. But they use risks to focus our attention on things they want from us. Two aspects of risks are used against us: our natural aversion to some risks and "risk + outrage." "Risk aversion" is a process through which we, as human beings, see two or more equal risks as being unequal because of psychological factors. "Risk + outrage" is when the risk may be low but, by its nature, it evokes outrage in individuals or groups. We need be aware of risks and how we think about them in order to avoid being tricked by politicians and businesses.

Perhaps the best example of risk taking is in how we tend to vote for the "devil we know" (the incumbent) rather than the one we do not know. Rather than try something new and unfamiliar to us, (even though it may be much better for us in the long run), we often do things we do not like simply because we are familiar with them. This is the essence of risk aversion. This is why well-known but perhaps unqualified individuals get elected or re-elected over others who are more qualified, and why politicians work to keep their faces and names before the voters.

Risk/Benefit Analysis

We consciously or subconsciously conduct a risk/benefit analysis many times each day. Risk/benefit analysis is the comparison of the risk of a situation to its related benefits. Intuitively, many of us understand what risk is. Risk is related to possible hazard consequences and the probability of the consequence occurring. For example. traveling is hazardous due to possible consequences such as death or injury from an accident. The probability of an accident depends upon the mode of travel and other factors. Driving a car is a health hazard due to the possibility of an accident causing death, however, one of its benefits might include the fact that, through driving, you get to see grandma. There is data that provides the number of automobile deaths per miles driven (as a probability). If you know this number every time you drive, you could assess your chances of being killed by multiplying this number times the number of miles you plan to drive.

Risk Aversion

Let's consider the trip to see grandma (say from San Francisco to Los Angeles) in terms of how we travel there and our chances of dying as a result of an accident. Common modes of transportation include automobiles, buses, trains, and airplanes. Let's assume that the costs for auto and airplane travel are about equal, and time is not a dominant concern. According to the National Safety Council, buses, trains, and airplanes have much lower death rates than automobiles, when the risk is expressed as passenger deaths per mile of travel. By automobile, one person dies per approximately every 125 million passenger-miles. By airplane, one person dies per approximately 5,000 million passenger-miles. To fill in the equation, buses and trains are safer than automobiles and worse than airplanes. Another way to state this result is that you are forty times more likely to die in your automobile than in an airplane when you go to see grandma. Despite this big difference, many people still fear air travel and prefer to drive. This is risk aversion: we are uncomfortable with certain things and would rather accept higher risk. The common psychological variables that cause us to be risk adverse are provided in **Table 5-1**.

Table 5-1: Risk Adverse Variables

- **Control – (voluntary vs. coerced):** We feel comfortable when we feel we are in control. You or a family member is driving the auto and some unknown pilot is flying the plane. More generally, "I control" and "I think I control" takes precedence over "they control" even when the risks are higher for "I" than for "they."
- **Space and/or size – (not memorable vs. memorable):** We tend to forget and accept smaller size, numbers and/or space over big size, numbers and/or space. Autos are small, few people die in an accident and they run on familiar ground. Airplanes are large, many people die in an accident and they float in the air. Think about what the public impact would be if 300 or more auto deaths all occurred at one time and in one location.
- **Familiarity vs. exotic:** We prefer what we know about, not the unfamiliar; you are much more familiar with autos than airplanes. You are familiar with your existing politician representative rather than someone you have known at best for a short time.
- **Time — (now vs. later):** We prefer taking risks that result in instantaneous verses delayed outcomes. This does not directly apply to our visit to grandma, but is an important variable. Generally, we rank time related risks "from ok to bad" as follows; instantaneous (driving, skydiving), controlled and delayed (smoking, overeating) and uncontrolled and delayed (nuclear power, big businesses and big government). Think about what the public impact would be if 50,000 auto deaths, 25,000 gun deaths or 350,000 smoking related deaths all occurred at one time, yet these occur annually.

Risk Aversion and Politicians

The psychological risk aversion factors listed above are often used in public policy discussions. Unfortunately, our political leaders frequently take the easy way out by simply avoiding proposals and possible good decisions because of these psychological variables. An example is using natural gas or coal electrical power plants that produce carbon dioxide (CO_2) versus nuclear plants that produce no CO_2. Why not use nuclear power? The answer is simple: the word "nuclear" evokes all of our risk aversions. Other energy sources, many of which still emit CO_2, do not have these adverse factors. Yet, nuclear energy is the source for a high percentage of electric power production worldwide, such as in Canada (fifteen percent), Europe (thirty percent), Korea (thirty-five percent), Russia (seventeen percent), Japan (twenty-five percent), and even the United States (twenty percent), but it is seldom part of the U.S. energy discussion. In 2007, fourteen percent of all the world's electrical energy was from nuclear power plants. Many countries have several nuclear plants under construction including China (sixteen), Russia (nine), India (six) and Korea (six). In the United States, President Obama is proposing we build two new reactors.[1]

Another example is health care. In this case, an individual can reduce risks by basic health improvements, such as maintaining a healthy weight and exercise, but ultimately the individual does not have control over diseases or death. Health care is highly personal, we have limited control, many die each year from diseases whose causes are unfamiliar, and some diseases result in prolonged or delayed deaths. We are generally averse to all of these death options. Most of us would prefer not knowing when we will die, but hope it will be fast. Like nuclear power, health care is a topic where politicians and businesses have played upon our risk aversions, because essentially all of them are evoked. Strong risk aversions can also evoke "risk + outrage."

Risk + Outrage

Closely related to risk aversion is "risk + outrage" as described in work done by Professor Peter M. Sandman. He noted that, when a list of environmental health risks is ranked in order of how many people are killed each year, then listed again in order of how alarming they are to the general public, the two lists are very different. One might conclude that the differences are a result of a lack of knowledge. Professor Sandman has studied the psychological aspects of the risk aversion concepts listed above and has added his own. He concluded that the public defines risk broadly, and noted that when these risk factors are in play, a risk may be perceived as high whether it is or not, and may lead to "outrage." [2] He states: "...*if you wonder why the public is responding as to some risk issue, and what you should do about it: 'It's the outrage, stupid.'"*[3] His twelve component sets for outrage separated into what is perceived as "safe" versus "risky" are[4]:

Table 5-2: Outrage Components

"Safe"	"Risky"
1. Voluntary	Coerced
2. Natural	Industrial
3. Familiar	Exotic
4. Not memorable	Memorable
5. Not dreaded	Dreaded
6. Chronic	Catastrophic
7. Knowable	Unknowable
8. Individually controlled	Controlled by others
9. Fair	Unfair
10. Morally irrelevant	Morally relevant
11. Trustworthy sources	Untrustworthy sources
12. Responsive process	Unresponsive process

Professor Sandman has published many articles for reducing outrage, effective communication to influence outrage, topical items, etc. For the purposes of this document, his conclusions about risk hazards and outrage are useful[5].

Table 5-3: Seven Conclusions About Outrage

1. The public responds more to outrage than to hazard.
2. Activists and the media amplify outrage, but do not create it.
3. Outraged people do not pay much attention to hazard data.
4. Outrage is not just a distraction from hazard. Both are legitimate and important.
5. When risks are high, risk communicators try to nurture more outrage.
6. When risks are low, risk communicators try to reduce the outrage.
7. Companies and (governmental) agencies usually cannot reduce outrage much until they change their own organizations.

Risk + Outrage and Politicians

These conclusions by Professor Sandman do not mention politicians, *per se*. However, my observations indicate politicians use the "risky" components column in **Table 5-2** to help lay blame and to evoke outrage. They use the "safe" components column to describe themselves and their actions. Let's look at the health care debate, again, in terms of **Table 5-2**:

1. We are told we can choose our health plans (safe), but some of us feel the government option would result in coerced coverage (risky) and, therefore, the government option is under fire politically.
2. The fact that we are not naturally taking care of our own health (overeating, smoking, etc.) (safe) is not discussed, because voters would have to own part of the problem (risky). Instead, we are told the insurance industry is bad and needs fixing which is safe for politicians because big industries are bad.
3. We are familiar with what we have (safe) and we fear the massive (or exotic) changes proposed may be worse (risky).

4. We do not remember the expected good things our present health care system has done for us (safe), but we remember all the bad stories about what they have or have not done to us or others (risky).
5. Common simple health problems are generally not dreaded since these are covered by insurance or emergency room visits (safe). No health coverage particularly for large, long-term, and catastrophic health problems is dreaded (risky).
6. The present system addresses most chronic problems (safe), but not all catastrophic problems are covered (risky).
7. We trust the knowledge of our doctors and are told we can keep them (safe), but insurers and government employees are unknowledgeable (risky).
8. We are told we can control our health care plans (safe), but some of us feel the government option would result in too much government control (risky).
9. It is fair the "wealthy" or a worker's employer pays for all health insurance (safe). It is unfair that all people able to pay do not.
10. Taking care of oneself is morally irrelevant (safe). Everyone being entitled to health care is morally relevant (risky).
11. Doctors are trustworthy (safe), but big insurance companies and big governments are untrustworthy (risky).
12. Doctors are responsive (safe), but big insurance companies and the government are slow and unresponsive (risky).

Politicians used these psychological risk factors to shape the health care act. As humans, most of us accept what is presented as safe. Perhaps we should learn to understand psychological risk factors and re-look-at what our politicians propose.

Chant: No risk tricks!

Adversary Truths and Legalese

Throughout history, many of our leaders have been trained as lawyers. The positive aspects of having lawyers as leaders are they must think logically, and they have experience in dealing with other people (either as adversaries or clients). A negative aspect is they frequently have little experience in business and capitalism beyond what they need for their legal business. Two big negative aspects of having lawyers as leaders are they have been trained to be "adversary truth tellers," and they write in "legalese." Naturally, this training is used in their leadership roles resulting in what appear as blame games, white lies, and confusion to we non-lawyer laypersons.

A countryman between two lawyers is like a fish between two cats.[6]
— **Benjamin Franklin**

Adversary Truths

Honest lawyers are guided by legal ethics, i.e., rules the profession has developed to guide lawyers' actions. These include the process of "adversary truths" wherein the lawyer representing Client 1 will present only those truths advantageous to Client 1; at the same time, it is up to the opposing lawyer (adversary) representing Client 2 to present only those truths advantageous to Client 2. In this process, all aspects of the truth seldom reveal themselves, leaving the general public feeling that lawyers are not truthful.

Making matters worse, lawyers represent clients by means of "zealous advocacy." Adversarial lawyers do not care about fairness or balance. Instead, they care disproportionately, and at times almost *exclusively*, about their clients' interests. Unlike individuals, juries, and judges, adversarial lawyers are not charged to provide a true account of the facts of a case and may apply the law with no regard to the facts. Instead, they try aggressively to manipulate both the facts and the law into a shape that benefits their clients. In each of these ways, adversarial lawyers commonly take (and are often required to take) actions that in their professional capacities would be immoral if done by ordinary people in ordinary circumstances.

Lawyers are the only persons in whom ignorance of the law is not punished.[7] — **Jeremy Bentham**

As citizens, we need to demand the whole truth both good and bad from our (lawyer) leaders, demanding that they inform us of all sides of issues. By doing this, they would let us decide what is best rather than prejudging what is best for us, and then using adversary truth-telling and other tricks to convince us to go along.

Legalese

Lawyers continue to write laws using old terms and linguistic concepts, arguing that it is necessary because law is based on precedents set earlier in time. Changing to modern language, they argue, would make use of precedents harder. This is a bogus argument and really is more about lawyers' egos, money, and power. Legalese works to politicians' advantage. Few laypersons even try to read and understand legal documents. Two quotes tell the truth about this situation:

Robert W. Benson, Professor of Law, Loyola Law School: *"Inertia, incompetence, status, power, cost, and risk are a formidable set of motivations to keep legalese. Their tenacity should not be underestimated. One observation must be made, however. These motivations lack any intellectually or socially acceptable rationale; they amount to assertions of naked self-interest."*[8]

Judge Lynn N. Hughes, U.S.. District Court, Houston, Texas: *"The common language of the law is not the product of necessity, prec-*

edent, convention, or economy, but it is the product of sloth, confusion, hurry, cowardice, ignorance, neglect, and cultural poverty."[9]

Those laymen among us who have read newly drafted laws must agree with these quotes. The Health Care Bill is a classic recent example, considering that it was 2,000 pages before any amendments were added. If you tried to read it as I did, you would agree with the above quotes. The entire bill would probably run about 200 pages if it weren't for the legalese garbage.

As citizens, we need to demand our (lawyer) leaders change the way laws are written to make them understandable to all. At a minimum, all laws written in legalese should be accompanied by a companion document written by non-lawyers explaining them in modern language, lay terms. This could also minimize lawyers' use of adversary truths.

Chant: Tell the whole truth!

The Religious Twists

There are at least two religious teachings that are exploited by career politicians. First, most religions strive to be *charitable*, feeling that believers should help those less fortunate than themselves. Second, religious expectations are clearly defined for believers and if these are not met then feelings of *guilt* are a result.

Being *charitable* is a fundamental virtue discussed in most religious documents (such as the Bible, the Koran, etc.), and religious leaders strongly encourage believers to be charitable to those who are less fortunate. Such admonishments are frequent in these documents. Thus, it is not surprising that U.S. citizens, who practice a variety of religions, are the most generous in the world. We frequently come to the aid of our fellow U.S. and world citizens. Individuals participate in charitable and religious organizations by giving their time and resources, as they feel appropriate. Favorable tax status is provided to charitable organizations to foster these activities. This generosity by individuals is part of what has made the United States great.

As Jews, Christians, Muslims, other faithful, and atheist individuals, we can all agree that helping others is important, but we need to ask ourselves a few questions: Who has the authority to take from some citizens and give to others, and for what purpose? Does a politician have the right to covet and take money from some of us so he or she can dole out money to the rest of us to garner re-election votes?

Unfortunately, we seem to have many career politicians who feel they have the moral right to force us to fund their political "charitable causes." Nowhere in any religious documents is the idea of "taking by force from some to help others" or the placing of future generations in jeopardy for our debts by "kicking the cost can down the road" stated or implied. Both of these actions by politicians are essentially stealing, which is a sin in all religions.

Interestingly in Judaism, Christianity, and Islam there are teachings, (for instance, Christian commandments #8 and #10), that explicitly forbid stealing and coveting. Yet many career politicians find breaking two commandments to be "the right thing to do."

Politicians exploit our religious charitable beliefs, using blame, divide-to-conquer wedges, "Isn't it awful?" and many other games and tricks to convince us that they have the moral high ground. They frequently say with great moral authority that they are "doing the right thing," implying they are satisfying some religious calling. Many politicians seem comfortable with coveting what many have worked hard to earn, taking the earnings from them and others, and indebting those not yet born to achieve their political objectives.

When religious expectations are not met, feelings of *guilt* often set in— another tactic exploited by the career politician. This religious twist is often used with the religious *charitable* twist. One dominant guilt feeling often used is an accusation of discrimination, whether it be in regard to race, gender, or sexual orientation. Discrimination is considered to be morally wrong in most, but not all, religions, depending upon the topic. We are being manipulated using guilt by the cries of discrimination whenever certain problems are discussed. For example, when inner-city or immigration problems and solutions are discussed, those who oppose the solutions cry discrimination or racism. They rely on the religious view that all people are created equal to invoke guilt feelings and avoid any action. Discrimination or racism has helped elect and re-elect many politicians, so keeping guilty feelings before the public is often more important to the politicians than finding rational solutions to problems. Why are those who literally break the laws by not entering our country legally not held to the same standard? The answer is found in guilty feelings experienced when others use the cry of racism. There are a lot of laws many of us would like to ignore, but know we would pay a penalty for doing so.

I am not an expert on religion, but I was raised as a Christian and am comfortable in saying that Christ's fundamental teaching is about individual responsibility and accountability with regard to how people should relate to each other. He was not a community-organizer socialist, progressive, or Marxist who attacked the government or other religions. He acknowledged the Roman government, rather than leading a rebellion against it. Christ did not advocate that the government should use taxes to implement his philosophy. Indeed his beliefs in individual responsibility, accountability, and freedom are reflected in *The Constitution of the United States.*

Later I will show that less than one half of the population (excluding public employees) pays income taxes. Does this mean that more than one half of our citizens are charity cases? Should we feel guilty that these people do not make more? Is balance possible when less than one half of the citizens of the nation carry the rest of the citizens? These and similar questions are what we need to ask ourselves whenever a politician tries to use a religious twist by asking for charity that results in guilt.

The bottom line is that our religious beliefs are being manipulated and corrupted by clever career politicians. We all need to rationally look at present and potential future problems and reset our priorities while keeping in mind the intent and impacts of our religious beliefs and how politicians try to exploit them. We cannot afford to address every one of the world's problems and every politician's causes. Let's provide charity as we feel we can and want to, but let's stop letting politicians lead us using their tricks to fund *their* causes.

Chant: Who pays? No coveting or stealing.

The Feds Versus Commoners
(What is good for average citizens is not good enough for the Feds)

While not a trick, *per se*, there is a continuing theme in Congress and many of our state legislatures that what's good for the goose, is *only* good for the goose. For example, congressmen can fly around in private jets, and can even buy brand-spanking new ones, even though they criticize those in the business world who do the same (remember the CEOs of the "Big Three" auto companies?). Congress does the same thing as the CEOs but with money they forcibly take from us. At least businesses spend money they earn by selling people something they want.

Congress excludes itself from laws that affect all of us, and federal employees are also frequently given special treatment. Congress does this by exempting itself from many of the laws the rest of us must follow. Some say congressmen are exempt from the "Ten Commandments." Some politicians apparently feel they are exempt from some of them. In addition to coveting and stealing, many are good at marital cheating and even crimes. *"Congress would exempt itself from the laws of gravity if it could,"* said Illinois congressman Henry Hyde.[10]

Congress has exempted itself from a broad array of laws covering civil rights, minimum wages, and safety requirements and discrimination.[11] They have exempted themselves from Equal-Opportunity and Affirmative-Action laws, Occupational Safety and Health Association (OSHA) regulations, the Freedom of Information Act and the Privacy Act, and much of the Ethics in Government Act, to name a few. And, many more exemptions exist or are being added all the time.

During the health care debate, President Obama promised that under his health-care proposal *"you'll be able to get the same kind of coverage that members of Congress give themselves."*[12] He repeated this statement several times. One instance was in June 2009 when President Obama repeated that promise in a speech to the American Medical Association. This statement is simply not true. The President barnstormed the nation, urging swift approval of legislation, which has now been passed by Congress. This legislation, that will likely push Americans into stingy insurance plans with tight, HMO-style controls, specifically exempts members of Congress (along with federal employees).

Members of Congress *"enjoy the widest selection of health plans in the country,"* according to the U.S. Office of Personnel

Management. They *"can choose from among consumer-driven and high deductible plans that offer catastrophic risk protection with higher deductibles, health saving/reimbursable accounts and lower premiums, or fee-for-service (FFS) plans, and their preferred provider organizations (PPO), or health maintenance organizations (HMO)."*[13] These choices would be nice for all of us, but they're not in the offering. Instead, if you don't enroll in a "qualified" health plan and submit proof of enrollment to the federal government, you will be fined. Knowing what they have all sounds good, but all politicians know the average citizen will not have the "Cadillac" plans and coverage available to members of Congress. They did not lie, we *deserve* a plan as good as theirs, but we will not get one.

For a health plan to count as "qualified," it has to meet all the restrictions listed in the legislation and whatever criteria the Secretary of Health and Human Services imposes after the bill becomes law. You may think you're in a "qualified" plan, but the language suggests only plans with managed-care controls will meet that definition.

Defenders of congressional exemptions point out that legislators face special pressures: they often need to employ home-district personnel or friends of supporters. Stanley Brand, a former general counsel to the House of Representatives, says Congress historically has not placed itself under the yoke of various laws to protect itself from inter-government conflicts. Imagine, he says, the Justice Department using charges of job discrimination to harass unfriendly congressmen. Besides, "the reality of going before the voters and seeking election should force congressmen to behave," he says. Unfortunately, since the election advantages strongly favor incumbents, they do not have to behave very well![14]

Also, health care and retirement benefits for federal employees are generally much better than what we commoners have. Yet, federal employees are seldom laid-off due to a shortage of funds or for any other reasons that would force the private sector to lay off workers. So why should Congress and federal employees get these outstanding benefits? The answer is because Congress can do it with your money! We should be outraged that this continues.

Chant: No more federal perks!

Politicians' Subtle Psychological Tricks Summary Bullets

✪ Subtler, less well-known tricks include Risk Aversion and Outrage, Adversary Truths and Legalese, Religious Twists, and Feds Versus Commoners.

✪ Subtle psychological tricks generally work on our deep-seated emotions and beliefs, a general lack of knowledge of our own personal concerns and preferences, or common misperceptions of the facts resulting from repeated misleading statements by career politicians.

Chapter 6:
Politicians' Financial Tricks

Government is the great fiction, through which everybody endeavors to live at the expense of everybody else.[1] — **Frederic Bastiat**

In this chapter, we will look at several financial or money-related distortions and tricks our career politicians use to get us to believe they have the "right cost" answers. Most of the time the financial tricks are not lies, but certainly they are "adversarial truths." Unless we challenge our politicians, we can expect more of the same in the future.

The financial tactical tricks used by politicians are often used together with psychological tricks. To get started, the next time you hear a politician use the words "billion" or "trillion" in a casual manner, think about whether you want that politician spending *your* money. A billion or a trillion are difficult numbers to comprehend, so let's put these figures into some perspective:

- ✪ A billion seconds ago was 1978.
- ✪ About a billion minutes ago Jesus was alive.
- ✪ A billion hours ago our modern human ancestors were just starting to evolve.

- ✪ A billion days ago the earth was undergoing an ice age.
- ✪ Given the rate our federal government is spending a billion dollars (about $10.5 billion per day), it takes politicians only a fraction of a day to spend one billion dollars.[2]
- ✪ About 1,600 billion or 1.6 trillion days ago the collapse of a giant "particle" cloud initiated the formation of our solar system.
- ✪ The U.S. budget and deficit forecasts for 2010 are a $3.55 trillion budget with a $1.42 trillion deficit.[3]/[4] We have in one year borrowed the equivalent of about one dollar per day since the formation of our sun, planets and other objects in our solar system.

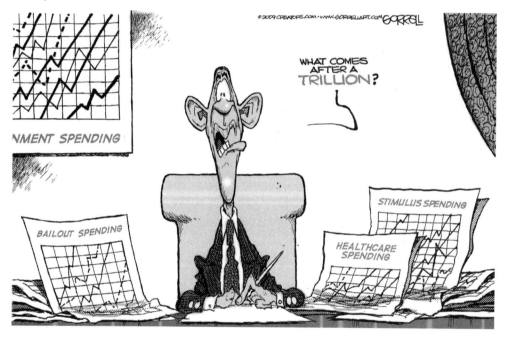

Free Money

A government which robs Peter to pay Paul can always depend on the support of Paul.[5]— **George Bernard Shaw**

All of us like free money! As we've already discussed, free money is cash, goods and/or services received that have not (yet) been earned. Like all things in life, some free money is good, but too much is bad. Let's look at free money topics and discuss why they are important to understand and control. Examples of voluntary or involuntary free money include money for those unable to earn money due to physical or mental disabilities (good), for long-term "welfare" paid to physically and mentally fit individuals without requiring any action in return (bad), and for illegal immigrants in the forms of emergency health care, education, and other services (bad).

Governments and individuals borrow money with the promise to pay the money back in the future, plus a profit. Borrowing for *investments* expected to result in increased value over time is not free money as defined here. Unfortunately, the money borrowed by our government can be considered free money since it does *not* increase in value over time.

Free money (for the government) comes from taxpayers and from foreign and U.S. citizen investor "loans." A monetary return or profit is expected by those who *loan* the money but it is free money for the government. So, what are the problems with this system? The first problem is that over time a smaller percentage of our citizens are paying federal, state, and local taxes, while we have an increasing number of handouts, bailouts, entitlements, and other expenditures adding to our debts. The second problem is that investors, particularly foreign ones, may decide to invest elsewhere. This decline in available free money may result in a significant financial system failure.

Types of free money are described below. We start with a few types of free money that are reasonable and continue with many types of free money that adversely impact our nation.

Voluntary

Money, monetary items, or services voluntarily provided by an individual or a charity is free money (under my definition). "Charities" include charitable foundations, religious organizations, and other voluntary, tax-free entities. Voluntarism is an excellent example of the American spirit and generosity. All of us should be proud of this kind of free money. Money voluntarily given is the only free money that is truly free.

Disasters

Money, monetary items, or services voluntarily given to people to overcome unforeseen disasters is free money (under my definition). Like voluntarism, disaster relief is another excellent example of the American spirit and generosity. All of us should be proud of this free money provided it is truly warranted and not a result of bad policies or practices.

Disasters may be natural or man-made. Most natural disasters such as hurricanes, earthquakes, floods, tornados, volcanic eruptions, or landslides are known to occur in various regions around the world and these hazards have existed for centuries. Plans and mitigating practices, that are frequently inadequate, are in place for most of these hazards. Free money support for these infrequent events is reasonable and should be provided quickly for maximum effectiveness.

Potential man-made disasters are too numerous to mention, but plans and mitigating practices are often but not always in place for these hazards. We should be particularly sensitive to free money spending for these types of disasters. The housing-driven financial crisis is one man-made example where bad government planning and management was a leading cause, but let's briefly discuss three other examples: the British Petroleum (BP) Company oil spill, failed government policies and systems, and the Hurricane Katrina impact on New Orleans. Comparing these examples will illustrate why being vigilant is important.

The BP Company had made plans to mitigate the spill but the plans were inadequate. The impact on individuals, families, and businesses was massive and demanded rapid actions. Appropriately, the government stepped in to help. The BP

Company took the technical and financial initiative to stop the leak and has started to compensate for losses of those affected. So long as the BP Company continues to be accountable and to compensate for losses, the use of taxpayer free money should be limited. Time will tell if this will continue, but holding those responsible for their man-made disasters is the model that should be used throughout our nation.

In contrast to the BP example, those politicians and government leaders responsible for the financial disasters caused by failed government policies and systems, as we shall see later, are not held accountable. Instead, free money from taxpayers is used for the bailout. Politicians frequently develop bad systems, implement bad laws and policies, fail to oversee the results of their actions, and then lay blame on others for any failures. This is a very poor use of free money yet politicians continue to scare, mislead, and seduce the public into accepting their stories. Politicians need to be held accountable, too.

Hurricane Katrina and its impact on New Orleans is an example of a disaster where the lack of *long-term* planning and policies was and is continuing to be a significant contributor to the crisis. New Orleans is a major port and the largest metropolitan area in Louisiana with a population of about 1.2 million. New Orleans is on average 1.5 to 3.0 meters (4.9 to 9.8 feet) below sea level and is sinking. Tall levees to the north and south keep the Mississippi River and Lake Pontchartrain from pouring into the center of the city. An intricate system of pumping stations and canals keep the land dry. Global sea-level rise is projected to accelerate two- to four-fold during the next century, increasing storm surge (to heights of more than twelve feet above sea levels) and shoreline retreat along low-lying areas in southeastern Louisiana. The combination of sea level rise and continued subsidence (sinking) will result in New Orleans being 2.5 to 4.0 meters (8.2 to 13.1 feet) below sea level by 2100.[6]

These facts about New Orleans coupled with the fact that major hurricanes are a way of life for New Orleans suggests cost effective long-term solutions are needed to minimize future disasters. In particular, how many billions of dollars should be spent to reinstate the status quo verses being spent to relocate many of those living underwater? Interestingly, this was not a significant part of the disaster discussions. The median asking price of a New Orleans Home is $174,900.[7] If ten billion - about ten percent of the costs to date – were spent on homes located above sea level this would pay for fifty seven thousand homes or about twenty-one percent of the total homes lost.[8] Later we will see that long-term solutions may be good for the nation, but are seldom useful to help career politicians be re-elected in the short-term. So politicians throw free money at the immediate problem only to have the problem reoccur again later as this example suggests. We need to hold politicians accountable if they fail to consider long-term solutions.

Government Borrowing

Government borrowing takes on many forms. The dominant ones are national debt, state and local debt, and entitlements. These monies some of us receive (or are spent by the federal, state, and local governments) are obtained through government borrowing and must be paid back by us or by future generations. Unfortunately, given the massive and growing debt, every government bailout, negative tax payment, war, welfare payment, entitlement payout, etc., is (at least in part) borrowed free money.

National Debt

The U.S. government incurs debt by issuing *treasuries* (bills, notes, and bonds) for unfunded entitlements (such as Social Security, Medicare, and similar obligations). Unfunded Social Security and Medicare obligations alone total over $40 trillion.[9] These are obligations not mentioned or considered when quoting the national debt.

As of August 2010, the total outstanding national debt, exclusive of mandated entitlements, is over $13.4 trillion[10] and is increasing at approximately seven percent per year. With unfunded entitlements, our debt totals between $40 trillion and $100 trillion— depending upon what is included. In December 2010, a $1.1 trillion omnibus bill covering everything except national defense and health care was passed. A large part of the bill will be paid through borrowing. The bill includes:

- ✪ Ten percent increases for programs under congressional control (i.e., exclusive of entitlements).
- ✪ Over 5,000 pork barrel projects totaling $3.9 billion. For the 535 House and Senate members this averages about ten pork barrel projects, amounting to over $7 million for each member of the House and Senate. Pork for politicians is alive and well!
- ✪ A two-percent pay raise for federal employees even though since inflation is zero they were not entitled to receive pay increases.

Again, this shows that even in a recession with high unemployment, politicians do not care about the debt despite what they may say. National debt and entitlements are potentially very serious and could lead to a new Great Depression.

Entitlements

Entitlements are federal programs guaranteeing a certain level of benefits to persons or groups who meet requirements, which have been set by law. Thus there is less discretion by Congress on how much money to appropriate, and some entitlements carry permanent appropriations. The most important examples of entitlement programs at the national level in the United States include Social Security, Medicare and Medicaid, most Veterans' Administration programs, federal employee and military retirement plans, unemployment compensation, food stamps and other welfare, and agricultural price support programs.

Entitlements are generally part free money, part Ponzi-schemes, and part slight-of-hand financial tricks by politicians. Once in place, they are politically impossible to eliminate and they generally get expanded. Let's look at Social Security as an example:

Example 6-1: Social Security — The History.

Franklin Delano Roosevelt (term of office: March 4, 1933 to April 12, 1945), a Democrat, signed the Social Security (FICA) Program into law in 1935. Under the 1935 law, what we now think of as "Social Security" only paid retirement benefits to the primary worker. A 1939 change in the law added survivors' benefits and benefits for the retiree's spouse and children. In 1956, disability benefits were added. Cost Of Living Adjustments (COLAs) were first paid in 1975 as a result of a 1972 law. Prior to this, benefits were increased irregularly by special acts of Congress. Originally President Roosevelt promised:

1. Participation in the Social Security program would be completely voluntary. (In 2010, this is mandatory for almost everyone.)
2. The participants would only have to pay one percent of the first $1,400 of their annual incomes into the program. (In 2009, an employee and his or her employer each pay 6.2 percent on up to $106,800 of income, self-employed workers pay 12.4 percent for Social Security, which does not include the additional payments for Medicare.)
3. Funds put into the program would be deductible from income for tax purposes each year. (So far this promise has not been broken, but if your income exceeds a certain amount, you do not get your full Social Security amount. In many cases, this is the same or worse than being taxed.)
4. The money the participants put in would go into the Independent Social Security "Trust Fund," rather than into the Federal General Operating Fund and, therefore, would only be used to fund the Social Security Retirement Program and

no other government program. (Funds are now part of the General fund.)

5. The annuity payments to the retirees would never be taxed as income. (Now, even if you paid into FICA for many years, your Social Security check is, or will be, taxed. The amount of tax depends upon your income from other sources.)

Looking only at promises three and four, the following is a listing of when, how, and who reneged on these promises:

✪ Dwight David Eisenhower (term of office: January 20, 1953 to January 20, 1961), a Republican, was president in 1958 when Congress voted to remove the funds from the Social Security Fund and put them into the General Fund for Congress to spend. Congress's logic at the time was that there was so much money in the Independent Social Security Fund that it would never run out or be used up for the intended purposes.

✪ Lyndon Baines Johnson (term of office: November 22, 1963 to January 20, 1969), a Democrat, actually took the Independent Social Security "Trust Fund" and put the funds into the General Fund for Congress to spend.

✪ James Earl Carter, Jr. (term of office: January 20, 1977 to January 20, 1981), a Democrat, decided to start giving annuity payments to all immigrants, so that, at age 65, they would receive Social Security even though many had not paid in a dime.

✪ William Jefferson Clinton (term of office: January 20, 1993 to January 20, 2001), a Democrat, and the Democrat-controlled Congress behind him, voted to tax Social Security, with Vice President Albert Arnold Gore casting the tie-breaking vote as President of the Senate.

Government leaders like to assume that continuing population and Gross Domestic Product (GDP) growth will allow payments for all future entitlements. For example, Social Security funds are paid to retirees, while being funded by those still working and/or through borrowing. In the financial world, this might be called a Ponzi scheme. How will we pay for Social Security if our growth slows or the number of payers decreases? History and population projections indicate that in 1945 there were 41.9 people paying into Social Security for each person receiving Social Security benefits. In 2009, that number dropped to approximately 3.3 people paying in for each person, and - by 2025 - the ratio will be approximately two to one. The Ponzi scheme is about to end but in this case no one is going to jail.[11],[12]

All entitlements, including Social Security, evolve similarly. They start out well-intentioned with relatively fair contributions by all, but quickly expand to the point where they are ultimately paid for through borrowed money and progressive taxation. Entitlements are approved for enactment because they offer free money for a significant number of our citizens. Unfortunately, all entitlements significantly change their funding priorities over time. All of them are funded by at least some borrowed funds.

Pressures are always present to expand or create new entitlements. Some citizens feel they are entitled to cash, goods, and/or services (perceived entitlements) simply because they are citizens. This is a false assumption, and is destructive to our society. Welfare that pays people who *can* work but *choose not to* falls into this category of a perceived entitlement. Welfare and other free money impact our economy and social values in many ways. Initially, potential investment funds are taken out of the market, decreasing jobs and wealth growth. We lose the productivity of those who can work, and the self-worth of those receiving the money declines, as does the public perception of them. We will explore later how the social consequences of this system are problematic. Why haven't our politicians worked on this problem? Providing free money is easier, buys more votes and power, and, of course, the money they are spending is yours - not theirs.

The extent to which every entitlement is required or earned needs to be carefully considered. Also problematic is that most entitlements have succumbed to progressive taxation. Too much progressive taxation will result in an unstable capitalistic system that may change our nation into a socialistic state. Unfortunately, a number of political tricks are in play and our political leaders likely are not telling us the whole truth.

States' Borrowing

Many state governments have fallen into the free money pit as well. California is a classic example. California has the tenth largest governmental economy in the world and the largest state economy in the United States. As of 2008, California's GDP was about $1.85 trillion which is thirteen percent of that of the United States GDP, while California has approximately twelve percent of the U.S. population. State and local government debt is estimated at over $340 billion (eighteen percent of the state's GDP)[13] and, unlike the federal government, California cannot print money. This amounts to over $9,000 more debt for each Californian, which will be added to their national debt load. In addition, the unfunded state employee pensions liabilities amount to $500 billion.[14] This is in addition to California's overall debt and is sinking counties and cities throughout the state.

When my wife and I came to California in 1963, the K-12 schools, state colleges, public universities, roads, weather, and many other features were great. The weather is still great. Everything else is in trouble. In 2009, California was ranked dead last by CEOs for business, 48th in business tax climate,[15] and a state report indicated regulations on small businesses cost about $500 billion, resulting in the loss of 3.8 million jobs.[16] California has the highest sales tax of the 50 states and has the second highest (and progressive) income taxes.

Free money and many system failures are bringing down California. Simply stated, a long-term lack of political balance has led to runaway public service employee growth far in excess of population growth and inflation, many forms of new public spending, over-compensated public employee unions, excessive public employee pensions, heavy taxation, and a high and quickly-growing debt. Within three years, approximately ten percent of the state's budget will be required to cover the debt burden. [17]

The standard state of California political leaders' budget mode of operation - independent of whether the governor is a Democrat or a Republican - has been the same. The state's constitution requires the governor propose a budget by January 10th that balances estimated revenues against expenditures. The constitution requires the legislature to approve a budget by June 15th. For many years the large majority of democratic politicians have rejected the governor's proposal without any suggested alternatives other than raising taxes, borrowing, or using financial tricks such as taking away funds normally allotted to counties and cities. For example, in 2010, the legislative leaders said, in essence "you've got to be kidding" to the budget proposed by Gov. Schwarzenegger. Republicans oppose higher taxes and borrowing and a two-thirds majority vote is required to raise taxes. The Democrats do not quite have a two-thirds majority, so they blame the Republicans for the fiscal problems. So June 15th is the start of the budget wars that continue well beyond the state's constitutional deadline until a near total meltdown occurs and some compromise is established

It is unclear how California will resolve its troubles. Major political changes or another federal bailout may be required. Unfortunately, the state is, and has been, controlled by one party, even though an occasional governor from the other party has been elected. Even so, all governors have been essentially powerless. There is nothing that looks likely to improve the balance. The dominant party came into power by doling out massive amounts of free money, catering to social groups and unions, and using many political tricks to accomplish their "successes." They have bought enough votes to assure their control for the foreseeable future unless Californians realize what is happening to them.

Personal Borrowing

Individuals or families may borrow money, either against an asset or by using a credit card, but they must pay the loan back in the future. If this money is spent based on a rational expectation of a future increase in value, then the money spent is an investment and is not free money. If the money is *not* an investment, then the money is being borrowed simply to "keep up with the neighbors" type of reasons.

Never spend your money before you have it.[18]— **Thomas Jefferson**

Given the free money recklessness of our federal, state, and local governments, it is not surprising that individuals do the same thing. All too often when the borrower of this free money is unable to make the payments, the debt is paid by others who have been willing to earn before spending their money. The housing crisis is a recent example where all taxpayers are contributing to a few homeowners who - for various reasons - have financially overextended themselves.

A root cause of this borrowing is the fact that many individuals lack any knowledge of basic financial processes and risks. Borrowing makes buying designer tennis shoes or expensive toys easy. All one needs to do is hand the clerk a credit card. Unfortunately, this root cause indicates a weakness in our educational system (which will be discussed later).

"Legal" Bribes

When the people find that they can vote themselves money, that will herald the end of the republic.[19]— **Ben Franklin**

A bribe is certainly free money. Free money is frequently doled out or promised by politicians, and/or written into laws that favor large groups of their constituents with the intention of garnering their votes. Politicians also take "campaign" money from individuals and corporations (acting alone or through lobbyists) in return for their votes on legislation. As part of the political process, money and favors are also traded among politicians. The key question is: When is the line crossed between horse trading or bargaining and committing a "legal" bribe? Our politicians are often so far beyond that line they cannot even see it.

While "robbing Peter to pay Paul" makes sense for those truly unfortunate who, physically or mentally, cannot take care of themselves, a law that results in taking money from hard-working, risk-taking people and giving this money to others who choose to not work as hard or take the same risks is not fair and is a direct contradiction to our Founding Fathers' trait for personal responsibility and their principle of individual rights.

Examples of these actions include selective tax relief for specific businesses, excessive public employee retirement programs, and laws favoring public employees and public unions resulting in advantages to their employees over those in the private sector. Here are the facts:

- Hundreds of corporations have contributed heavily to selected politicians and have gotten tax relief for their corporations. If this occurred in a foreign country we would call it a bribe.
- Many of the entitlement programs and assistance programs are used to garner votes and some are abused, but no action is taken. If this occurred in a foreign country we would call it vote buying.
- Public employee job loss risks are low, public retirement programs and union labor costs generally exceed similar private sector costs. The funds for these public employees come from taxpayers and the easy way out for politicians is to yield to public employee demands. Politicians use your money to ob-

tain votes and to be sure they will be treated well by public employees. This is wasteful and is unfair to private sector employees. If this occurred in a foreign country we would call it vote buying.

✪ Political horse-trading such as committing to provide free coverage of Medicare increases forever to a state for a senator's vote on the Health Care Bill is a classic example of using taxpayer money to buy a congressman's vote. Is this horse-trading or a bribe? I believe this horse-trading is as bad as or worse than those stated above. If this occurred in a foreign country we would call it a bribe.

The evidence is clear that free money is used to buy votes and the process seems to be working for the politicians. We are at the point where about one half of U.S. households pay income taxes to the government. The government uses a large portion of these taxes as free money to buy off the other half of the population. While our Founding Fathers understood the need to bargain and compromise, they probably did not see today's "legal" bribes situation coming and would not have approved of it. How long can this continue? If only ten percent (or even thirty percent) of the population pays for the government and the rest of us take free money, do you believe the nation will survive? We need to stop the bribes.

The bottom line is that we have become a free money society where much of the free money is borrowed. Continuing to borrow and accumulate debt is not sustainable. We had better wake up soon or we will become a socialist country.

Chant: No free money!

Number Manipulations
"Rate Versus Total" and "Low Versus High"

A set of tricks frequently used by politicians and other leaders involves carefully selecting words they use to provide estimates or numbers that suit their interests. If we do not listen closely, we can be misled by what is said.

One set of tricks used is to use the word "rate" instead of "total." For example, when we hear the "rate" of unemployment has declined or the "rate" of the national debt is decreasing this does *not* mean the total unemployment or debt has declined; indeed the "totals" have continued to increase but are simply doing so more slowly. A clearer – and more correct - statement would be to say, "Unemployment is growing at a *slower rate* (than last year)."

A second set of tricks is the use of a "low" or "high" estimate of costs. Any credible group asked to estimate costs that have any uncertainty will provide a range of costs. This type of estimating is generally true for state and federal agencies. For example, a new law may be estimated to have a savings ranging from $100 billion to $300 billion depending upon the assumptions used, and have an expected (or "best guess") savings value of $125 billion. Politicians typically only discuss one of the three numbers. They might say "save $300 billion" for this example if they favor the law and "save $100 billion" if they oppose it. President Obama and others used this approach when discussing the savings estimated for the Health Care Bill. A more "transparent" approach would be to give the actual stated *range* of the estimates. As pointed out earlier, for the Health Care Bill, ten-year estimates were used to show a savings.

Obviously the reasons these tricks are used are to mislead, misdirect, or confuse us into believing something. Politicians are not lying when they use these tricks, but full transparency does not serve their political agenda. So what should you listen for to get clues to the real issues? Any time a leader mentions a "rate," ask yourself the meaning in terms of the "total." Any time a leader uses a phrase like "up to," "as little (or as much) as," or similar phrases, ask what the range of values is; often the differences are several times more (or less) than the number stated. Do not let politicians try to define success as the "slowing of failure," or as an improvement in the rate of decline.

Chant: Numbers do lie!

Kick the Can Down the Road (KCDR)

This phrase is a take-off of an old children's game, "kick the can." The longer "kick the can down the road" (KCDR) version is commonly used as a delaying strategy, or a means of buying time for a problem. The hope is that the problem will go away or be addressed by somebody else. Politicians use KCDR in several ways. First, borrowing money to be paid by future generations is a KCDR process. Second, Ponzi-like schemes such as Social Security are KCDR processes since the number of workers paying into the fund has dropped from the initial forty to three for each person receiving Social Security money. Third, outgoing administrations frequently KCDR to pass unresolved issues on to the new administrations.

A fourth subtler, but important, KCDR is to pass costs or resource requirements to other lower-tier governments. This trick is often played by administrations and Congress, and sometimes by the states. Politicians simply pass a law requiring some lower-tier government actions without providing sufficient funding to meet the requirements. This happened with the new Health Care Bill. Total state costs were not considered in the cost calculation presented by its federal supporters. Nevertheless, states will pay out more than the federal government provides. The big advantage to the federal politicians is that they look like they are spending less, or using fewer employees, but it is just another trick to fool us.

The number of federal employees has held about even for some time, while lower-tier government employees have continuing to increase. Many of these increases are a result of federal KCDR to lower-tier governments. When states are required to spend resources, they have to either increase taxes, or pass down the costs of the required actions down to counties and cities. Guess who is at the bottom of this chain: we citizens.

Chant: Kick the can — no you can't!

Inflation and Progressive Taxation

Inflation

A common trick used by our politicians is to take advantage of the fact that progressive taxes are rarely tied to inflation. We seniors remember when gasoline was about ten cents per gallon, a hot dog was about ten cents, a car was $850, and a new house was $3,920. We never dreamed that today's prices would ever happen, but they did thanks to inflation and improvements in productivity. When we are told taxing the rich will be used to pay for something, most of us think, "I am not included." This is true if the taxes are inflation-adjusted, but few of our federal, state, or local taxes are inflation-adjusted. Even lower-wage earners are impacted as they move into higher income and other progressive tax brackets over time. Most progressive taxes such as income taxes have several tax brackets, the first of which is relatively low. For 2010, taxation starts at $8,375 for singles and $16,750 for married couples filing jointly. Let's look at the high threshold level health care tax and top-level income tax brackets being debated that would affect the "rich" or "wealthy" to see the impact of inflation on progressive taxes. Let's answer the question: When will you be rich or wealthy enough to have to pay these new taxes?

Example 6-2: Health Care and Income Taxes

One source of funding for health care is to increase taxes on "rich" individuals making more than $200,000 per year (or $250,000 for couples filing jointly). These same dollar levels are being debated for the top income bracket for the "wealthy." Since most of us earn much less than this amount, we tend to say, "I will not be affected" and move on to the next issue. Let's look at history and see how soon you, or you and your spouse, might be making $200,000 and $250,000, respectively.

The history of the average wages (and their percentage increase) has been listed and modeled using Social Security Administration data from 1951 through 2008 by Political Calculations.[20] These past and estimated future numbers for the end of each decade are shown from 1960 through 2060 in **Table 6-1: Average U.S. Wages by Decade.** Future estimates were calculated by averaging two rate numbers. The first rate number of fifty-six percent per decade is the average wage data by decade from1960 through 2010. The second number of forty-five percent per decade is the predicted average using the Political Calculations model. In **Table 6-1** future decades were calculated using fifty percent (an annual rate of 4.138 percent) as a reasonable estimate compromise. Actual rates in the future will depend upon inflation, productivity improvements, and other factors.

Table 6-1: Average U.S. Wages by Decade

Decade End Year	Average Wage	Decade Rate (%) increase	Decade End Year	Estimated Average Wage	Decade Rate (%) Assumption
1960	$3,744	15.5	2020	$64,629	50.0
1970	$6,307	68.4	2030	$96,943	50.0
1980	$12,393	96.5	2040	$145,414	50.0
1990	$20,863	68.3	2050	$218,121	50.0
2000	$31,065	48.9	2060	$327,182	50.0
2010	$43,086	38.7			

If you are not making $200,000 now should you worry? *YES!* Working the math backwards allows us to determine how many years it will take until you (or you and your spouse) to reach the $200,000 and $250,000 tax brackets. Let's see what happens if you now make the average $43,086, or $50,000, $75,000, $100,000, $150,000, or $200,000, and file your taxes either as a single or as a joint couple. **Table 6-2: Tax Rate Changes for Progressive Taxation** shows what year - and how many years from 2009 until - these present incomes will reach the $200,000 and $250,000 income tax brackets.

Table 6-2: Estimated Tax Rate Changes for Progressive Taxation

Present Wages for Single or Couple	Approximate Year at $200,000 for Single	Approximate Year at $250,000 for Couple	Approximate Years to $200,000 for Single	Approximate Years to $250,000 for Couple
$43,086	2048	2053	38	43
$50,000	2044	2050	34	40
$75,000	2034	2040	24	30
$100,000	2027	2033	17	23
$150,000	2017	2023	7	13
$200,000	2010	2016	0.0	6

Table 6-2 shows a single taxpayer earning $100,000 in 2010 will reach the $200,000 tax bracket in seventeen years, and a couple earning $100,000 will reach the $250,000 tax bracket in twenty-three years. Based on these and the other examples in **Table 6-2**, you can estimate when you will reach the higher tax brackets. For example, if you now make $125,000, you will reach $200,000, in about ten years. You will be considered "rich" and "wealthy" and pay more health care and income taxes even though you may be doing the same job.

So, before you jump to the conclusion that you will not have an income that will require paying health care taxes, higher income taxes or any other progressive taxes, you should determine:

✪ How long you are going to work?
✪ What will your inflation-adjusted retirement income be?
✪ Do you believe you will do better or worse than the historical averages with regard to income increases?

✪ What will your spouse and you together make now, and possibly in the future?

Two things well known to every politician are evident in this. First, taxes, particularly progressive income taxes (and the taxes on business profits discussed earlier), are great cash cows. "Tax the rich or wealthy" is good for generating votes since the perception is that those paying the taxes can afford them, but you may soon be in the "rich" and "wealthy" category. Second, the fact that inflation quickly moves middle and lower-income persons into ever-higher tax brackets is good for politicians. The example shows that our politicians have played us as suckers for years. Perhaps we must demand all taxes be tied to inflation.

Progressive Taxation

Progressive taxation is a system of taxation by which the tax rate increases as the taxable amount increases. The term is most frequently associated with personal income taxes, where people with more income pay a higher percentage of income tax than those with less income. It also applies to the adjustment of tax bases, such as tax exemptions or credits, or a sales tax on luxury goods (goods which are not basic necessities).

Many tax laws are not accurately indexed to inflation. In a progressive tax system, failure to index the brackets to inflation eventually results in more taxes since wages increased due to inflation move individuals into higher tax brackets with higher percentage rates. One example of a tax not indexed to inflation in the United States is the Alternative Minimum Tax. A large number of upper-middle-income taxpayers have been finding themselves subject to this tax each year. The great visibility of this tax and public outrage has forced politicians to periodically increase the dollar amount where this tax kicks in.

Some history of personal income taxation is relevant to our discussion. Prior to the adoption of the 16th amendment to *The U.S.*

Constitution in 1913, the federal government was constrained from directly taxing personal income by Article 1, Section 9 of *The U.S. Constitution*, which reads as follows: *"No Capitation, or other direct, Tax shall be laid, unless in Proportion to the Census or Enumeration herein before directed to be taken."* A careful reading of this clause reveals the federal government actually could levy a personal income tax (which is a direct tax) prior to the 16th amendment, but income tax collection had to be in apportionment to population, in other words, only if each person paid the same amount.

The 16th amendment negated the apportionment clause written in Article 1, Section 9. The 16th amendment reads as follows: *"The Congress shall have the power to lay and collect taxes on incomes, from whatever sources derived, without apportionment among the several States, and without regard to any census or enumeration."* The 16th amendment was passed by Congress on July 2, 1909, and ratified on February 3,1913.

Congress's option to levy a federal income tax does not itself imply that government will grow, but only that government has another source of revenue on which to finance growth. It must be noted, however, that the U.S. government growth during the past 100 years since the passage of the 16th amendment to *The U.S. Constitution* has been significant. The growth of both the U.S. federal government, as well as state and local governments, has increased taxes dramatically.

Several tax growth theories can be divided into two categories: citizen-driven demand, and government-driven demand.

Citizen-driven demand growth includes voters:

✪ Deciding what the government should provide or correct (e.g., homeland security and health coverage for those unable to work)
✪ How wealth should be redistributed (e.g., progressive taxation)

✪ The merits of special interest groups (e.g., public employee unions, Sierra Club, the National Organization of Women, and the National Rifle Association) arguments

Government-driven growth includes:

✪ Leaders seeking power and money (e.g., politicians)
✪ The inherent inefficiencies in the public sector
✪ The personal incentives of bureaucratic officials (e.g., for recognition and monetary rewards; not for efficiency)

The governmental growth needs to be carefully assessed and balanced against our successful economic model, capitalism. Capitalism strives for higher levels of productivity that equate to a higher level of income, and the higher income increases consumption and wellbeing. Big government does not improve productivity, and robs investment funds for idea development and job creation. Voters need to understand we cannot have government do everything for us and still continue with our way of life. Our economic system is even more important to protect in the new more-global world. Perhaps our Founding Fathers once again did understand that progressive taxes would upset the balance, and therefore, exclude them. Their wisdom was overcome by desires of later politicians with the 16th Amendment.

Chant: Adjust for inflation or no taxes!

We contend that for a nation to try to tax itself into prosperity is like a man standing in a bucket and trying to lift himself up by the handle.[21]
— **Winston Churchill**

Government: Cheaper or Better

The only thing that saves us from the bureaucracy is inefficiency. An efficient bureaucracy is the greatest threat to liberty.[22] — **Eugene McCarthy**

How many times have we heard that government can do something "more efficiently or cheaper" than the private sector? Most recently this was claimed for health care. This presumption is based on the belief that because the government "does not make a profit," they can do things more efficiently. History shows us governments exploit their national resources and people, sometimes through wars to attain wealth (and power), but creative people who are relatively free of government controls are much more efficient in creating wealth (and jobs).

The average profit margin for corporate America over the last twenty-five years was approximately 8.3 percent[23] with slight variations depending upon the nature of the goods or serviced rendered. For example, the health insurance industry profit margin is stated as less than four percent.[24] As discussed earlier, if profits are too low, any company will go out of business since stockholders will simply invest elsewhere for better profits. Higher profits tend to attract competition, thereby controlling profits. If there is no competition, there is something wrong with the capitalist system.

So, is the government eight percent more efficient than the private sector? If so, where is the evidence? How many things are you aware of where the government is efficient? The government's efficiency claim may be proven to be true if the costs for the bureaucrats to run the program or service are not included. Certainly there are many things the government can and should do for its citizens, such as managing our national defense. These are things we cannot do as individuals and should not do through private sector businesses.

Why isn't a government-run activity more efficient than any other activity? Private businesses constantly seek to be more efficient to help them to produce more with less, which is the definition of productivity. Government employees may be as bright and as hard-working as others, but efficiency is not a major goal of bureaucrats. Government staffing is seldom rewarded, reduced, or consolidated to improve productivity and they have no competion. In addition, many of the public union employees have salaries and benefits (including medical and retirement) that exceed those in the private sector for similar jobs. Reasonably well-regulated private sector businesses can always do an effective good job for all of us and with the highest of efficiency.

You will find that the State is the kind of organization which, though it does big things badly, does small things badly, too.[25] — **John Kenneth Galbraith**

Chant: Government never cheaper or better!

Politicians' Financial Tricks Summary Bullets

- ✪ Financial tricks include Free Money, Number Manipulations, Kick the Can Down the Road, Inflation and Progressive Taxation, and Government Cheaper or Better
- ✪ Free money is cash, goods and/or services received that have not (yet) been earned. Some free money is good, but excessive government borrowing, debt, deficits, and entitlements are bad.
- ✪ Passing costs to future generations and/or down to lower tier governments is bad.
- ✪ Historically wages have increased about fifty percent per decade due to inflation and other factors.
- ✪ As wages increase individuals move into higher progressive taxes brackets and pay more taxes even though an individual may be doing the same job. This is a way politicians' obtain more tax money they can spend.
- ✪ Productivity improvement (efficiency and effectiveness) is always sought by the private sector as a means of maintaining or growing their businesses. Government workers are seldom rewarded for productivity improvement.

Tricks Game

You might want to develop a game of listening to politicians. Such a game may be more fun if played with family members or friends. It's a great way to educate yourself, your family, and your friends. Items you might include:

✪ A listing of the promises a politician makes during a speech.
✪ After the speech, ask which promises are potentially real and might be achievable or which ones are, in your opinion, simply the politician telling people what they want to hear while he or she is unlikely to do anything about them.
✪ Ask how each promise might be achieved and what obstacles (political, fiscal, constitutional, or even physical) will stand in the way.
✪ Ask about the cost and consider where the money will come from; is it free money, pay as you go, etc.
✪ Ask if this is something we, as a nation, really should do, or if it would simply be nice to do, or if you are interested because it is in your personal self-interest.
✪ Make one list of the results you expect, including the promises that are real, achievable, cost-effective, and desirable; and make another list of those promises that are just a politician telling you what you want to hear. Generally, most promises will be in the latter list.

Have fun!

PART III: THE CASUALTIES OF CAREER POLITICIANS' LEADERSHIP

Our governments have thousands of processes and functions that constitute systems[1]. Our career politicians are the architects for these systems. Now that we have knowledge of politicians' tactical tricks and modes of operation that were used to develop, oversee, and manipulate these systems, we need to understand how complex systems work and which key ones are failing or deficient. "Failing" refers to a system that is not working or is very poor, and could soon become unstable. An unstable system would significantly impact our way of life and future. "Deficient" refers to an important system that is presently "stable-but-deficient." If these systems continue down the path they are currently on, they, too, could become unstable. All systems selected for analysis are critical to the future success of our nation.

Chapter 7: Complex Systems Analysis

Chapter 8: Failing Financial System

Chapter 9: Failing Capitalistic Economic System

Chapter 10: Failing Social Systems

Chapter 11: Deficient Education and Low-Skilled Jobs Systems

Chapter 12: Deficient Corporate Compensation and News Media Systems

Chapter 7:
Complex Systems Analysis

There are many major and minor governmental systems that are vital to our nation. Furthermore, many of these systems are intertwined, so changes to any system needs to be well controlled and tested to ensure any proposed changes cause no unintended consequences. Unfortunately, our political leaders seldom consider the impacts of their system changes on other systems.

The key major national systems I think about (and what I often become concerned about within each) are:

- Socio-economic system (balance between capitalism and socialism)
- Financial system (spending and debt controls; personal responsibility versus corporate or government responsibilities)
- Labor-management system (job opportunities and creation; public versus private sector unions; management-labor teams)
- Tax system (amount, kinds, and fairness)
- Social welfare system (Welfare, Social Security and other entitlements; costs; responsibilities)

✪ Health care system (health improvement; care costs and responsibilities)
✪ Educational system (curriculum utility to nation; costs)
✪ Legal system (laws for laymen)
✪ Crime and punishment system (fairness; costs)
✪ Public communications system (value and utility to nation; fairness)
✪ U.S. Political system (failure causes; change; power balance)

… and many more others.

The intertwining of these systems is fairly obvious. Our socio-economic system is impacted by most, if not all, of the other systems. The financial, labor-management, and tax systems are the underpinnings of the socio-economic system. The social welfare, health, and educational systems are all important to the wellbeing of our society, and their costs and benefits need to be balanced against the nation's economic health since we cannot afford to do everything. Our legal, and crime and punishment systems provide stability and control of the other systems. A fair media and other forms of public communications are a vital source of information for all of us. The glue holding everything together is our political system. Most of these systems - or subsets of them – will be discussed later.

Before we start analyzing specific systems, let's address the fact that most large systems are complex, but can be explained in simple terms such as bounds, stability, oscillatory, tipping points, and feedback (loops). Understanding how complex systems work and how they are controlled teaches us why and how some systems fail.

Complex Systems Concepts Overview

Large physical and governmental systems are complex due to many possible influencing factors such as many different beliefs or perspectives, psychological and emotional factors, past experiences, world events, and scientific and economic principles. These systems, however, are generally "time varying" and "nonlinear" in nature. They have controls or "bounds" to keep them stable and if they become unstable they fail— often catastrophically. There are many examples of systems that have become unstable and failed. The Soviet Union's communist socio-economic system is one example. Our use of "greenhouse gases", including CO_2 from burning fossil fuels is an example of a potentially failing environmental system that could cause significant global warming, and could have catastrophic effects for our planet and all of its inhabitants.

Fortunately, in recent U.S. history, few systems have failed irreversibly or catastrophically. Nevertheless, many systems on which we depend are deficient and need to be changed or improved in order to avoid future failures.

I will use simple examples to help explain the system concepts of "time varying," "nonlinear," "bounded," and "feedback loops."

Time Varying Example

You turn on your TV and adjust the sound to your liking. Sometimes, however, it increases when the TV station turns up the volume for ads. This higher and lower volume over time makes your TV a time varying system. The volume is bounded by "no sound" at one end of the spectrum and the maximum sound output of your TV audio amplifier at the other. Systems variations are typically bounded and, as a consequence, a time varying system is often oscillatory, meaning that it moves up and down over time within the bounds. This example also points out that you are not in complete control of this system. The TV station has some control, too. In the same way, many of our national governmental systems are impacted by unexpected events and actions our government does not control.

Linear - Nonlinear Example

Suppose you are interested in having your house painted as quickly as possible. You check with painters and find a good one who can paint your house in 100 hours. Using linear thinking how long does it take more painters to do the job? Consider these numbers:

Number of Painters	Hours to paint — Linearity Assumed
1. Two painters	50 hours
2. 20 painters	5 hours
3. 200 painters	30 minutes
4. 2,000 painters	3 minutes

Physically 2,000 painters would not be able to simultaneously paint the house in three minutes and, most likely, 200 painters could not paint it in thirty minutes. So linear thinking does not describe plausible results because of the physical bounds of the situation. Thus, as the number of painters increases, at some point, the result becomes nonlinear since the number of painters is not proportional to the reduced time to do the painting.

Bounded Systems and "Tipping Point" Example

It is important to understand that systems without bounds fail. Most systems have man-made or natural bounds. For example, our *Constitution*, our laws, and nature's laws provide bounds. These bounds provide system stability in our governmental systems, though, deviations from our Founding Fathers' intents due to greed or other factors could lead to irreversible or even catastrophic consequences to our way of life. We need to look for clues to potential or impending failures and determine how to adjust the system before the system fails.

An incandescent light bulb is a simple physical example of a bounded system with a tipping point. If the voltage is too low, the bulb generates some heat and no visible light— but it may last for centuries. If the voltage is higher than the bulb is designed for it will burn brightly, but will fail early, if not immediately, in a flash of light. Thus, upper and lower voltage bounds are placed on power the utilities supply to customers by utility regulatory agencies.

Catastrophes may evolve from systems that becoming unstable. The dashed wiggly line in **Figure 7-1** shows a system initially oscillating between an upper bound (1st) and a lower bound (zero in this case) and, as such, it is stable. Later in time the upper bound (2nd) is moved higher and the system continues to oscillate between the bounds. One might believe it possible to keep moving the upper bound up, but there is a limit to this in all systems. At some point, the system reaction time quickens and, before a new bound can be established, a "tipping point" is reached. This tipping point can be caused by a variety of reasons either man-made or natural. When the tipping point is reached, actions to stabilize the system may not be possible and then the system will fail, perhaps catastrophically. It may either "stop" or "blow up" or something about the system may be changed forever. This, of course, can have a dangerous ripple effect on other systems, as well.

Figure 7-1: Stable System Becomes Unstable

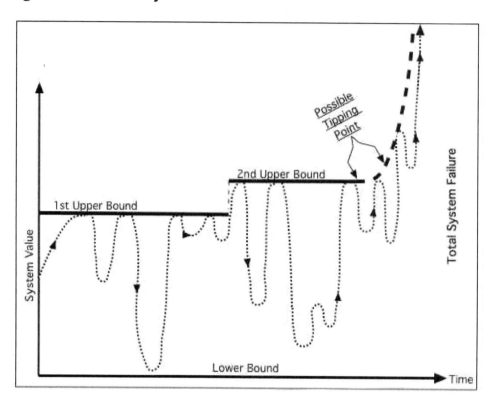

Feedback Loops Example

Simple systems such as a light bulb do not have feedback loops and must rely on some external mechanisms such as our electric power company's control of the voltage in order to function properly. Large systems, however, generally require one or more feedback loops to maintain control of the system. Feedback involves monitoring the output of the system, or some system indicators and characteristics, and using this monitored information to take actions necessary to maintain or return the system to the desired functional state. An example of this is the way feedback is designed to happen for our governmental systems as defined in *The Constitution*. Congress has the primary responsibility through its "overseer role" to monitor and correct our governmental systems. Unfortunately, Congress frequently does not do its job until after a system is in deep trouble. Instead, Congress tends to wait until a system is at the tipping point before reacting. In other words, our Congress, of mostly career politicians, is a poor feedback mechanism.

System Concepts Examples

Four brief examples are provided to show system concepts before we start analyzing our failing systems. The first example is a simple macro-level national system that uses a simplified model to show how very complex systems can be explained in simple terms. The second example explains why the Soviet Union's socio-economic system failed. The third example explains how "greenhouse gas" may cause an environmental failure. The last example is a more detailed analysis of health care that demonstrates how using the information in this and earlier chapters would have resulted in a completely different solution.

Simplified National System Example

A nation is a system comprised of a set of processes that provide goods and services to its citizens. The system input is the total of all goods and services citizens' need and want. The system output is the goods and services actually provided by the system.

The system feedback loop compares (subtracts) the actual output of goods and services produced with the goods and services citizens' need and want. If the difference is zero or a small positive or negative value, then the system is generally doing what it needs to do by providing the needed and wanted goods and services. If the difference is large and positive then the system must have the capacity (gain or amplification) to produce more goods and services to reduce the difference. Over time the nations' needs and wants change due to population increases, technological and other advances, and world events. The system must have the capacity to adapt to these changes as well. A system best able to quickly adapt to input changes must have lot of capacity.

For this simple model let's assume money is the means that provides the goods and services that citizens need and want. The national system can generate this money by taxation, sale of the nations' natural resources (assets) or borrowing, and through job creation. Jobs provide citizens with money to obtain what they need and want, and additional taxes for the national system. The money flowing in this system is either spent by the government or by individuals for goods and services.

The national system may pay citizens directly for entitlements such as for Social Security and Welfare, military service or other commitments, or for doing work sponsored by the government. In a communist or socialistic national system the government provides most of the money for the system including for new jobs, but in a capitalistic national system the private sector has a dominate role particularly in the generation of new jobs. Job generation is important for any growing national system.

If money is not adequate to allow the system to adapt to the increasing inputs then the nations' standard of living declines. As this decline starts, a nation can try to sell more of the nations' natural resources, borrow money from other nations, increase taxes, or put in place policies that foster job growth. Assets and borrowing have limits (bounds) that eventually make them no longer available. In Chapter 1 we discussed capitalistic systems and learned that per dollar spent the private sector is much more effective and efficient at producing goods and services, and jobs than the government sector. This is why the system capacity (gain) is much greater in capitalistic systems than in other systems. Excessive taxation (moving money from the private to the public sector) reduces the ability of the system to produce jobs and the system collapses (catastrophically) to a new system state unless the government takes quick often-drastic actions. (Unfortunately, history shows another way some nations have reacted is to go to war with others.)

As we will show in later chapters, the wrong policies such as excessive entitlements, borrowing, taxation of the private sector (both businesses and their employees), and other poor policies will cause our national system to collapses to a new system state.

Soviet Union's Socio-Economic Example

The Soviet Union's communist socio-economic system failed catastrophically primarily because their system was unable to compete with our Western capitalistic socio-economic system during the Cold War. The tipping point was economic because they could not match the West in war preparation expenditures. They could have saved their system by making significant changes, but they did not and perhaps could not. Their citizens had become dependent upon their government for sharing the wealth of the country and had little motivation or opportunity to work hard and take risks to get ahead. Interestingly, China (a communist country) has been willing to slowly allow capitalism to creep into its system. This has resulted in significant increases in China's wealth.

"Greenhouse Gas" Example

The concerns about "greenhouse gasses" in the atmosphere are based on many observations, studies, and computer models that suggest these gasses are deviating from what have been observed in the past and may cause global warming. The suspected cause for the deviations is fossil fuel burning by humans. Scientists are concerned a global warming tipping point may be imminent. For example, some continents have large areas of frozen permafrost (tundra). This permafrost contains vast quantities of organic matter. While frozen, the microbes (called methanogens) that would cause the decay of the organic matter are relatively inactive. Once the microbes warm up and become active they release methane, a "greenhouse gas" that is twenty times more effective at trapping heat than carbon dioxide. As the permafrost continues to warm, the microbes will cause the organic matter to decay faster and faster, thereby generating ever-larger quantities of "greenhouse gases", resulting in very fast global warming.[1] For this environmental system, the permafrost melt could be a tipping point, with potentially catastrophic consequences. Most of the current debate revolves around what needs to be done and on what timeline.

Health Care Example

All human situations have their inconveniences. We feel those of the present but neither see nor feel those of the future; and hence we often make troublesome changes without amendment, and frequently for the worse.[2] — **Benjamin Franklin**

Health care's escalating costs are another example of a failure of government leaders to act in a timely manor. The Health Care Bill also demonstrates other political tactics at work. In addition to the blame game and other tricks, politicians allowed problems in the health care system to evolve into a crisis and then used them as an opportunity to re-engineer a whole new system to their liking. Politicians chose to ignore the feedback and indicators provided to them. Most of the features now enacted to "save the health care system" could have been done under prior-existing laws by simply adding in new standards and regulations. Unfortunately, our political leaders seem to favor crisis management over logical systematic improvement. Crises allow excellent opportunities for career politicians to institute their common mode of operation for political gain.

A key stated goal of our politicians is to reduce health care costs without affecting quality. Political leaders inferred quick action was required to control costs (keep the system stable). But nothing enacted by the government is likely to lower costs or improve quality, and total costs will likely increase. There is a fundamental difference between reducing costs and simply shifting costs around, like a pea in a shell game at a carnival.

Instead of focusing on the root causes of costs or quality, the politicians' focus was primarily on those "bad guys in the insurance industry." While the insurance industry has earned some of the blame - in particular since they could have developed their own standards - the causes of the crisis are far more complex. Cost savings resulting from new regulations and standards for sharing information (some in the bill), controlling frivolous litigation (not in the bill), and other topics were not adequately addressed.

Unfortunately, the overarching goal was not the correct one. To determine the root causes, I used root cause analysis and asked myself why the costs of health care are so high. I derived many cost-related answers including a lack of personal responsibility and accountability for costs, unhealthy lifestyles, unneeded testing to avoid lawsuits, new medical procedures, drugs and equipment, and others. The "why?" root cause analysis questions lead to the conclusion that the cost of health care is a *symptom*, not a cause of the crisis. The goal should have been how to improve the health of *all* citizens.

This new goal led to three key root causes: 1) a lack of individual responsibility and accountability; 2) failure to reduce the onset of diseases (disease avoidance); and, 3) insufficient controls on lawsuits. New medical procedures, drugs, and equipment add costs, but if they improve health sufficiently we may want to pay for them, which means this is a cost-benefit issue and becomes a second-tier cause of the crisis.

Reasonable solutions for these causes exist and are doable. Below are some suggestions to get us started.

One root cause for high costs of health care is inadequate individual responsibility and accountability for our and our family's health. This can be logically addressed by requiring individuals (rather than employers) to pay for minimum standard family health insurance. After all, we require individuals to pay for minimum standard collision and liability automobile insurance for each vehicle. Employer health insurance payments now leave some employees feeling health care is a "free" entitlement. This perceived lack of ownership drives up costs. Employers who have provided health care funding for their employees should initially increase each employee's pay to compensate for their health care costs. Employers can and should continue to help employees by providing information about employee options and continuing to pay wages that reflect realistic living expenses, including health care.

The health care bill that was passed did just the opposite by requiring *more* employer payments. This "political solution" garners votes since many people do not want to be responsible or accountable, but it is not the right thing to do for individuals, families, or our nation.

The self-employed or unemployed should pay for minimum standard insurance, too. A carefully crafted assistance program should be provided to aid those who are unable to make full payments to a minimum standard health insurance plan. Some of these assistance features are in the bill.

A second root cause of high and escalating health care costs is poor lifestyle habits that result in early onset of diseases. Let's look at what kills us and see what the government might do to help us improve our living and health habits.

Centers for Disease Control data for 2006 provides the six leading causes of deaths in the U.S.A.:

All Causes: 2,426,264   (Percent of Total)

1. Heart disease 631,636   (26.0)
2. Cancer 559,888   (23.1)
3. Stroke (cerebrovascular diseases) 137,119   (5.7)
4. Chronic lower respiratory diseases 124,583   (5.1)
5. Accidents (unintentional injuries) 121,599   (5.0)
6. Diabetes   72,449   (3.0)

Major risk factors for each of the top four diseases - that account for 59.9 percent of all deaths - have some common causes or risk factors. For heart diseases, the major risk factors include:

1. High Blood Pressure (Hypertension)
2. High Blood Cholesterol
3. Diabetes
4. Obesity
5. Smoking
6. Lack of Physical Exercise
7. Gender
8. Heredity
9. Age

This shows that the first six major risk factors for heart disease are intertwined with five of the top six causes of deaths! (Accidents are independent contributors to death.) For example, a lack of physical exercise, poor diet, and smoking can lead to obesity and some cancers. Obesity itself increases the likelihood of heart disease (high blood pressure and cholesterol), cancers, strokes, and diabetes. Most important, all of the first six risk factors can be greatly influenced by good public policies and practices.

Let's focus on reducing the incidence of obesity as one example of how to improve our national health, thereby reducing health care costs. This is a health cost issue not addressed by our political leaders. Obesity in the United States has been increasingly cited as a major health issue in recent decades. While many industrialized countries have experienced similar increases, obesity rates in the United States are among the highest in the world, with 64 percent of adults being considered to be overweight or obese, and 26 percent being categorized as obese. Estimates of the number of obese American adults have been rising steadily, from 19.4 percent in 1997, to 24.5 percent in 2004, and to 26.6 percent in 2007. Should current trends continue, 75 percent of adults in the U.S. are projected to be overweight and 41 percent obese by 2015.[3]

While there are many causes of obesity, one or more types of refined sugars[4] are in most processes food we eat. These sugars, and the fats and salt prevalent in fast and processed foods, are major contributors to our overweight and obese population. As some have proposed, the United States might want to consider a tax on the consumption of sugar, as we have done for cigarettes. Cigarettes are heavily taxed because they are a health risk and drive up the cost of health care. The federal tax on cigarettes now comes to about $10.10 per carton, or $1.01 per pack. State taxes per pack, in 2009, ranged from $0.30 in Virginia to $3.46 in Rhode Island. Thus, on average, smokers are charged taxes of approximately $3 per pack and many smokers smoke one or more packs per day.[5]

All refined sugar products should be taxed for the same reasons as cigarettes. Let's look at the numbers and apply a tax only to carbonated and non-carbonated sugary soft drinks. Such a tax would both improve public health and easily pay for the uninsured. If the tax was effective in lowering consumption of sugary soft drinks, we might get less tax money, but would have a healthier population. It would be a win-win for lowering health care costs.

What might a "soda tax" contribute? Per capita consumption of sugary soft drinks in the United States, for 2008, averaged more than one twelve-ounce-can-sized serving per day per person.[6] The United States Department of Agriculture (USDA) recommended daily allotment (RDA) of added sugars is ten teaspoons as part of a 2,000-calorie diet.[7] Most soft drinks contain more than this amount of refined sugars. High caloric sugar intake contributes to obesity when it is not balanced with significant exercise. Shouldn't a canned drink containing ten teaspoons of sugar be taxed at least $1? This is only one-third of the daily tax the average smoker is charged. Using this formula would yield approximately $113 billion per year (assuming a population of approximately

310 million multiplied over 365 days at $1 of taxes per can) or approximately *$1.1 trillion over ten years*! This amount would likely be much higher if all sources of refined sugars were taxed. Taxing unhealthy fats, salt in processed foods and other unhealthy food items or practices would add billions of more dollars per year.

We could also reduce medical costs by other means, such as by limiting frivolous lawsuits. Many high-cost tests, medications, and procedures are instituted now to protect doctors and hospitals from ruinous lawsuits, rather than as a cost-effective way to help patients. Liability insurance and legal fees for doctors and hospitals are outrageously high as a result of lawsuits. These costs need to be controlled through legislation that puts dollar bounds on individual medically related lawsuits, and stringent requirements for the initiation of class action lawsuits.

This simple example shows the stated health care goal (a reduction in costs) is secondary to the overarching goal of improving health, and the root causes of health care costs were not addressed in the 2,000+ pages of the Congressional Health Care Bill. Yet, in November 2009, Senate Majority Leader Harry Reid indicated there is an emergency and it exists now. Again he implied that the system is near a tipping point, however, this bill is not scheduled to be fully implemented until 2014 well after the presidential election in 2012.

Why was there such urgency to pass a bill before 2010? The answer: the politicians want the ten-year cost assessment by the Congressional Budget Office (CBO) to show a net savings. According to FactCheck.org, the revenue measures (such as a surcharge on the wealthy) kick in right away, but major cost components, like subsidies to help people buy coverage, will not be implemented until 2014.[8] This means that the 2010-2019 period - during which the Congressional Budget Office says the bill would decrease the deficit by a net $109 billion - includes at least three more years of revenue-collection before significant spending begins!

There are some ways in which the real costs of medical care can be reduced as suggested above, but the people who were leading the charge for a government takeover of medical care are not really interested in reducing those costs. They are more interested in shifting the costs around or just refusing to pay them entirely. This is a case of those in power seeking more power for the government, rather than protecting the people.

When politicians, with a gift for rhetoric and free money, tell us the government can reduce the costs of healthcare without consequences, we tend to believe in such political miracles. But the political agenda in passing the Health Care Bill was to pass something fast before the public got wise and changed the balance between the two major parties. Obviously there were other agendas in play. Addressing the true costs was a secondary priority.

Interestingly, as a result of the "Massachusetts 2010 explosion" wherein Independents and Republicans voted in a Republican senator to replace the longtime liberal Democrat and universal health care advocate, Ted Kennedy, the urgency for quick passage was almost lost. The Health Care Bill under discussion at the time was a major factor in the election in a state with a three-to-one democratic advantage. A more rational law might have been the result. Instead, thanks to proposed rate increase actions by Anthem Blue Cross of California, the Democrats and President Obama were given another "Isn't it awful?" moment they could use to push through their bill without any Republican support. It may be a bad bill but it protects the politicians' egos and provides their needed arguments for re-election. They can now tout all the good features and ignore the bill's longer-term negative consequences.

In my view, the bill is bad enough that it will have several failure modes, thereby allowing the career politicians to again repeat their "mode of operation" to "improve" it with the underlying liberal goal of a full government take-over of health care. They will try again using the failures of this bill as their justification.

Doing Health Care Over

Let's briefly discuss what a "do over" of the health care system might look like if we started with the goal of improving the health of all citizens. Other important, yet secondary, objectives would be to reduce costs, widen coverage to include the uninsured, and address pre-existing conditions. Below, I offer three acts (bills or enactments) to systematically achieve these objectives. These three acts should be developed, debated, and enacted individually and in the sequence shown.

Act 1: Health Improvement Act of 2010

A key root cause of our health problems is bad eating habits. A secondary root cause is a lack of adequate exercise that makes the impact of our eating habits even worse. These problems are not unlike the smoking habit, but probably are easier for individuals to deal with since food addiction is not regarded as a big problem. This act would raise revenue through taxes on harmful dietary substances such as processed sugars, undesirable fats used for cooking, excessive use of salt in processed foods, etc. Unprocessed foods such as meats, nuts, vegetables, and fruits would not be taxed. Some of the revenues raised would be spent on the psychological and physiological issues associated with appetite control to help individuals' transition away from unhealthy foods and lifestyles. The rest of the revenues would be used for other health care causes that need fixing, per the two acts that follow. This act would require changes in the food industry, but motivated by profits, these changes would be rapidly implemented. I believe this act alone would improve the health of most citizens, cut health care costs, and take less than one generation to show significant improvements in both the health of our citizens and reduced health care costs.

Act 2: Health Care Modernization And Efficiency Act of 2010

Much can be done to reduce the costs of our health care system through existing technologies. This act would establish four fundamental sets of standards. First, a set of standards for secure data and information would be established to allow electronic transfers of patient data, digital record keeping, etc. For privacy, an individual's data could be provided on a flash card that each citizen would control, with local doctors or hospitals holding back-up data. Second, this act would establish a set of standards for minimum or base-line insurance coverage and standard "shopping list" definitions for insurance policy coverage in excess of the minimum standard. (Pre-existing condition solutions would be part of these standards.) Third, this act would establish standards for portability of information and insurance across state lines, and between medical facilities and insurance companies. Finally, this act would establish litigation standards and limits for lawsuits against the medical profession and the drug industry. I believe this act would fix many of our healthcare issues and reduce costs substantially.

Act 3: Health Care Insurance Improvement and Accountability Act of 2010

Given the revenues and standards generated by Acts 1 and 2, insurance needs can be addressed with this third act. Minimum standard health insurance would be mandated and, per Act 2, so would pre-existing condition coverage. Insurance portability from job to job and across state lines would be allowed. To make citizens responsible and accountable for their health, insurance would be paid for by individuals rather than by the companies for which they work. There should be no exceptions.[9] Initially, companies would provide the funds they now provide for insurance to each employee as part of his or her pay. At a specified time in the future, insurance would revert back to being part of a salary discussion where insurance funding could be a personal trade off, but employees would be required to purchase at least the minimum standard insurance. The government should still exempt funds provided by employers for health care from personal income taxes. To make the insurance industry responsibilities and accountabilities clear, guidelines would be part of the act. I believe this act would allow increased personal flexibility, while holding individuals accountable for their own and their family's health. It would create a more level playing field for health care competition, and control the health care insurance industry.

Complex Systems Analysis Summary Bullets

✪ Complex systems are generally time varying and nonlinear, and rely on bounds and feedback loops to maintain stability.
✪ Systems may reach a tipping point and become unstable.

✪ Careful monitoring and controls of systems are required to avoid catastrophic failures.

✪ A system with a large response capacity (gain) is best able to respond to changing system inputs.

✪ We have near-catastrophically failing governmental systems that have been provided by, overseen by, and, in some cases, mismanaged by our career politicians and governmental leaders.

✪ Our health care system is an example of political mismanagement.

✪ Knowledge of how our systems work, and how our leaders think and act can help minimize failures of our country's important systems.

Chapter 8:
Failing Financial System

The actions taken to date by the Bush and Obama administrations have not fixed our national financial system. Some financial institutional problems which contributed to the recent mortgage and lending crisis are being addressed, but these actions will not remedy our financial system's primary problems' root causes: national debt and annual deficits. If these primary root causes are not addressed, we can be assured that another much bigger crisis awaits in the not-so-distant future.

The 2010 national debt of $13.4 trillion[1] alone amounts to about $43,000 for every citizen and it continues to grow rapidly. (Estimates state that every citizen will owe $48,500 by the 2012 election.)[2] Adding the minimum 2010 estimated $40+ trillion for unfunded entitlements, this number skyrockets to a *minimum* of $171,000 per citizen! Of the $13.4 trillion national debt, approximately thirty-six percent are intra-governmental holdings borrowed from the U.S. Federal Reserve, and approximately sixty-four percent has been borrowed from the U.S. public or from foreign sources. Presently, about thirty-two percent (or about $4.3 trillion dollars) of debt is owed to foreigners. China, Japan, and oil-producing countries dominate this list, with China holding over $875 billion, and Japan holding over $760 billion of the debt.

The Problems

Figure 8-1: National Debt History shows the inflation-adjusted history of the national debt as a percentage of the GDP. Note the 100 percent horizontal line on the graph indicates when the national debt has exceeded the GDP, which has happened only once (for a few years following WWII).

A billion here, a billion there, pretty soon it adds up to real money.[3]
—Everett Dirksen

Figure 8-1: National Debt History[4]

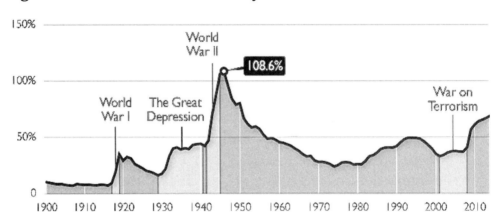

Figure 8-2: National Debt Projections, shows two projections of future debt growth. The most likely one is the "Alternative Fiscal Scenario." Again, the "100 percent" horizontal line on the graph indicates when the national debt will exceed the GDP. For the most likely scenario, this will occur by 2023, and likely it will be even sooner with the present debt growth. Even the best-case scenario puts this as happening just thirty-two years from now.

Thus, **Figure 8-2** suggests our financial system is nearing an unstable *tipping point*.

Figure 8-2: National Debt Projections[5]

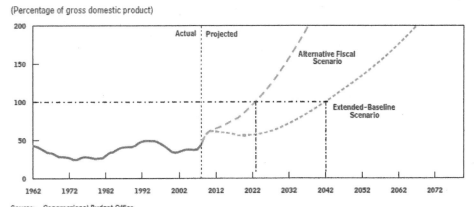

(Percentage of gross domestic product)

Source: Congressional Budget Office.

Notes: The extended-baseline scenario adheres closely to current law, following CBO's 10-year baseline budget projections from 2009 to 2019 and then extending the baseline concept for the rest of the projection period. The alternative fiscal scenario deviates from CBO's baseline projections, beginning in 2010, by incorporating some changes in policy that are widely expected to occur and that policymakers have regularly made in the past.

Many politicians (and a few economists) argue that the U.S. debt is not a problem. They cite the fact that the national debt, as a percentage of the nation's GDP, is lower than during the world wars, etc., however, they are overlooking a significant distinction: those debts at the time were almost completely owed to U.S. citizens, the dollar was gold-based, and U.S. consumption was predominantly from U.S. companies using U.S. laborers.

Now a large and growing portion of the debt is foreign-owned, the dollar is not tied to any standard such as gold, and much of what the U.S. citizenry consumes is imported from *foreign*-based sources using *foreign* labor. Thus, most of the arguments made by those believing the nation's debts are not a problem fail to acknowledge that today's economy is not the same as it was in the 1940s. We play in a changed global theater, and the results from our own government (shown in **Figure 8-2**) strongly indicate we are in trouble.

Those same U.S. politicians who are not concerned about our debt are ignoring what is happening in the world, such as Greece's near socio-economic failure. Years of unrestrained spending have lead to a Greek national debt estimated at $413.6 billion, which is bigger than the country's gross domestic product (GDP). Some estimates predict a 120 percent debt versus Greece's GDP in 2010. Greece's annual deficit (how much more is spent than taken in) is 12.7 percent of their GDP. Greece's credit rating has been significantly downgraded, meaning it will likely scare away foreign investors. This leaves the country struggling to pay bills while interest rates on existing debts rise.[6]

Comparisons to the United States suggest we are on a similar path as Greece. Years of unrestrained spending have lead to our national debt in 2010 of $13.4 trillion. From **Figure 8-2**, it can be extrapolated that the U.S. debt as a percent of GDP will be at Greece's 120 percent in about seventeen years. The U.S. deficit forecasts a $1.42 trillion deficit in 2010, or 9.9 percent of the U.S. GDP, so we are rapidly approaching Greece's 12.7 percent.

The Greek government has started slashing away at spending and has implemented austere measures aimed at reducing the deficit. The government has hiked taxes on fuel, tobacco, and alcohol, raised the retirement age by two years, imposed public sector pay cuts, and applied tough new tax evasion regulations. Greek citizens (predictably) are unhappy, and there has been resistance from various sectors of society. Workers nationwide have staged strikes closing airports, government offices, courts, and schools. These actions and public reactions are expected to continue.

Predictions are it will take at least a decade before Greece returns to its 2008 economic level. The rest of Europe is attempting to help bail them out, but other European countries are also near failure. Unfortunately, our present administration seems to be following the Greek/European model. Who will bail out our nation? Will the world come to our rescue? I do not think so.

Those U.S. politicians who are not concerned about large debt also point out debt is not bad because, due to inflation, we will be paying our future debt with less-valuable dollars. While this sounds good, the truth is that a larger debt will ultimately result in higher inflation, leading to higher interest rates and stagflation. "Stagflation" is an economic situation in which inflation and economic stagnation occur simultaneously and remain unchecked for a significant period of time. Stagflation occurred under President Carter where interest rates started at approximately eight percent in 1977 and topped out at 21.5 percent in December 1980.

Some politicians also imply the ongoing Iraq and Afghanistan wars are the reason we have such a high annual dept. Independent of whether or not you are for or opposed to these wars, this implication is not valid. On August 31, 2010, President Obama announced a future date for ending combat in Iraq. At that time the cost for the Iraq portion since 2001 was $745 billion. The spending deficit for 2010 is $1,420 billion.[7] So the total *multiyear* war costs are fifty-two percent of the *one-year* spending deficit. Adding the total Afghanistan war costs of $329 billion to the cost of the Iraq war shows the total of both wars from 2001 until September 1, 2010 is seventy-five percent of the 2010 spending deficit.[8] Hence, blaming the debt on the wars is simply another misleading trick politicians are playing to mask their deficit spending.

A *tipping point* exists in the United States today that may cause another financial crisis and would make the 2009 financial crisis - or even the 1929 stock market crash - seem mild. Let's discuss a possible and perhaps likely scenario. Presently, much of our debt is owed to foreigners like China, Japan and India - all of which have large populations. These countries are now dependent on the United States because much of their growth is the result of U.S. consumers buying their products, goods and services, so they may continue to buy our bonds for a while. If these countries succeed with their policies many, if not most, of their products, goods, and services will soon be for consumption by their own citizens.

(For example, in 2009, the Chinese purchased more cars than U.S. citizens.) These foreign governments will likely seek to borrow from their own citizens if they need funds, as we did in the past, or will invest in their own countries', rather than U.S. notes. In either case, U.S. foreign borrowing will dry up, the dollar value will drop quickly, and interest rates will go through the roof, resulting in a very unstable system likely to fail catastrophically!

Stabilizing the System

There are three key problems (root causes) needing attention. The lack of dollar limits or controls on the debt size is the most fundamental problem. A debt related problem is the selling of our debt paper (bonds and other U.S. securities guaranteed by the U.S. government) to foreign countries and foreign nationals whose self-interests do not serve our national interests. This form of borrowing must stop. A set of hard bounds[9] on the national debt must be established and adhered to by Congress. The second problem is spending. The upward spiral of spending as a percent of our national output is not sustainable. The two financial-ly linked systems, the national debt and annual spending, need controls imposed as soon as possible to avoid a catastrophe. The controls I propose are what I believe are the minimum controls to avoid a catastrophe. More stringent controls would be even bet-ter. The third problem is tax responsibilities and accountabilities. We must address the continuing burden of new taxes and changes to existing tax codes.

National Debt

At present, the only bound on the national debt is one set by Congress. This bound is useless since Congress simply increas-es the limit whenever they want to spend more money. A high national debt is a "no win" for the nation, despite what some poli-ticians might tell you. Raising taxes to pay off the debt will create even bigger problems, such as fewer jobs, unless free money is curtailed.

Two key changes are needed to control the national debt. The first is to implement a set of hard upper bounds. The second is to stop selling debt to foreign governments, and perhaps even to foreign nationals.

Hard Bounds: A rational approach to setting boundaries on the debt is to establish a hard limit or bound tied to the actual GNP and to force Congress to abide by that bound. This bound could only go up in case of war or a globally catastrophic event. When the event is over, the debt would have to be repaid in fifteen years - five years longer than it took following WWII (see **Figure 8-1**). If budgets are bound and Congress wants to spend more money, they would have to cut something to make their goal. The debt could and should be reduced during good economic times thereby creating a "nest egg"— a margin between the actual debt and the maximum allowed debt as defined below, for future downturns.

I propose an upper bound on the national debt of sixty percent of the GNP as a starting point. This is about the same as the 2000 ratio (See **Figure 8-1**). Within ten years, by 2020, this bound must be reduced to fifty percent debt as a fraction of GNP. This fifty percent debt value is still above the historical average before and after WWII. For significant wars, these bounds might need to be raised, but following the wars we must return to these bounds within fifteen years.

For a congressionally approved regional or non-conventional war (such as a "war" on terrorism), I propose a maximum hard bound not to exceed seventy-five percent of our GNP. In this situation, the non-war portion would remain at fifty percent and war costs (separately accounted for) would be bound at twenty-five percent of the GNP. Finally, for a major world war, the bound is not to exceed 100 percent, which is slightly lower than during WWII. Again the non-war limit would remain at fifty percent.

Currently, the national debt is already over the sixty percent limit and will soon be past the seventy-five percent limit, but we have no ongoing, *congressionally approved*, regional, or non-conventional wars! Given the present world economies, at no time - including during a major war - should we exceed 100 percent of the GNP.

Selling Debt to Foreign Governments: During WWII, when the national debt was at its highest, the debt was essentially all carried by U.S. citizens, many of who bought "war bonds." In other words, U.S. citizens bought our debt to help the nation in a time of crisis. Now, foreign entities and governments buy much of our debt paper even without any declared crisis. These foreigners are not buying our debt paper to help our nation. Instead they are looking out for themselves. We already see the debt carried by some countries being used as leverage against us. For example, China has financial policies that are not favorable to the United States, but the United States can do little about them. If we apply too much pressure, China can stop buying our debt paper, or even sell what they currently have. Either situation would likely cause another major financial crisis.

We need to immediately stop selling national debt paper to foreigners. This would have three immediate effects. First, the leverage already gained by other countries would stop. Second, if only U.S. citizens can buy these papers, any returns on the investments would be more likely to be utilized within our country, adding to our wealth and jobs— not some foreign country's wealth. Third, U.S. citizens would greatly influence the size of the debt and how borrowed money is used since the U.S. citizens who are debt paper buyers would be deciding if they wanted to carry the debt. I doubt "war bonds" would have been purchased by American citizens during WWII if they thought the money would be spent on some unneeded items or a cause trumped up by career politicians' to garner re-election votes.

Spending

There seems to be no limit when it comes to politicians' spending money for any and all constituents who might support their re-election. There is no need for these politicians to limit spending to match income. All they need to do is promise some free money, or sponsor some law that requires money, and the money will be there via either more taxes or more debt. Unlike the rest of us, they do not live within a limited budget. If Congress members are our leaders and we are the followers, many of us have been following them by ourselves living beyond our means through unwise borrowing. That is exactly how the recent financial crisis was launched.

Congress has made half-hearted attempts to live within a budget by requiring identification of the revenues that will fund new legislation. The Gramm-Rudman-Hollings act that applied until the year 2000 (then lapsed) is one example. Its proposed actions only addressed new legislation and not the rising costs of entitlements. In 2008, Congressman Paul Ryan (R-WI) proposed a bill to control entitlement costs, but the bill was not widely publicized. Recently, Senate Budget Committee Chairman, Kent Conrad (D-ND), and past Chairman, Judd Gregg (R-NH), introduced new legislation to create a bipartisan fiscal task force to address the nation's long-term budget crisis. The bill establishes an 18-member task force comprised of currently-serving members of Congress and Administration officials. Everything would be on the table, including spending and revenues. Congress would consider the task force recommendations under expedited procedures with a required vote. A bipartisan outcome would be ensured, with 14 of 18 task force members needing to support the report. The recommendations and supermajorities would need final passage in both the Senate and House.[10]

The Senate rejected this proposal. To his credit President Obama created a similar bipartisan debt and deficit (spending) commission co chaired by Democrat Erskine Bowles, Clinton's chief of staff, and Republican retired Senator Alan Simpson with a mandate to look at *everything*. The co chairmen recently discussed their initial thoughts and many of their thoughts are similar to some of mine contained herein. Reactions were predictable with most

Democrats including President Obama, and some Republicans expressing concerns or opposition. Unfortunately, we may never see a final report since 14 of 18 commission members must agree before a final report is released. Past history suggests this proposal, too, may become another joke played on us. In truth, most career politicians do not want debt and spending controls. These politicians always have some lame excuse for not having such controls, establish some way to convince us it is not in our best interest, fake a solution to con us, or continue to kick the problem down the road for others to fix.

Spending has two components: mandatory spending and discretionary spending. The percentage (and non-inflation adjusted dollar) changes from 1965 to 2009 in total mandatory and discretionary expenditures are:

1965 Total	$595.7 Billion	2009 Total	$3.52[11] Trillion	With Interest
• Mandatory	29% ($172.8 B)	• Mandatory	59% ($2.09 T)	[65%]
• Discretionary	72% ($422.8 B)	• Discretionary	41% ($1.43 T)	[35%]

This continuing percentage growth of mandatory versus discretionary spending cannot continue. Thus, I propose a bound not allowing mandatory spending to exceed sixty percent of our total annual spending. We are already exceeding this value when the debt interest is included (last column) as part of our mandatory spending, but we need to set a goal of reducing mandatory spending to this level within ten years. This will require tough decisions since, for example, Social Security costs are presently projected to go from 4.3 percent to 6.3 percent of our GNP in twenty-five years. All the medically related entitlements have even faster projected growths and these do not include anything for the new health care legislation.

The bottom line is that, when our government spends more than it has collected in revenues, the difference must come from borrowing. Unfortunately, borrowing required for annual spending raises our national debt. An actual "spending as a percentage of GNP hard limit" (of say, twenty percent) could also be established for annual spending, but it may over-constrain the system and is not necessary if both the national debt and mandatory spending bounds are enforced.

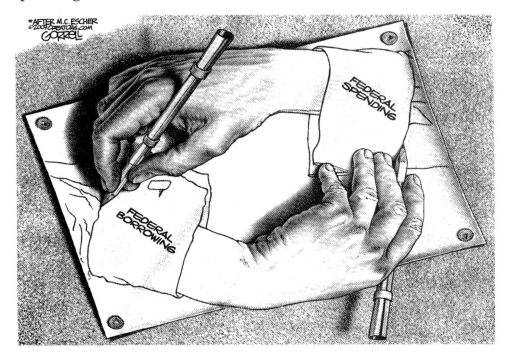

What would be the benefits of such debt and spending boundaries and controls? First, our politicians would have to become responsible spenders and could no longer pass costs to future generations. Second, our government would have to address runaway entitlements, even though reductions or controls on entitlements will impact all of us. Third, the true costs of wars would be highlighted since returning to the fifty percent debt-to-GNP bound will require belt-tightening during and after a war. Finally, we would be free from being held hostage by foreign governments since they would not hold any of our debt paper.

A constitutional amendment to require these bounds and controls, although highly desirable, would take too long, and catastrophic failures could result before an amendment could be enacted. So what might we be able to do? A grassroots approach is a strategy that can work. If most states passed legislation demanding controls on federal spending, the federal government would likely be forced to act. For example, look at the increased interest in the problem of illegal aliens as a result of Arizona's immigration law. If a state's actions work for immigration they should also work for spending controls. Ultimately, a major voter uprising may be required where "DRIP" ("Don't Re-elect Incumbent Politicians") becomes the rally cry.

Taxes

I do not pretend to be a tax expert, but I do consider myself a reasonably good observer of the past, and a logical thinker. A key observation of mine is that all taxes sought by career politicians have done the same thing: they provide more funds that are used by these career politicians to garner re-election votes without sufficient consideration of future consequences. Thus, any proposed changes to the tax code by career politicians must be seriously examined. There is ongoing discussion about adding or changing existing tax codes "to make them fairer" (suggestions include adding a national sales tax and a value-added tax). These and other tax ideas will only add to the tax burden of our citizens one way or another unless they replace existing tax codes.

Logically, individual accountability can best be achieved by making sure all citizens "own" some portion of what our federal, state, and local governments impose upon us. To ensure that this will happen, taxes - particularly progressive taxes such as income and capitol gains taxes - need to be paid by *all* citizens, including those receiving entitlements and other free money funds from our federal, state, and local governments. Charities should continue to be excluded since they are likely more creative and efficient than government-run programs and they provide individuals with opportunities to be charitable by giving either their money or time.

The question is: how do we make these taxes fair, and not allow political manipulation?

Assuming we keep progressive taxes and want to fairly apply them so every one owns a piece of the costs for our government, then our discussion must focus on what the progressive tax formula is that ensures wealth and jobs-growth. Once this rate structure is established, several other requirements need to be added to ensure minimal political manipulation in the future. I believe the following approach would work.

First, any progressive tax structure should be part of an exponential function formula. Here's an example for those of you who are mathematically inclined: rates for single wage earners could be set using: %-rate = $7 \times e^{N/3}$ where "e" is a real number constant that appears in some kinds of mathematics problems[12] and N equals the number of rates (or tax brackets) used for the tax code. For a six-rate structure (where N equals 1 through 6), these rates are shown in **Table 8-1** column two [Tax Rates (%)]. Whereas the formula yielding the rates for one through five, in column two, approximate 2009's rates, formulas can be debated that are more or less progressive. Column five is an example of a more progressive tax structure. Both rates top out at about 50 percent (where N equals 6). These highest rates would reflect a new higher tax on the super-wealthy.

Second, these rates need to be applied to income amounts based on percentages from the actual statistics of what U.S. citizens earn, including entitlements and not on fixed dollar amounts. One plausible percentage application is shown in **Table 8-1** column four [Income Ranges For $ Amounts], but other choices can be debated. In this example for N = 1, the top dollar amount earned by the lowest five percent of the population sets the income tax rate threshold; for N = 2 the top dollar level earned by the lowest twenty-five percent of the population sets the income tax rate threshold; and so on up to N = 6 where the lowest dollar amount earned by the highest five percent of the population sets the tax rate threshold. These dollar amounts will change from year to year to reflect earnings by everyone.

The actual income amount to which a rate applies should be tied to the income ranges for the year preceding the tax year, giving plenty of time to determine the actual numbers. The bottom 5 percent earners (including any entitlements as income) would pay a 9.77 percent tax (N = 1); those in the 5 percent to 25 percent range would pay the 9.77 percent for the first dollars earned up to the income of the first 5 percent, then pay 13.61 percent tax (N = 2) thereafter; and so on for N = 3, 4, 5, and 6. This is the normal way progressive income taxes have been applied, but those have been without a fixed exponential formula being used thereby allowing politicians to freely change the ratios.

Table 8-1: Suggested Progressive Tax Formula

N	Tax Rates (%) $7xe^{(N/3)}$	Plus 10% Increase	Income Ranges For $ Amounts	Rate More Progressive $2.5xe^{(N/2)}$
1	9.77	10.75	< 5%	4.12
2	13.63	15.00	5-25%	6.80
3	19.03	20.93	25-45%	11.20
4	26.56	29.21	55-75%	18.47
5	37.06	40.77	75-95%	30.46
6	51.72	56.90	>95%	50.21

What makes this approach different is what can be done to avoid political tricks. First, by requiring use of a fixed formula, any increase or decrease in taxes would be applied across the board. So if taxes were raised ten percent for some program or purpose, *all* rates would go up ten percent as shown in **Table 8-1** column three [Plus 10% Increase]. For example those individuals in the bracket of earnings in the bottom five percent would see their taxes go up from 9.77 to 10.75 percent. Everyone would feel the pain of the increase in taxes and there would be no impact uncertainty. Conversely, if the spending decreases so fewer tax dollars were needed, everyone would have more to spend resulting in increased wealth and more jobs.

Second, entitlement and other handouts must not be increased (at least no faster than the cost-of-living index) because otherwise politicians could simply add funds to entitlements to offset any tax increases, thereby continuing to maintain their ability to use our money to garner votes.

Finally, by using percentage ranges of incomes (rather than fixed dollar amounts) the inflation "bonus" that politicians get today would be taken away. Currently, an inflation bonus results because taxpayers' inflation-related income increases move them into ever-higher tax brackets. (See Chapter 6, "Inflation and progressive taxation.")

The actions to implement these changes are to establish a fixed formula with fixed (percentage-based) income ranges, avoid readjustments to entitlements, and tie everything to inflation. We must also beware of any new taxes proposed to ensure they are not riddled with political tricks that may help some in the short run while hurting our nation's ability to develop jobs and create wealth in the future. We must aggressively demand politicians carryout these actions.

Failing Financial System Summary Bullets

✪ Hard debt bounds need to be imposed:
  ★ Without war, less than fifty percent of GNP.
  ★ With declared regional or non -conventional wars, less than seventy-five percent of GNP.
  ★ With declared worldwide war, less than 100 percent of GNP.
  ★ Stop selling debt to foreign countries.

- ✪ Hard annual spending bounds need to be imposed, such as, holding mandatory spending to less than sixty percent of all annual spending.
- ✪ Fair taxation policies need to be imposed that encourage individual responsibility, such as, requiring all citizens with income from any source, including governmental sources, to pay income taxes.
- ✪ Use a fixed formula for progressive tax rates, and apply rates based on population income percentages, thereby accommodating inflation increases.

Chapter 9:
Failing Capitalistic Economic System

Every country has a working economic system. At one extreme, is a "free enterprise" or *capitalistic* system where most resources are privately owned. This system is maximized when all members of society are free to pursue their rational self-interests. Capitalism has been dominant in the Western world since the breakup of feudalism. In capitalism, most of the means of production are privately owned. Production and income distribution is handled by the operation of markets. At the other extreme, is a *communist* system where most resources are publicly owned. This system is based on the belief that public ownership of the means of production (and government control of every aspect of the economy) is necessary to minimize inequalities of wealth and achieve other agreed-upon social objectives. No nation exemplifies either philosophy in its most extreme state.

Between capitalism and communism is *socialism*. Socialism is a social organization in which private property and the distribution of income are subject to social control (through a government body). Because "social control" may be interpreted in widely divergent ways, socialism ranges from "Marxist" to "liberal." Karl Marx and Friedrick Engels saw socialism as a transition state between capitalism and communism, and appropriated what they found useful in socialist movements to develop their "scientific socialism." In the 20th century, the Soviet Union was the principal model of strictly centralized socialism.

As a nation moves from capitalism through socialism to communism, a greater share of the nation's productive resources is publicly owned and a greater reliance is placed on centralized economic planning and control that also requires greater control of the citizenry and, thus, less individual freedom.

The inherent vice of capitalism is the unequal sharing of the blessings. The inherent blessing of socialism is the equal sharing of misery.[1]
— **Winston Churchill**

Our capitalistic economic system has been a driving force in making our nation great. Individuals have the freedom to choose their financial destinies, and the opportunity to get ahead by working hard and taking risks in the hopes of improving their lives. Anything that greatly diminishes or suppresses our capitalistic economic system, I believe, will result in a failure that will forever change our nation for the worse. I see signs that we have allowed our political leaders to manipulate us into accepting policies and doing things that have the potential to make our capitalistic system fail.

Looking at world history, every socialistic nation has failed. I believe we are slowly but surely becoming a socialist nation. In this section, I will show that there is a gathering storm that has the potential for catastrophic failure unless we stop a lot of what we have been doing. How this is happening is clearly stated by a well-known socialist, Norman Thomas, U.S. Socialist Party presidential candidate in 1940, 1944, and 1948, who said:

The American people will never knowingly adopt socialism. But, under the name of 'liberalism,' they will adopt every fragment of the socialist program, until one day America will be a socialist nation, without knowing how it happened.[2]

The Problems

The gathering storm is a result of several things happening simultaneously:

✪ Increases in funding for mandatory social programs at rates much faster than the growth of our population or GNP, and over 100 percent faster than the rise in median household income.

✪ A continuing proliferation of new taxes - and increasing rates for some existing ones either by raising rates or through inflation's impact on progressive taxes.

✪ Fewer and fewer citizens paying more of the federal and state income taxes, which is a fairness issue.

✪ Increases in total number of federal, state, and local government employees at rates faster than the growth of our population or GNP.

✪ An attitudinal shift away from our Founding Fathers' belief in self-sufficiency and personal responsibility towards more citizens believing they are "entitled" to free money.

Collectively, all of these things eat away at our capitalistic economic system and any one of them by itself may cause a strong shift toward socialism. If you factor in the impacts of a failing financial system, we have, at minimum, a great potential for disruption of our way of life and, possibly, something much worse. Let's look at some of the trends making this gathering storm such an important problem and we will see we are nearing an unstable *tipping point* for our socio-economic system.

Federal Tax Expenditures

Let's start by looking at where are tax dollars go. Tax expenditures for 2008 are shown in **Figure 9-1.** Years 2009 and 2010 are atypical years due to the financial and unemployment crises making the problems discussed worse. The 2008 data are used in this section to avoid clouding the historical information and providing arguments for critics. Figure 9-1 shows that social programs including Social Security, Medicare, Medicaid, Children's Health Insurance Program (CHIP), Safety Net Programs, and debt interest constituted about sixty percent of the expenditures and were increasing (to sixty-five percent in 2009). These are legally "mandatory" expenditures, or entitlements, and the remaining forty percent were mostly "discretionary" expenditures.

Figure 9-1: Tax Expenditures For 2008[3]

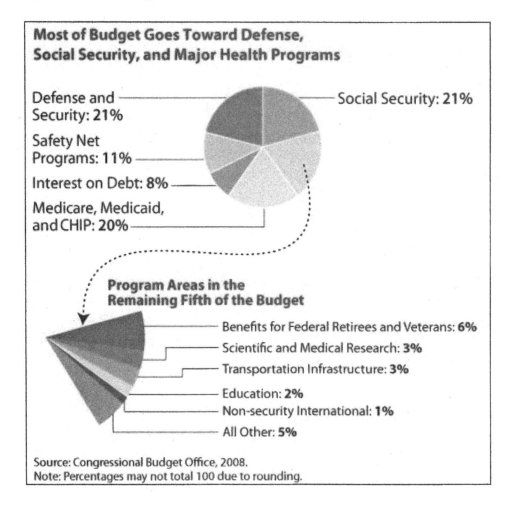

Most of Budget Goes Toward Defense, Social Security, and Major Health Programs

Defense and Security: **21%**

Social Security: **21%**

Safety Net Programs: **11%**

Interest on Debt: **8%**

Medicare, Medicaid, and CHIP: **20%**

Program Areas in the Remaining Fifth of the Budget

Benefits for Federal Retirees and Veterans: **6%**
Scientific and Medical Research: **3%**
Transportation Infrastructure: **3%**
Education: **2%**
Non-security International: **1%**
All Other: **5%**

Source: Congressional Budget Office, 2008.
Note: Percentages may not total 100 due to rounding.

Social Security and medical entitlements are the major expenditures. Expenditure projections for these entitlements shown in **Figure 9-2** indicate a continuing upward trend that will result in the thirty-year average tax rate of approximately 18.5 percent of GNP by 2052. This means in less than forty-two years there will be no discretionary funds available unless drastic actions are taken.

Figure 9-2 Entitlement Expenditure Estimates (2008)[4]

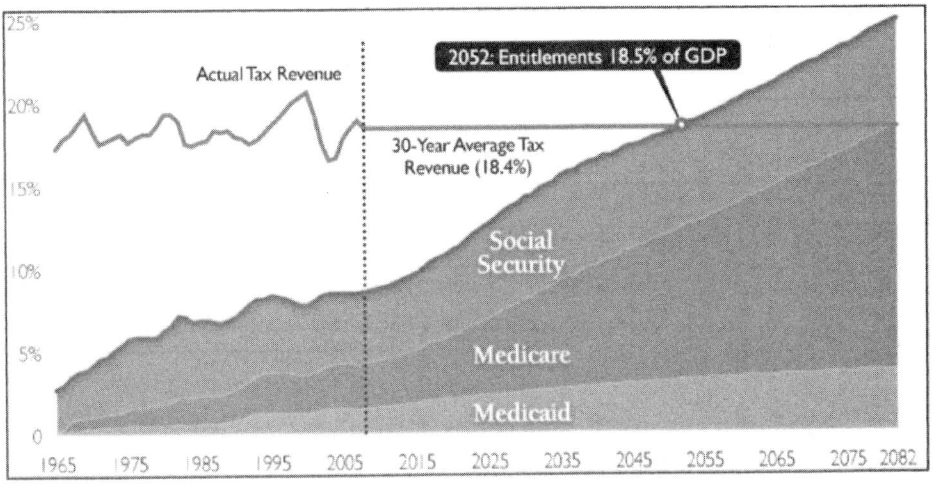

According to the U.S. Census Bureau, the U.S. population is approximately 308 million in 2010 and will be approximately 392 million by 2050, which is a twenty-seven percent increase. The projected increase in entitlements over this same period is over 100 percent— about four times higher than the projected population growth, even though these data do not reflect any potential entitlement increases for health care or illegal immigrants. In the financial system section, mandatory spending as a percentage of annual budgets was shown to be increasing rapidly from twenty-nine percent in 1965 to fifty-nine percent— or sixty-five percent when debt interest is added in 2009. We cannot allow this to continue; it is not sustainable!

Tax Sources

Our politicians continue to hand off our problems to future generations, or simply create new taxes. This is not the answer. (Remember: *people* pay taxes *not* businesses.) Businesses must make a profit to stay in business, so the burden of any taxes is passed on to the people who buy their products and services, or else companies will have to outsource materials and labor to less expensive foreign sources. **Figure 9-3** shows the two major inflation-adjusted tax sources - individual income and corporate taxes - from 1965 through 2009. (Note that the total inflation-adjusted tax dollars have *tripled* since 1965.)

Figure 9-3: Major Federal Tax Revenue Sources (Inflation-Adjusted Dollars, 2008)[5]

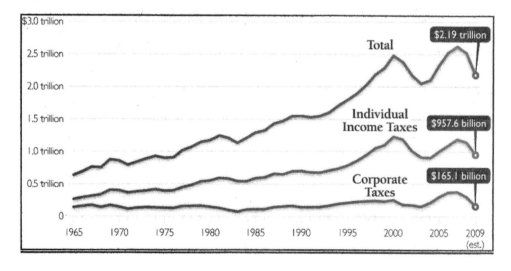

Tax the Rich

A popular rallying cry, which exploits many of the tricks discussed in Chapters 4, 5, and 6, is to "tax the rich." The amount and percentage of citizen's who paid income taxes in 2008 are shown in **Table 9-1**. The next-to-last column shows that the top fifty percent of our income tax paying citizens pay 97.11 percent of the taxes collected by the IRS. Are one half of all of us "rich?[6]"

Table 9-1: Summary of Federal Individual Income Tax Data

	AGI* Income Taxes Paid ($ millions)	Group's Share of Total AGI	Group's Share of Taxes	Average Tax Rate
All Taxpayers	$1,115,504	100%	100%	12.68%
Top 1%	$450,926	22.83%	40.42%	22.45%
Top 5%	$676,293	37.44%	60.63%	20.53%
Top 10%	$794,432	48.05%	71.22%	18.79%
Top 25%	$965,875	68.71%	86.59%	15.98%
Top 50%	$1,083,243	87.74%	97.11%	14.03%
Bottom 50%	$32,261	12.26%	2.89%	2.99%
Source: Internal Revenue Service				

* Adjusted Gross Income (AGI)

One way to address the entitlement estimates in **Figure 9-2** would be to increase the percentages in each income tax and corporate tax bracket. **Figure 9-4** shows what would need to happen to cover the costs of only the *mandatory* entitlements. The problem gets worse when the discretionary spending is added. Also, given these tax rates, it would appear that investment funds would largely dry up, businesses would go under, and we would likely have massive unemployment.

Figure 9-4: Tax Rates Needed To Cover Projected Entitlements[7]

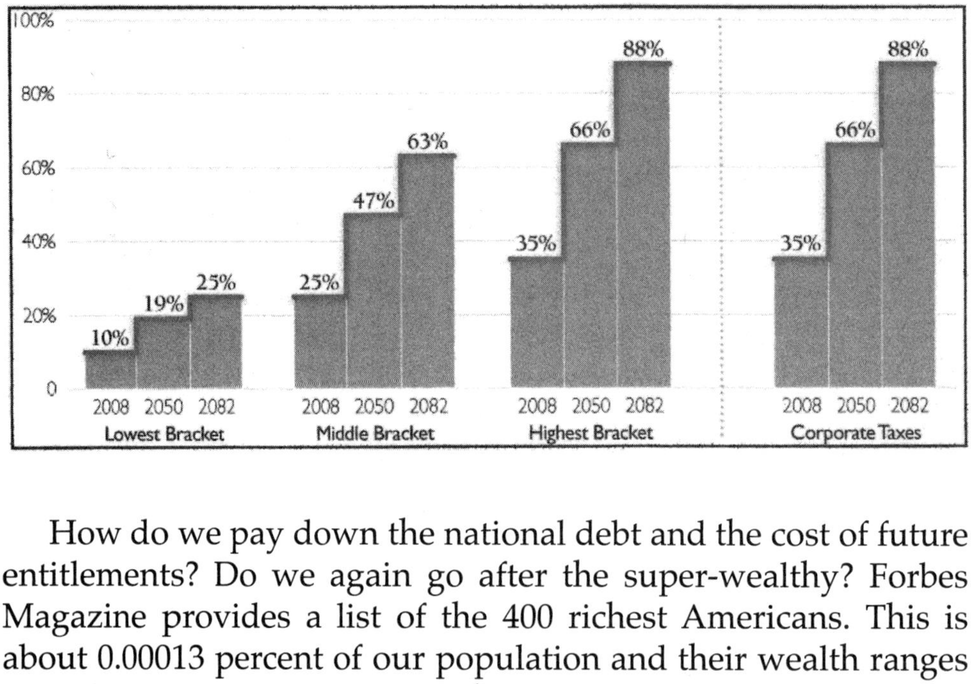

How do we pay down the national debt and the cost of future entitlements? Do we again go after the super-wealthy? Forbes Magazine provides a list of the 400 richest Americans. This is about 0.00013 percent of our population and their wealth ranges from $50 billion down to less than $1 billion. Let's suppose we took *all* of the wealth of the top ten to pay down our debt, leaving them paupers. A rough calculation shows the top ten are worth about $246 billion, which does not make much of a dent in the debt. If we take *all* the wealth away from all 400 of the wealthiest Americans in 2010, we would have about 1.3 trillion dollars or about ten percent of the national debt, but this would be nowhere near the total debt when entitlements (minimally estimated at between $40 trillion to $60 trillion debt) are included.[8] You would have to steal all of the assets of a great number of our citizens to break even. And, if you did, who would pay for the jobs lost by such actions and pay the taxes they are now paying? Every one else's taxes would need to increase substantially.

Another hypothetical scenario for paying down our debts would be to put a "wealthy flat tax" of $100,000 on the top ten percent of all taxpayers in addition to what they pay now. There were 142 million federal income tax (both single and joint) filings in 2008, but only 90.4 million actually paid income taxes.[9] The added $100,000 tax paid by the 9.04 million existing taxpayers would be a $904 billion. This still does not pay one year's worth of deficit spending.

How much to tax the rich is an ongoing debate, but much of the debate is political rhetoric not supported by the numbers. For example, Treasure Secretary Geithner proclaimed on ABC's "This Week" (on July 25, 2010) that the Bush tax cuts should be allowed to lapse for the top 2 to 3 percent of the wealthiest population. He said, *"We think that is the responsible thing to do."* He went on to say, *"We need to make sure we can show the world that we're willing as a country now to start making progress bringing down our deficits."*[10] In September 2010, President Obama made several pre-midterm election speeches repeating similar statements.

This sounded good to those of us interested in lowering the deficits and debts, but let's look at the numbers without taking sides on the issue. The increased taxes proposed for the wealthy would generate about $700 billion over ten years or $70 billion per year.[11] While this may help, it is not even a drop in the bucket of our debts! The Obama Administration's *deficit* alone for 2010 is estimated at $1,420 billion so $70 billion is about five percent of this total. All of the projections for future deficits I have seen are much larger than $70 billion.[12] In addition, the annual interest alone on the *national debt* (not including entitlement debts) is many times higher than $70 billion. Do Treasure Secretary Geithner and President Obama really believe the world will be impressed by their proclamations? I doubt it. This is really all about U.S. politics, increasing taxes while trying to waylay our debt fears. Spending is the problem, not taxes!

So, the next time a politician tells you he or she will have the rich pay for something, think about what he or she really means. Most of the time this is a ruse to make you believe you are getting free money or, as in the example above, that the government is fixing a problem. The bottom line is that a small percentage of our wealthiest citizens can and perhaps should be tapped for more taxes, but they are not a bottomless money pit and even stealing all of their wealth will not solve our problems!

New Taxes

Politicians are good at finding new ways to tax us. One hundred years ago, our nation was the most prosperous in the world, we had absolutely no national debt, we had the largest middle class in the world, and paying for government was done through relatively simple taxation policies. Since then, many positive things have occurred such as improvements in equality and quality of life. Unfortunately, now almost everything is taxed and some of these taxes do not seem to correlate with the added benefits. Here are a few of the tax sources that have evolved in the last one hundred years. Remember: we left British Rule to avoid so many taxes. Perhaps we should all again join the Tea Party.

A Few of Many New Taxes Over Last 100 Years

Accounts Receivable Tax	Real Estate Tax
Building Permit Tax	Service charge taxes
Cigarette Tax	Social Security Tax
Corporate Income Tax	Road usage taxes
Dog License Tax	Sales Tax
Federal Income Tax	Recreational Vehicle Tax
Federal Unemployment Tax	School Tax
(FUTA)	State Income Tax
Fishing License Tax	State Unemployment Tax (SUTA)
Food License Tax,	Telephone federal excise tax
Fuel permit tax	Telephone federal universal service fee tax
Gasoline Tax	Telephone federal, state and local surcharge taxes
Hunting License Tax	Telephone minimum usage surcharge tax
Inheritance Tax	Telephone recurring/non-recurring charges tax
Interest expense	Telephone state and local tax
Inventory tax	Telephone usage charge tax
IRS Interest Charges	Utility Taxes
IRS Penalties (tax on top of tax)	Vehicle License Registration Tax
Liquor Tax	Vehicle Sales Tax
Luxury Taxes	Watercraft registration Tax
Marriage License Tax	Well Permit Tax
Medicare Tax	Workers Compensation Tax
Property Tax	

Note this is not a complete list[13] but the list does show that politicians would tax everything if we would let them. I am sure you have heard your politicians talk about the need for new taxes and new ways of generating them. As a citizen of California, I hear more taxes are needed every year.

Taxpayers to Non-Taxpayers

There are many taxes that almost all citizens pay, but income tax is not one of them. There were 142 million federal income tax (both single and joint) filings in 2008, and 51.6 million of the filers had no income tax obligation. Thus 90.4 million filers paid income taxes. Given the economic situation in 2009 and 2010 the number of income filers that actually paid is likely to be even lower for these years. A good portion (forty percent or about twenty-one million) of those not paying income taxes actually received money from the government in the form of a "negative" income tax.[14]

Most of our federal, state, and local employees likely paid income taxes. There are approximately twenty million total federal, state, and local employees. In 2009, the federal rank and file employee base pay (without benefits) ranged from $17,540 to $127,604 for employees classified GS 1, Step 1 through GS15, and Step 10, respectively, and top federal executives got more.[15] A reasonable assumption is that most of these government employees paid income taxes. The taxes they paid went toward their own and their fellow employees' income.

Subtracting income-tax-paying government employees from the pool of 90.4 million income tax payers shows the number of private sector income tax payers is 70.4 million. Private sector income tax payers are less than fifty percent of all income tax filers. The percentage of private sector income tax payers is much less than fifty percent of the adult population (about 235 million over the age of eighteen) since citizens who did not file income taxes and illegal immigrants are not included in the calculations. The fact that so few private sector taxpayers are carrying the load for all citizens and immigrants is fundamentally unfair and is not sustainable if the trend continues.

If you are not a government employee and you are paying income taxes, you are a member in good standing in the "Under Fifty Percent" club. (Congratulations to those who pay!) There is also an "Over Fifty Percent Free Money" club for those who do not pay income taxes. The group that does not pay income taxes includes those receiving free money in some form from their federal, state, and local governments.

What happens as the ratio of taxpayers to non-taxpayers continues to drop? In the extreme, there would eventually be no income tax payers. The result would be a totally socialistic (or communistic) country. We would then most likely join the other past failed socialistic countries.

At present, over one half of all U.S. citizens (the members of the "Over Fifty Percent Free Money" club) are free to ask for - and vote for those politicians who advocate - more free money from the "Under Fifty Percent" club. Is this fair to the "Under Fifty Percent" club members? Do the "Over Fifty Percent Free Money" club members have the right to dictate (through their votes) how taxes are spent when they have no ownership? They do not need to care about what something costs, and are not responsible or accountable for what is done. Is this situation in the best long-term interest of the nation? To be fair, perhaps only members of the "Under Fifty Percent" club should decide how their money should be spent. This was the case before the 16th Amendment to *The Constitution* was enacted; therefore, our Founding Fathers may have had it right.

A better alternative is to institute policies that create a feeling of ownership and responsibility so every citizen is invested in how our government spends our money. A simple fix was discussed earlier: require everyone to pay some income taxes on whatever they earn (including income received from federal, state, and local governments). By holding the ratios of the progressive rates fixed, all individuals would "feel the pain" of government spending. This is one way to improve individual responsibility, control career politicians' free money spending, and re-establish a fairer taxation of all citizens.

The question is: "What is the system 'tipping point' for our nation to become socialist?" Given the mammoth burden we have already placed on future generations for entitlements and other debts, our already high taxes, fewer individuals carrying the tax load, the rapidly increasing national debt, and the rapidly changing global environment, *we are at that tipping point*. We must address these problems in the next few years; otherwise, disaster will be here before today's newborns have children.

Stabilizing the System

If you are a member of the "Under Fifty Percent" club, you should be outraged. Yes, the super-wealthy can afford to pay more. For example, a higher inflation-adjusted progressive tax rate on the top layer of capital gains may be appropriate for our most wealthy citizens since this is a major source of income for most of the super-wealthy. But looking at **Figure 9-4** shows that the golden goose has (or is about to) hit its egg-laying limit.

If you are one of the "Over Fifty Percent Free Money" club you need to critically think about how you vote to spend the money others earn. You are eating the golden goose that creates your jobs and allows you to take risks to create wealth. If you do not select wisely, your children and all of your future relatives will suffer. I ask you to think about one question: Do you really believe continuing to add national debt (now at least $43,000 per citizen), expanding entitlements (now at least $128,000 per citizen), eating the golden "wealthy" goose one bite at a time, and creating an ever-smaller "Under Fifty Percent" club is in your, your children's, your grandchildren's, or our nation's best interest?

Unfortunately, we are in this mess so deep, there are not any magic bullets for this system's problems. Any solutions will be painful and will last a long time, but we must make changes now. Here are a few thoughts on solving the problems (more details will be provided later).

First, we must start now to curtail free money, government spending, and personal, local, state, and federal debt, as well as reverse our current reality that fewer individuals are paying more and more taxes. Spending policies need to be focused on how to create and maintain jobs and should not be implemented unless they provide a solid return on investment. The hard bounds proposed for our financial system are an excellent start.

Second, there needs to be a major attitudinal change that restores our Founding Fathers' traits of hard work and personal responsibility to replace the all-too-often stated: "I am a citizen of the U.S.A. and (therefore) I am entitled to _____" (you fill in the blank). Hard work and our capitalistic structure are the keys to greater personal and familial rewards. Personal responsibility includes both being responsible for obeying our laws and doing what is perceived as "the right thing to do." Blaming others is easier than taking personal responsibility. Committing to spend money that someone else earns is also easy. Making everyone an income tax payer, thereby owning a part of all expenditures, would start fixing the problem.

Third, the super-wealthy *can* afford to pay some more. I believe no more than the top five percent of our population can be considered super-wealthy— not the fifty percent that our politicians like to call "rich." Capital gains are a major source of income for most of the super-wealthy. Capital gains tax rates (for investments held longer than one year) are fewer in number and lower than ordinary income tax rates. These rates are important, since lower rates can encourage savings and investing and lead to more jobs and wealth. Capital gains progressive tax rates need to be adjusted using at least six capital gains brackets. I propose a very progressive inflation adjusted rate schedule such as shown in **Table 8-1** (column five) with a fifty percent value applied to the top five percent super-wealthy earners and near zero for the lowest rate. To ensure maximum investments by all citizens (from the poorest through the upper-middle-class) the remaining rates should drop dramatically with the second highest rate being at or lower than it was in 2009. This approach would encourage investment savings by lower-income individuals, make the wealthiest among us pay significantly more, and allow everyone else in-between to invest more. Income percentages established for both capital gain rates and ordinary income tax rates need to be annually adjusted for inflation in order to avoid inflation related wage increases pushing citizens into higher tax brackets.

Finally, an essential part of stabilizing this system is to understand what is happening, and demanding rational solutions and honesty from our political leaders. Anytime one of your politicians uses any of the tricks discussed herein, suggests a free money solution, or addresses problems in ways that are aimed at his or her re-election, call him or her on it. Become outraged and let him or her know it! If he or she wants to continue as-is, plan to vote for someone else next time even though he or she might be less well known. We do not want to change the name of the nation to the United Socialist States of America (U.S.S.A.).

Failing Capitalistic Economic System Summary Bullets

- ✪ Spending by all governments - federal, state, and local – needs to be limited to what is affordable and sustainable by:
  - ★ Reducing free money handouts
  - ★ Limiting the amount of taxes
  - ★ Allowing more progressive capital gains taxes on the top five percent (super-wealthy) and lower rates for lower income investors.
- ✪ Policies are needed that focus on jobs and wealth generation. Return-on-investment rather than the number of votes that can be bought should be the criteria used to establish these policies.
- ✪ Individual responsibility needs to be reinstituted in our policies. Entitlement policies should be changed to reflect individual responsibilities.
- ✪ Institute the federal bounds and taxation policies presented for the financial system.
- ✪ Aggressively hold politicians to the above principles.

Chapter 10:
Failing Social Systems

S everal social systems are failing and many of them have life-altering impacts on our citizens. Unfortunately, some of the impacts are subtle and may go unnoticed. Since we already covered the health care system in Chapter 7, we will now analyze the public employee system, and the corporate/business and labor system.

Public Employees System

Early on in our nation's history, businesses commonly abused employees, leaving unskilled workers with inadequate wages to support themselves and their families. This can still be found in some existing low-skilled jobs. Unions were effective in evolving these mostly private sector jobs (many in manufacturing industries) into reasonable middle-class jobs. There are still private sector jobs where unions could again help develop low wage jobs into reasonable middle-class jobs. I suggest such a possibility in the section "Jobs For Low-Skilled Workers" in Chapter 11. For those readers favoring unions, please know that I am not opposed to unions. What I am opposed to is the present lack of bounds on public employee unions and the ultimate impact this lack of adequate bounds is having on our nation.

The Problem with Public Employee Unions

Union workers made up thirty-five percent of the workforce in the 1950s, a percentage that went down to 12.3 percent in 2009.[1] The number of union members began to drop in part because the number of manufacturing jobs was decreasing, in part because unions had been successful in achieving livable wages for relatively unskilled workers, and in part because the increasing service jobs were less amenable to unionization. Realizing these facts, union leaders started a big push to gain access to public (government) workers. In 1960, there were only 900,000 public union members. In 2009, 37.2 percent (7.9 million) of the approximately twenty-one million government employees belonged to unions, compared with just 7.2 percent of private sector workers.[2] With the help of Democratic politicians, many public workers are now unionized. As shown in **Figure 10-1**, unionized public workers constitute fifty-two percent of unionized workers in 2009.

Figure 10-1: Percentage of Union Members — Public vs. Private Sectors[3]

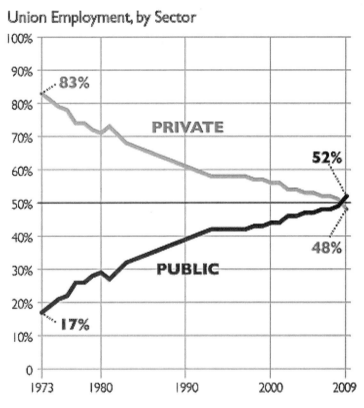

Note: 1982 figures not available.

In California, a so-called "progressive state", public unions essentially own the state. Fully fifty-four per of state government workers – that's almost 1.8 million people – are unionized. Public sector unions in California gave $38.2 million in 2008 to selected state and national political candidates and political committees mostly in an effort to guarantee exorbitant wages and benefits from the state.[4] Deducting contributions to committees drops this number to about $23 million. In this discussion I am unable to estimate the equivalent costs of this free manpower public unions demand of their members to support their selected politicians. This free effort is likely many times higher than the dollars given.

Further analysis of the dollars given indicates Democrats received about ninety-two percent, Republicans received about six percent, and others received the rest of the money. This is consistent with 2004 data and the results determined by others.[5] California is a state that has been dominated by the Democratic Party for many years. Guess which party rules? Public unions rule in California.

Each election, unions spend tens of millions of their members' dollars and likely many millions of hours supporting local, state, and national politicians, whether the union members like them or not. This means that, in just California, citizens are paying out tens of millions to unions who pass the money along to politicians. In this indirect way, politicians get *public* funds.

How, you may ask, is this different from business support to politicians? The first important fact is we have no choice but to rely on government employees, because we have no other options. If we are unhappy with Wal-Mart's or Nordstrom's service or politics, we can go elsewhere to shop, but we cannot do that with government entities that have union employees.

Second, we pay public employees' wages and benefits and their mandatory union dues. Certainly, as public employees, each one has the right to support whomever they wish, but support should be out of their pockets or time, not ours. Why should we pay public employees extra for their unions to give to politicians who are "incentivized" to gain votes and not to control costs? Private sector unions do not cause the same problem because their company is incentivized to control costs. Private sector unions and businesses should be treated equally, but there are problems with both union and business special interest funding of politicians, which we will discuss later.

The lack of adequate bounds on public unions is a significant problem for the general public in several ways. First, the number of public employee union members is increasing as a percentage of the total government employees. Nearing election time, politicians will happily hand out "free money" to secure large amounts of union money, and, more importantly, the manpower resources generated at election time by unions. Union leaders and peer pressure have considerable control over members' actions. I see nothing that will change this situation unless "we the people" take action.

Figure 10-2 shows that local and state employees have increased in number while federal employees have decreased as a percentage of the total U.S. population. Adding the two percentages together, we see that the total percent of government employees has risen slightly. This bodes well for public unions since unionizing smaller local groups is easier than larger ones. Most of the public union growth has been at the local and state levels.

Figure 10-2: Government Employees as a Percentage to Total Population[6]

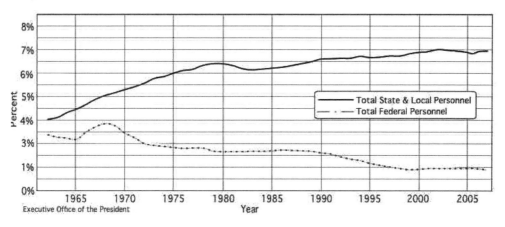

Second, in the public sector there is no labor-management "give and take" like there is in the private sector. "Management" in this case is some set of politicians who are willing (and in a position) to give the unions what they want. The politicians simply pass present and future costs along to the rest of the population.

The impact of having politicians as managers is hitting home in almost every city, county, and state in the country. Unionized city, county, state, and federal governmental employees - whose jobs are seldom at risk and whose benefits exceed those in comparable private sectors - are a large portion of the government's costs. Ironically, in the private sector managers must control labor costs to stay in business while in the public sector politician managers must allow increases in labor costs to be re-elected.

In California, jail guards get large salaries, lots of overtime, and big benefits, as do most of the rest of the union members in the state. This is not consistent with all California unions, however. For instance, jail guard wages and benefits are higher than those of teachers. Also, some state employees have been allowed to use their overtime and perks as part of their base calculation for retirement benefits. Since most retirement benefits are calculated using the last few (typically three) years, it is not surprising that many state employees greatly increased their overtime prior to retiring. Some retire at significantly higher rates than their base pay.[7]

Third, most of these jobs are service jobs with considerable interactions with the public and/or are important to safety and health. Strikes have a large public impact, and as indicated above, the public has no alternative ways to fulfill the needs left behind. In the private sector, businesses usually have alternatives when a strike occurs. Businesses can wait to build commodities, or to use managers to fill in for a while as negotiations continue. In some cases, they can switch to offshore labor sources.

We are at a *tipping point*, where public employee unions are capable of "buying" enough politicians to get everything they want. Certainly we do not want to continue with the status quo of letting these union members make more in wages, benefits, and perks than do their counterparts in the wealth and job building private sector. And the use of public money controlled by public unions that is provided to "union compliant" career politicians needs to be stopped.

Stabilizing the System

Public unions may be reasonable or desirable if properly bounded. Without proper bounds we are almost certain to be held hostage and will have to pay high prices for the failures of our politician "managers" who have more motivation to give in to public unions than to challenge them. Many states and localities are already beyond the tipping points and a few have gone bankrupt. So how do we set the bounds?

Ideally, public unions should be abolished and replaced by formalized wage and benefit systems tied to comparable private sector jobs. This would isolate workers' pay and benefits from the irresponsible or inept career politicians. Individuals then would be free to support whomever they like for public offices. These jobs would still attract good people since they are relatively risk-free in that seldom are government employees laid off. Unfortunately, this is probably too much to ask. So what bounds might be possible? At least two fundamental principles, if implemented, would help.

First, public unions as an entity must not be allowed to contribute funds to politicians or political parties. They are using public money when this happens. If they can do this why not let other governmental entities use some of their "discretionary" funds for political purposes? This would quickly change our nation, as we have known it, to a socialistic state. While individual public union employees can do what they please with money out of their own pockets just like any other citizens, public union leaders must not be allowed to dictate how much support individual members must provide or to whom this support is to benefit. Laws establishing this change should also carry fines for public union members who violate this principle. This one law would address both vote-buying and irresponsible political "management." Politicians would still be responsible for policies as they are now, except for wage and benefit policies.

Second, public unions need some type of leverage, and strikes are one of their more effective forms of leverage. However, public unions need to have bounds placed on striking since the public has no alternatives but to use their services. If strikes occur, they should be limited to a fixed maximum duration (say, less than one week in any year). After the specified maximum duration, workers must go back to work and an "arbitration board" would provide a fair and balanced solution based on wages and benefits for similar jobs in the private sector. This board should be comprised of twelve members: at least seven citizens from the private sector who actually use the services provided, up to four government employees, and one judge, a non-voting member, to lead the process. If the public union did not accept a proposed solution, the public union would be dissolved and could not be reinstituted for a fixed time (say, six months).

We have some choices. We can either be held hostage by ever-increasing governmental costs for public workers or we can act to bound public unions. I vote of the latter.

Failing Public Employees System Summary Bullets

✪ Stop allowing public unions (but not individual members) to contribute to politicians or political parties, so that public money is not being spent for partisan political purposes.
✪ Fine the public unions and their leaders for any and all political activities, including coordinating union members in support of political functions. Individuals may act on their own as citizens, as the rest of us do.
✪ Limit strikes and institute arbitration boards dominated by citizens who use the affected public services.
✪ Disband any public union that does not agree to arbitrated recommendations, but allow members to vote to reinstate the union in six months time.

Corporate/Business and Labor System

There has always been, and will always be, tension between "labor" and "management." Obviously, some of the two groups' objectives are conflicting. In recent history, private sector businesses and unions have worked well to establish and maintain a reasonable private sector balance. The evolving world's economic environment has changed that dynamic. Labor, management, and politicians now need to change their strategies and actions in light of new realities. We need "team play" now to survive. A few fundamentals of capitalism discussed earlier should be enough motivation to foster team play. Briefly stated, here are some of the fundamentals:

✪ Insufficient business profits or growth means no one invests in the business.
✪ No investors ultimately means no business.
✪ No business means no jobs and no business taxes.
✪ No jobs means no income or income taxes and more entitlement payouts.
✪ No business and income taxes means no money for:
  ★ Social entitlements.
  ★ Necessary government functions.
  ★ Politicians to dole out to garner votes.

The Problems

In 1940, there were four million Americans working for our governments (federal, state, and local) and eleven million working in manufacturing. In 2009, there are approximately eight million more Americans working for our federal, state, and local governments (twenty-one million, total) than in all U.S. manufacturing industries (twelve million, total).[8] Manufacturing jobs peaked in

1979 at 19.5 million.[9] We have shifted from an economy of people who make things, to an economy of people who provide services, and government agencies that tax, regulate, subsidize, outlaw things, and hand out free money.

Corporations and businesses have new worldwide competition, but also have potential new markets and labor options. Survival requires them to become ever more efficient to increase productivity. Productivity improvements resulting from automation and access to lower-cost materials and labor sources worldwide are but one of the major contributors to the decline in manufacturing jobs in the United States. Politicians' use of blame games, labor-management wedges, and bad self-serving business policies are the second major contributor to the decline in both manufacturing and some service jobs in the United States. These political actions and policies force more businesses' to outsource if they wish to survive.

Most economists agree resurgence in manufacturing jobs is unlikely, but private sector service-related jobs will continue to grow, and all high-skilled jobs should remain in demand. With close cooperation between labor and management, a new balance may be possible. If not, we can expect more manufacturing, service and many high skill jobs to be outsourced to foreign countries.

Unskilled citizens' jobs have reached a *tipping point*. Unfortunately, educating and training tens of millions of people in a short time frame to overcome what is happening is not possible. While certainly education and training are long-term objectives, is there anything we can do in a shorter period of time? Two solutions come to my mind. One involves changing the labor-management system in the United States as discussed below, and the second is covered in the "Jobs for Low-Skilled Workers" section of Chapter 11.

Stabilizing the System

How can we change the labor-management system to save as many private sector jobs as possible? Labor, management, and politicians all need a paradigm shift. I will discuss what some labor-management teams are pursuing, despite politicians' efforts to divide them. I would like to see a call for more action and dialogue among all three parties and greater awareness by the public. My goal is to raise awareness of this problem to a national level without the usual use of the political blame games and other futile rhetoric.

Management Paradigm Shift

Despite the perceptions of some, most business managers I have met would prefer to use U.S. workers rather than outsource to foreign workers. After all, U.S. workers are easier to train, and eliminate a lot of problems associated with long-distance communications and product delivery— both of which cost money.

But management must overcome all temptations to take the easy road of continuing to feel superior or more knowledgeable than those doing the day-to-day work. Those "on the floor and behind the desks" know more about how to work efficiently than their managers. A large part of management's responsibility is to facilitate ways to obtain input from all labor and make work a team effort. Management must also cut itself to the bone, if necessary, to accommodate employees whose jobs are eliminated as a result of effective cost, product, or service improvements.

A significant paradigm shifting "team" policy should be established by every U.S. business— the goal of which is to protect productive employees from being laid off as a result of productivity improvements. Certainly some situations may require lay-offs, but an employment policy that retains productive workers who contribute hard work and worthwhile suggestions to receptive management would be a significant management paradigm shift at many businesses.

Lincoln Electric Company sets a good example of this policy concept[10]. They have an incentive performance system that among other things guarantees employment after three years of service. The company has not exercised its layoff options in their U.S. operations since post-war 1948. To help save U.S. jobs, every business should strive to match the Lincoln Electric Company.

The American public should be rightfully angry at what appears to be greed or abuse of power by some business executives. In the next chapter, I will discuss corporate leader compensation. Good compensation should be provided to managers, but the criteria should also include incentives, i.e., stocks, and how they address the long-term wellbeing of both the business and all its employees. Just like politicians, some corporate leaders "talk the talk, but do not walk the walk." They need to do what they say instead of just idle boasting. So team play is the only way!

Labor Paradigm Shift

One of the biggest assets a labor force has is a lot of people, which translates into a lot of brainpower. One of the things I learned early as a youngster and again as a manager is that we all have, more or less, the same intelligence. Thus, if we can get all of this brainpower focused on common goals, the impact can be enormous. We all have different experiences and attributes we can draw upon to solve problems; therefore, making the sum of a business's laborers' knowledge much greater than that of an individual or a few managers. Labor can offer this resource to receptive management. Individuals who do not accept these facts should not be promoted to management or labor leader positions in this 21st century world.

Before this happens, labor must recognize the industries for which they work have worldwide competition and must be constantly trying new, innovative approaches to improve productivity, marketing, and sales. Labor must understand the industry's margin of profit is limited by competition. Each laborer should strive to provide strategic help to the industry (and, thus, survival) by continuously looking for and offering suggestions to improve productivity, even if in some cases laborers will no longer be needed. Labor can benefit from such actions provided management first establishes a paradigm shifting "team" policy. At a minimum, labor should seek such a policy from the business. Labor also needs to stop demonizing management in public forums. This, too, is counterproductive.

Making these strategic changes is even more important for labor that is unionized. Their adversarial strategies need to be replaced with cooperative strategies. This may not be easy to do, but it can be done and is being done in a few businesses. Big-labor unions of unskilled workers, and the politicians who support them, cannot pass legislation that makes the worldwide competition go away. So team play is the only way!

Politicians Paradigm Shift

Political parties have chosen sides, one party demonizing labor and the other demonizing management and businesses in general. This might be what they think is needed to get re-elected, but it is really counterproductive to the nation, as well as to both labor and management. The result is divisive, killing any form of team effort. This, in turn, leads to more job losses and outsourcing. The latest political ploy is to blame business for outsourcing jobs and to promise fixes to the outsourcing problem. The truth is politicians have forced outsourcing with their policies. Once again the politicians are trying to sucker us into blaming others for what they have done.

If politicians were truly interested in representing all of their constituents, they would instead work to foster labor-management team efforts. Nothing will happen until both labor and management fully understand why teaming up is vital to their survival. Nothing will happen if politicians continue to use wedges and other tricks to divide labor and management for their own personal gain. Both labor and management must demand political change. Politicians must take the high road to foster team efforts, or be voted out.

Failing Corporate/Business and Labor System Summary Bullets

✪ Labor, management, and politicians must work as a team rather than as adversaries.
✪ Managers must recognize and seek survival ideas from labor while also seeking to maintain laborers' jobs, as well as their own.
✪ Labor must understand their company's need for profits to stay in business and for providing the brainpower of the working masses to help ensure the company's survival.
✪ Politicians must stop being partisan and become team-builders instead of dividers.

Chapter 11:
Deficient Education and Low-Skilled Jobs Systems

Not all systems are about to fail, but numerous other systems in our federal, state, and local governments should be analyzed for their *potential* to fail. Needed analyses cannot be done by one person or in one book. So how should it be done? According to *The Constitution*, this is one function of Congress. Members of Congress are charged with the responsibility of making laws and associated standards and overseeing what they have imposed. Unfortunately, they frequently fail to do their duty. As we have seen in previous chapters, they are masters of blame evasion. In this chapter we will analyze two of these stable-but-deficient systems that greatly impact many individuals and our nations future, education and jobs for low-skill workers.

Educational System

Accountability

We have heard and read about problems with our educational system involving a shortage of funding. This certainly is one cause that has adversely affected our educational system, but is not all that is wrong with it. There are at least two additional significant educational deficiencies.

First, I believe people cannot be held accountable unless they have been provided with clear expectations, and the knowledge and tools (education) to meet those expectations. Individuals who have been provided an education that is both practical and useful in their daily lives will have the knowledge and tools they need to meet expectations for being good citizens. Only then can they be held accountable to be good citizens. Our younger citizens' education does not provided what they need to live and thrive in our capitalistic economy and politically driven society.

Second, our citizens, young and old, do not know what skills they should obtain and sustain to maintain employment over time. Our current national system fails to determine the professions and trades needed to help the country compete in future global markets. Our school systems should be informing all citizens (particularly young people and their parents) of future professions and trades needs and ensuring that our educational system provides the knowledge and training required for these professions and trades.

These are complex issues, but one thing is clear: our K-12 and governmental education system does not do an adequate job of meeting these needs. The present lack of educational funding is in part linked to these two failures, and vice-versa. If our students were more knowledgeable in practical and political terms, and understood future job prospects, they would be better prepared for making quality decisions about their future. Over time the financial shortfall for education would be reduced since informed citizens would be more likely to demand our leaders' priorities become congruent with theirs.

Socio-Economic and Political Systems Knowledge

Daily living uses money as a primary ingredient for business and survival in our society, yet most students, and some adults, do not know, and cannot explain:

- ✪ How to develop a budget
- ✪ How to use and balance a checkbook, either on paper or electronically over the web
- ✪ What compound interest is and its impacts
- ✪ The risks and responsibilities of accumulating debt
- ✪ The basic economic principles and practices of capitalism
- ✪ Why companies must make a profit and how much profit is needed for them to stay in business
- ✪ How new jobs and wealth are created
- ✪ How government job creation may reduce the number of private sector jobs and the total number of jobs
- ✪ There is no such thing as free money despite politicians' insistences to the contrary

Years ago, according to old school records, many of the items on this list were formally taught, but they are no longer emphasized. Civics, government, and U.S. and world history curricula are taught in our schools. Perusal of some of these curricula indicate what is taught is useful, but does not provide the details and discussion necessary for understanding political strategies and tactics for living in our present and future world.

In a practical sense, how our country operates is very complex. Covering U.S. history and the three branches of government is a start. However, politics and what politicians do is essential knowledge for our citizenry to understand. Politics has a major impact on individuals and the country. Many politicians would likely prefer not to educate our citizens about their modes of operation and their other tactical tricks, since they rely on the ignorance of voters to get themselves re-elected. But students and adults need to know how our political system really works in practice, and be exposed to the political punches to which they could become a victim. All of us need to be more aware of the likely impacts the evolving world economy will have on each citizen and our nation.

We have changed curricula to reflect environmental topics and other important social awareness issues. Political and daily life knowledge and skills are at least as important. If these skills had been taught, the financial problems of our government (and of many of our citizens who are now heavily in debt) could have been avoided. We need curricula changes as soon as possible.

Fixing the Problem

Two or more semesters of coursework that teaches what is needed for daily living and how politicians operate should be mandatory for every high school student before they begin their senior year. These courses could be made "fun" and educational by use of "fast forward" societal role-playing with "real life" examples. These simple, required curriculum additions would have enormous long-term impacts. If required, other governmental and socio-educational programs should be reduced to accommodate these two new educational requirements.

Future Professions and Trades

The freedom to choose a career path is a precious one. Making a bad career path decision can result in a lifetime of struggle. How is a young person or adult wanting a job supposed to know what professions or trades to choose that will be in demand over a few years - or a lifetime? Professions and trade skills training selected by young people is vital to the future of the nation, yet there seems to be no clear guidance to help with these critical decisions. Many of the countries we are and will continue to complete against in the next few decades are not as cavalier. They are aggressively educating and training their younger citizens.

The Bureau of Labor Statistics (BLS) compiles a variety of data and provides some ten-year projections. These are helpful, but not adequate, since what is needed over time, when the need will exist, and the likely future global (economic) environment is not defined.[1] These weaknesses in the data make them difficult for interested individuals to use for answering questions like:

❂ What professions and trades will likely be in demand in five-year intervals for the next fifty years?
❂ What quantities of each of these professions and trades will be needed and when will they be needed?
❂ What training or education is needed for each profession and trade?
❂ What national and international factors drive, or might significantly change, these requirements?

Years ago, planning a future was a problem but not nearly as critical as in our 21st century global environment. For example, I was born and raised on a farm in Ohio. Back in 1954, when I was a high school sophomore, a realization struck me that after graduation I would need a job. My options were to stay on the farm, work in a factory, become a bum, or go to college and get a degree. I was too lazy to be a farmer, and factory work did not sound like fun, so those were ruled out. I like good food, so being a bum was out. A college education was the only option left and I started taking education much more seriously.

The next question was "what would be a good field of study?" I had no idea what profession would have great future potential for stable employment. I really liked physics and math, so I decided upon physics even though I knew little about the actual job operations of a physicist. In 1957, as I was about to head off to a nearby university extension center, Russia put up *Sputnik I*. Our government realized, and publicized, that we were behind in the space race and we needed engineers as soon as possible. I asked an extension center counselor, who happened to be a physicist, what branch of engineering was most like physics. He scratched his head and said: "I guess electronics." I became an electronics engineer.

After talking to many working people, I find many have similar stories. I also have talked to young people who seem to be groping for direction. Not surprisingly, a lot of younger people learn about careers by watching TV and movies. Throughout history, some professions have been glamorized. The newer media, namely TV and the web, have greatly enhanced this glamorization. For example, lots of TV shows glamorize athletes and other entertainers, lawyers, policemen, and doctors. No doubt we will need some of these professions, but let's ask the question "How will each of these professions benefit the nation in the likely global environment twenty years from now?" Very few athletes or entertainers make it big, so planning to be one is not realistic for most young people. According to the American Bar Association there are about 11 million licensed lawyers practicing in the United States. That is approximately one lawyer for every 300 people. There are far more with inactive or retired status that substantially lowers the 300-to-1 ratio.[2] The result is that we have more lawyers per capita than any other country.[3] What and how will our lawyers contribute to the nation in the likely global environment twenty years from now? We likely do not need a lot more lawyers. Of course, we will always need policemen and doctors. The few shows that highlight technical professions - such as the sciences and engineering - paint a picture of geeks or geniuses, neither of which "the average Jane or John" would necessarily like to or aspire to become.

Counselors help give some guidance to students by identifying student's skills and attributes. The real problem is, given the global economic environment and world problems, the United States can no longer be cavalier about what we teach our young people. We must help our young people select careers which are both useful to the future of the nation and consistent with their skills, attributes, and interests.

Fixing the Problem

What do we need to do to correct this problem? Starting at the top, Congress and the President should establish a broad-based commission of futurists, a "Jobs Futures Commission," to brainstorm this problem with the goal of providing a ranked list of professions and trades essential to our future success. This is an important task for the long-term future of our nation.

This commission cannot be left up to the politicians; however, they must help implement the commission's recommendations. This commission should be made up of individuals appointed by universities, corporations, and other strategic entities outside of the government. The commission should make available to the public their thinking and discussion points. The commission members themselves must be leaders in "futuristic thinking and planning" and should be replaced periodically. Given the importance of this task and the fact they will likely have full-time jobs, they should be paid a government stipend for their participation.

Once the commission has made its first recommendation, K-12 school, trade school, college, and university educators around the country should re-evaluate their curricula and train their counselors to determine if they are meeting these future needs. Finally, a national educational program is needed at all levels to bring the public up to speed. The web or a telephone "app" could easily disseminate information needed by the general public. This media can provide lists of jobs in demand, the skills a person needs, examples of the daily work the job entails, and typical "up sides" (i.e., promotional and other opportunities) of the jobs.

Education Funding

Last, but not least, funding for education is a significant issue and I do not want to make light of this problem. The fight for education must continue. Ironically, in California we pay our unionized teachers less than our unionized prison guards.

Thanks to generous overtime rules, thousands of prison guards make over $100,000 per year.[4] Which jobs require more training, and which are more valuable to our nation? Of course the answer is our teachers. Why do we have such an imbalance? Do we have our priorities right?

In California, nearly 307,000 teachers worked in public school classrooms in 2008-09.[5] Each district's governing board sets a schedule for teachers' salaries through the collective bargaining process negotiated between the district and the teachers' representatives. The salary schedule is based on levels of education and years of experience. Teachers' threats generally carry little weight since they care about their students and do not want to hurt them. As a consequence of smaller unions negotiating with many entities and teacher loyalty to their students, teacher unions are less powerful than other public unions. Meanwhile, the state prison guards basically only deal with one entity and can threaten to walk off the job, which would instantly become a safety issue.

Education, in general, has been trapped by too little money chasing too many social programs, and an unstable public employees system where union priorities seem not to reflect citizen priorities. Our educational system as a whole may be near failure, which would significantly impact the future of our nation. We must change our priorities now.

Fixing the Problem

To reset our priorities, I believe we need to adopt bounds on public unions, including teachers unions, per the discussions in Chapter 10. Then, salaries and benefits of teachers need to become one of our highest public employee priorities - higher than anything except perhaps local public safety. A fair merit-pay system should be adopted. If my "Future Professions and Trades" solution is adopted, then specific teaching skills, such as math and science, might become more valuable. Teacher salaries should have ranges based upon what the teacher is capable of teaching, what the private sector would pay for similar "technical" skills required, as well as other teaching performance capabilities. Finally, much can be achieved by utilizing active and retired experienced experts in private and public sectors jobs in limited teaching settings. Presently, they are excluded or over-constrained because they have not had training to be a teacher. There is no better way for students to learn about occupations than to hear about professions and trades from someone actually doing the work. Unfortunately, we can expect the public employee unions to be a major obstacle to any of these changes.

Deficient Education System Summary Bullets

✪ Our high school curriculum needs to provide young adults with the expectations and knowledge needed for daily living, political awareness, and civic responsibility.

✪ Our federal government needs to provide families with targeted career resources and guidance so young adults can make informed educational decisions in order to meet our future job needs.

Jobs for Low-Skilled Workers

Inner Cities Versus Immigration

During the Great Depression, public works programs funded by taxpayer-borrowed money were used to employ millions. These jobs were scattered around the country so many breadwinners had no choice but to go where the work was, such as to where the Hoover Dam was built. This was tough on the families involved, but did provide food for the families, while the acquired skills helped many workers to find future jobs, and their work contributed to society and the economy. They worked hard and were grateful to have the work, despite poor working conditions.

We have millions of individuals who have entered our country illegally, most of whom have traveled thousands of miles and taken great risks to get here. They continue to take risks after arriving here, but still generally find work and many send money home to their families. They work hard, and are generally grateful to have the work. Most are filling jobs that do not require great skills.

According to the Homeland Security Department, the number of illegal immigrants in the United States fell for the first time in four years in 2008, as the nation's tough economy discouraged people from sneaking into the country. The decline still left the country with 11.6 million illegal immigrants in January 2008, down from a record 11.8 million a year earlier, according to a Homeland Security report. There were about four million illegal immigrants in 1990, according to federal agencies and researchers.[6] While not all of these illegal immigrants have jobs, a reasonable assumption is that more than half of them are filling jobs that could be filled by U.S. citizens. We have about 150 million working citizens (over 16 years of age),[7] and about 6 million illegal immigrants employed, meaning that about four percent of our workforce is illegal immigrants. A four percent drop in unemployment for our U.S. citizens, I believe, is worth working on.

A downside of illegal immigration is shown by separate research by George Borjas, Robert W. Scrivner Professor of Economics and Social Policy at Harvard University, and Paul Samuelson, Nobel Prize-winning economist from MIT. They have shown that illegal immigration had a substantial effect on *reducing* the economic status of the American poor while *benefiting* middle-class and wealthier Americans.[8]

A second downside is that we U.S. citizens are taking risks by having a largely uncontrolled illegal population. If all of these illegal people can easily cross our borders, how long will it take for terrorists to learn how to do the same thing using the same techniques? Let's hope this has not already happened. In addition, what do we know about those who have crossed the border? The answer is virtually nothing, other than that, as a group, they seem to be hard-working, honest, inexpensive to hire, and available when needed.

Also curiously, we have millions of jobs for those here illegally, but still have many U.S. citizens (mostly living in our cities) who are without jobs. What is wrong with this picture? Why do our unemployed citizens not fill the available jobs held by those here illegally? Some might say that our unemployed citizens do not want to do the jobs the illegal immigrants do for our society. This may be true in some cases where significant governments assistance is provided, I do not believe this assumption is correct for the majority of the "employable unemployed." I believe many have simply given up looking for jobs due to the lack of job opportunities available to them.

I was born and raised on an Ohio farm in the 1940s and 1950s. The first money I earned was for picking strawberries. I was young and probably ate more than I picked for sale. I also spent a lot of time doing various farm work that included working in sugar beet fields. For sugar beets, we hired part-time labor to hand-hoe-out the excess small beets so that no two were close enough to interfere with each other as they grew. The people we hired were U.S. citizens, Mexicans, American Indians, and others. These workers were amazing. They worked very hard with a common bond to their families. Observing these workers, and the many others I have had the opportunity to know from around our nation and the world, has convinced me that almost all human beings want to work, to be self-sufficient, and to improve their lives and the lives of their loved ones. What unemployed people need most are opportunities and motivation.

Some leaders at all levels of government have worked the "jobs opportunity and motivation" issues. Their answers have been to try to get companies with jobs to move to where the people are located by providing tax breaks or other incentives, and provide some form of free money until jobs become available. Politicians have, more recently, added incentives for those receiving free money to seek a job.

Specifically, in 1996, the Welfare Reform Act was passed into law with the promise to end welfare as it had existed since its inception (approximately sixty years earlier). A new era of welfare benefits and provisions was on the horizon, and the Welfare Reform Act was the catalyst needed to begin these much-needed changes. One of the reforms under this act was the Welfare-to-Work initiative, which required work in exchange for time-limited financial assistance. Recipients of Temporary Assistance to Needy Families (TANF) were required to work at least twenty hours per week, and the reform statute listed twelve authorized activities accepted to meet this requirement. According to reports, within three years of the reforms enactment, millions of Americans had moved from being dependent on welfare to being self-sufficient. In addition, agencies reported a reduction in the number of social welfare cases.[9]

Congress passed the Welfare Reform Agenda of 2003, and the 2003 reform's goals were built on the foundation of the 1996 Welfare Reform Act. Essentially, the goals of the 2003 Agenda were to provide assistance to individuals and families in achieving financial independence from the government. Protecting children and strengthening families were important aspects of this reform measure, and state and local governments were asked to assist these individuals and families in gaining this independent status. In 2004, the Welfare-to-Work program ended, but during the time this program was active millions of Americans' lives were changed for the better. TANF was reauthorized in 2005, and this social welfare program continues to help millions of struggling families. While Food Stamps, Medicaid, Supplemental Security Income and TANF are still common social welfare services, Earned Income Tax Credits (EITC) are also being offered to low-income families to help create financial stability. For eligibility, the individual or family must meet certain requirements.[10]

These past approaches worked reasonably well but problems still exist - particularly in the inner cities. It is vital to the health and economy of the nation for the individuals in these areas to have the opportunity, ability, and desire to support themselves and meet the needs of their families, ultimately without economic assistance from the government. We need to again think "out of the box" for solutions.

Job Opportunity Limitations

What are some of the root causes for the limited successes to date? There are, no doubt, many causes. Here are some causes that are not adequately addressed by our federal, state, and local governments: (1) an inability to match people to available jobs near where they live, (2) ineffective utilization of free money, and (3) inadequate attention to transporting the workers to where the work is located. Some of our citizens simply stay put and take whatever little money is provided by government sources, since pay is low for the available jobs in their neighborhoods. A change in strategies and tactics is needed.

First, what and where are the full and part-time jobs for modestly skilled and unskilled citizen workers? Our government provides some statistics for this information, but not enough to be easily helpful. Given the global economy, manufacturing and service jobs that once provided a middle-class income for millions of American families are disappearing and will not likely come back. These manufacturing and service jobs generally did not require highly skilled workers. Most economists acknowledge that people are having a hard time finding jobs which pay as much as the lost manufacturing and service ones. Yet our lower-end manufacturing and services industries account for thirty to fifty percent of our workforce! Non-manufacturing, lower-wage service jobs (including childcare, nursing aides, security guards, teachers' assistants, janitors, home health aides, retail sales, routine maintenance, food processing, and food preparation) are among the country's fastest-growing employment opportunities. There are large and growing numbers of these jobs.

Second, we need to establish ways to assist potential workers to get to where the jobs are located. Do these jobless citizens need to move to the jobs, as was done by some during the Great Depression? Looking at the available jobs indicates that this should not be necessary for many of the new jobs being created. Many of the new jobs are near where the jobless citizens live, so transportation cost assistance may be required but the costs should be minimal.

Third, and most importantly, these lower-skilled jobs are essential to our economy and skills are not a great problem. This is why illegal immigrants are able to find and fill these jobs. U.S. citizens have the requisite skills (or could, with on-the-job or simple training) for jobs such as childcare providers, nursing-home aides, food processors, and janitors. Labor-intensive employers will continue to demand larger numbers of these relatively unskilled workers. Many of them are not prospects for outsourcing because the jobs must be done in specific locations, face-to-face with patients or customers. These jobs are ideal for millions of our unemployed citizens, including those in our inner cities.

Finally, the pay unskilled workers receive must be adequate to support U.S. citizens and their families. About twenty-five percent of our nation's workers earn less than $20,000 a year, before taxes or health insurance, which puts a family of four under the federal poverty level. For the people who hold these jobs to be in a position to support themselves and their families, the rewards of their jobs must be improved. We need to re-engineer the Welfare-to-Work program and related programs to address these needs.

Without question, better education and fluency in new technologies are essential to improving job options for this and the next generation of working men and women. People in virtually any positions should receive training throughout their careers to increase their opportunities for job and social mobility. But how do we dig ourselves out of this hole? We need to reset out priorities and redirect resources to make these low-skilled jobs available for U.S. citizens.

Fixing the Problems

The federal and state governments, with private sector help, need to develop a new system to find and fill private sector jobs that can be done by unskilled workers. The general goals should be to provide jobs to U.S. citizens by addressing the location, transportation, and living wage issues encumbering our low-skilled unemployed citizens.

A key to turning this around is understanding what makes "good" private sector jobs "good." There is nothing inherently skillful in welding bumpers onto cars or manufacturing electronic components that makes those better jobs than caring for children or cooking our food at our favorite restaurant. Even so, workers in manufacturing received higher wages, obtained paid leave, established retirement benefits and healthcare by the passage of social legislation and through private sector union actions. Thus, these initially "bad" manufacturing jobs turned into "good" middle-class jobs. These jobs provided an opportunity for families to succeed and for their children to have brighter futures.

The government seems to intrude upon many aspects of its citizens' lives. One myth some politicians perpetuate is that government creates jobs. The fact is that every dollar the government spends in this way reduces funds for a greater number of private sector jobs. I believe our government needs to become an employment *agency* rather than an employer.

The following is a sequence of steps that should allow new policies to develop that will turn "bad jobs" into "good jobs". This would have broad benefits to the nation. The U.S. Department of Labor (DOL) or, preferably, a joint task force could lead execution of these steps, along with members from several agencies, states, and the private sector.

Steps to employ low-skilled unemployed citizens:

1. Estimate type, number and locations of jobs (including those presently held by illegal immigrants).
   a. Determine the types of low to modest-skill jobs likely to be needed (child care, nursing aides, security guards, teachers' assistants, janitors, home health aides, retail sales, routine [lawn and other] maintenance, food processing, food preparation, etc.).
   b. Estimate the number of potential vacancies in each type of job versus when they will be needed (will they be needed now, or in two, five, ten, or twenty years?).
   c. Estimate the likely locations for present and future openings for each job type.
2. Determine where the "employable unemployed" are located.
3. Determine suitable jobs for each unemployed person by considering his or her strengths, life experiences, and other individual considerations. Also ask if he or she has job preferences from the list in 1.a. Using 1. and 2. above, establish two (or more) job opportunities that are physically close to where each unemployed person lives.
4. Determine the various sources and amounts of funds each of the unemployed is presently receiving, factoring in medical coverage, welfare, unemployment, food stamps and other federal, state, and local funds.
5. Develop criteria for a minimum "living wage" for each job type using existing comparable wages and regional cost of living information.
   a. The wages for the lowest value jobs should be at the poverty level (approximately $10 per hour in 2009) and become higher as the job values increase. This is reasonable, since starting higher would place more hardship on the approximately twenty-five percent of our citizens already employed who are at or below the poverty line.

    b. As necessary, initially subsidize these wages for a period of time. Since many of these jobs involve personal interactions with employers, it is likely the employer will willingly increase wages to keep qualified workers they know, rather than hiring unknown people.

    c. Ensure the criteria used are tied to inflation so that they do not lose ground as inflation and other factors impact the nation.

6. Establish family status and funding criteria (these already exist through various entitlement programs).

    a. Establish the family status for each unemployed worker, i.e., whether they are married, single, with children, two unemployed adults, etc.

    b. Develop criteria that add funding to encourage maintenance of the family unit, i.e., these criteria should encourage maintaining family units by addressing possibilities and needs for two-earner families and families with children without discriminating against single persons. The present welfare criteria are a starting point.

7. Determine transportation options and costs.

    a. Determine costs for transportation to/from the jobs identified in 3. with emphasis on public systems, walking, or carpools for workers (including any public transportation subsidies) to get to the two jobs determined in 3.a., above.

    b. If transportation costs exceed, for example, three percent of the wage value determined for the job type in 6.a., then provide an added subsidy for transportation.

8. Using the two jobs identified in 3., calculate the wages and subsidies, by adding up the results from Steps 5., 6., and 7.

9. Calculate the new taxpayer cost of this program by subtracting the total subsidy costs (in Step 8.) from the results for Step 4. to determine the savings or added costs to the taxpayer.

10. Require each "employable unemployed" person to seek and take one of the jobs available as a requirement for any of the above subsidies. They must strive to become self-sufficient to be

a part of this program. The Eligibility Requirements of Welfare Programs[11] provides an excellent start toward self-sufficiency. If the unemployed fail to accept a reasonable job, then a reduction or limit on their free money should be imposed. (As with any large group of people, a few of them may be just plain lethargic and would rather be "couch potatoes" getting carpel tunnel syndrome from using the TV remote. These few must pay the price for their inaction through reduced welfare.)

All of the above steps should be assisted via computerized software and a database system that links federal and state data. A web-based system and telephone app should be used to disseminate the information and allow rapid connections between employers and the available unemployed.

Example:
(Note: The following is a realistic, but hypothetical, example since the numbers vary greatly by region.)
   Suppose Mary is a single mother of two children living with her mother, who is physically unable to work. They both receive various subsidies. Mary, for unknown reasons, has no funds from the father of her children, but is healthy and unemployed. She has no unique skills, but it is likely that she could fill many of the job types in 1.a. She likes working with people, especially children. Jobs are available within her city for a childcare assistant paying the lowest wage of $10/hr. ($1,733/month), and for a home health care aide, which pays $11.54/hr. ($2,000/month) (Steps 2. and 3.).
   Mary is receiving welfare, health care (to be determined by the new Health Care Bill and not considered in this hypothetical example) and other subsidies totaling $850/month (Step 4.). The actual wage paid to a childcare assistant where she lives is $8.50/hour requiring a $1.50/hour wage subsidy, and for a health care aide is $10.50/hour requiring a $1.04/hour wage subsidy (Step

5.). Being unmarried with two children, she gets a $260/month subsidy, as part of her $850/month welfare (Step 6.). Mary can take public transportation to the childcare assistant job at a cost of $4/day, which is more than 3 percent of the wage value and adds a $26.27/month subsidy. She can walk to the health care aide job (Step 7.). These options and conversions of hourly to monthly dollars, etc., are provided in **Table 11-1: Example Dollar Amounts For Low-Skill Workers.**

Table 11-1: Example Dollar Amounts For Low Skill Workers

Job Title	Childcare Assistant		Health Care Aide	
	Hourly	Monthly	Hourly	Monthly
Local hourly wage	$8.50	$1,473.33	$10.50	$1,820.00
New Minimum pay schedule for job	$10.00	$1,733.33	$11.54	$2,000.27
Continue Child subsidy		$260.00		$260.00
New Monthly income		$1,993.33		$2,260.27
New yearly income		*$23,919.96*		*$27,123.24*
Present subsidies		**$850.00**		**$850.00**
New Wage subsidy	$1.50	$260.00	$1.04	$180.27
Same child subsidy		$260.00		$260.00
Transportation subsidy		$26.27		$0.00
Total New Subsidies		**$546.27**		**$440.27**
Taxpayer Savings (Present minus New Subsidies)		**$303.73**		**$409.73**
Taxpayer Savings Per Year		*$3,644.76*		*$4,916.76*

Given Mary's options, she could earn $1,993.33/month ($23,919.96/year) working as a childcare assistant, or she could earn $2,260.27/month ($27,123.24/year) working as a health care aide. After reviewing the two options, Mary decides to take the childcare assistant job even though this job pays less money and requires transportation time and costs. She has two reasons for her decision: she feels she will enjoy working with children, and she is thinking about opening a child day-care center in her neighborhood sometime in the future.

Without strong encouragement to work or assistance to help our unemployed citizens to find jobs, they will never have opportunities for improving their or their families' futures. The gap between the "haves" and the "have-nots" will continue to grow, straining an already divided nation. When income gaps become entrenched, as they have in our inner cities, breaking free is increasingly difficult for individuals and their families.

We must make the jobs we believe need to be done (and are often currently filled by illegal immigrants) available to millions of U.S. citizens. If we do not, we are undermining one of our nation's most fundamental ideals: if you work hard, you can support yourself and your family. As a nation, we have the power to ensure that the people who are able to work secure jobs that create self-sufficiency, making service jobs the "good jobs" of the 21st and 22nd centuries. We must not simply label certain jobs "unskilled" and sentence a quarter of our population to a life of poverty when valuable jobs can be made available.

Finally, other new jobs will evolve by establishing the proposed new jobs system. For example, childcare businesses will be needed to take care of the children of the newly working fathers and mothers, and employment agencies will need to be formed to match employees to employers, and to assist in managing processes. Also, over time and without illegal immigrant labor competition, government policies and unions can make these jobs into good middle-class jobs for our citizens just as was done in the manufacturing sector decades ago.

There is a sad irony associated with *The Constitution's* 14th Amendment, Section 1, regarding illegal immigrants and the employment of many of our low-skilled citizens. This amendment was adopted to ensure that the freed slaves – mostly born in the United States - would be U.S. citizens. This made a lot of sense at the time. As written, it also applies to any children born in the United States even if their parents are here legally or illegally for just a few seconds. No other country in the world has such a law. As a consequence of the 14th Amendment, some estimates indicate there are tens of thousands of pregnant women already living in our country illegally or coming into our country that give birth every year resulting in these children being U.S. citizens. This problem is made more complicated when those here illegally (or legally) are expected (and sometimes forced) to return to their own countries and they already have U.S.-born children. Some U.S. citizens may feel we are "showing no compassion by breaking up families" or are "discriminating against people of color or origin." The irony is that many of the jobs filled by these illegal immigrants are jobs that could be starting point jobs for many U.S. citizens, many of whom are descendents of freed slaves that the 14th Amendment was originally intended to help.

I wish there were a way illegal immigrants would not be hurt by the proposed program, but they will be hurt. Most are great people and sometimes we do not treat them well. One "tough" solution would be to enforce our existing laws and deport all foreign individuals when they are in the United States illegally or when their visas or other time-limited visiting papers expire. If they have children who were born in the United States while they were here they would have the choice of either taking their children with them or putting them up for adoption. No doubt this would significantly decrease the number of foreigners who attempt to take advantage of our laws.

Worth noting is the fact that several presidents deported millions of illegal immigrants during their terms to allow more U.S. citizens to have jobs. These presidents were Hoover (Great Depression), Truman (WWII veterans) and Eisenhower (WWII and Korean war veterans). What we should do is develop policies that allow foreigners to enter our country to work legally when jobs are available, or when there are no able-bodied citizens available to fill the jobs. If this program is implemented, the future will be much brighter for millions of our citizens and foreign workers would be more fairly treated. Laws against the hiring of illegal immigrants need to be strong and enforced, and our borders need to be secured.

Deficient Low-Skilled Jobs System Summary Bullets

✪ The federal government needs to become an employment agency rather than an employer or free money provider.
  ★ Match people to available jobs near where they live.
  ★ Address transportation needs of workers to work location.
  ★ Determine what jobs illegal immigrants are doing that can be done by unemployed U.S. citizens.
✪ Utilize existing free money more effectively and efficiently.
✪ The process proposed needs to be implemented by our federal, state, and local governments to improve opportunities for low-skilled workers to obtain jobs to support themselves and their families.

Chapter 12:
Deficient Corporate Compensation and New Media Systems

Whereas the topics in Chapter 11 discussed the impacts on individuals, this chapter discusses the impacts of two national systems: our corporate compensation system and our new media system. Here we will explore how these systems are deficient, and what we may do to ensure they don't fail us entirely.

Fair Corporate Leader Compensation System

Criteria, Standards and Principles

Boards of directors need criteria and standards to help guide them when creating corporate compensation packages for their top leaders and selected specialists. Corporate boards trying to get the best of the best think they have little choice but to outbid potential competition. The result has been a fast-accelerating set of wage and benefit packages. Almost all contracts contain great "golden parachutes" to make it easier for corporate boards to get rid of failing corporate leaders. Without some agreed-upon standard, there are no bounds to CEO compensation short of handing ownership of the whole company to the CEO.

Even before the current financial meltdown, those in the public who were aware of the compensation issue and the associated golden parachutes were concerned about the disparity between the highest and lowest paid workers. The high salaries being paid in a failing financial industry simply served to educate more citizens about the situation and led to some citizens becoming outraged. The fact that there were pre-existing contracts with many of these employees made the situation even more difficult to correct and further outraged the public. Overcoming the outrage will require visible actions. The intensified public scrutiny on corporate practices regarding executive compensation and should not and will not stop until there is a rational solution.

For a capitalistic economic system, a government mandate is not the best answer; however, if this compensation disparity is not fixed by corporate America, the politicians will surely step in. Publicly traded companies must take immediate and credible action to restore trust in the ability of their boards of directors to limit, control, and oversee executive compensation.

Some corporations have recognized the problems and are interested in solutions. The Conference Board, a global independent membership organization working in the public interest, is a not-for-profit organization and holds 501(c)(3) tax-exempt status in the United States. A Conference Board Task Force on Executive Compensation lays out five guiding principles:

1. *Paying for the right things and paying for performance.* Compensation programs should be designed to drive a company's business strategy and objectives and to create shareholder value, consistent with an acceptable risk profile, through legal and ethical means.
2. *The "right" total compensation.* Total compensation should be attractive to executives, affordable for the company, proportionate to the executive's contributions and fair to shareholders and employees, while providing payouts that are clearly aligned with actual performance.

3. *Avoid controversial pay practices.* Companies should avoid controversial pay practices, unless specific justification is present.
4. *Credible board oversight of executive compensation.* Compensation committees should demonstrate credible oversight of executive compensation. They should be independent, experienced, and knowledgeable about the company's business.
5. *Transparent communications and increased dialogue with shareholders.* Compensation should be transparent, understandable, and effectively communicated to shareholders.

This Task Force further states:

It recognizes that a "rules-based" (criteria and standards) approach cannot provide the essential flexibility required to accommodate the disparate industries, strategies, business models, and stages of development represented in the more than 12,000 U.S. public companies. If executed correctly, in furtherance of a company's business strategy and shareholder value and consistent with the company's values, the Task Force recognizes that attractive executive compensation is vital to the economic health of America's business sector.[1]

These guiding principles, I am sure, look great to corporate boards, but as a common citizen I believe some corporations will simply ignore them when times are rough. There needs to be some "teeth" through oversight and peer pressure to make any guiding principles work and to restore fairness and public confidence.

Fixing the Problems

First, let's take a page from the public sector. Large federal entities with multi-billion-dollar annual budgets establish task forces or oversight boards to address complex social, safety, financial, or technical problems - or combinations thereof. The task force members typically have access to all needed information and are paid a stipend for their time.

Why not set up a small corporate entity, Corporate America Management Compensation Oversight, Inc. (CAMCO), owned by its members, which provides support to a two-tier oversight task force structure? This two-tier task force would develop and monitor guiding principles (like those shown above) for corporate compensation. Given the large number of corporations involved, one task force could not address all the complexities.

The top-level, overarching task force would provide the general criteria and guidelines for executive compensation and seek to balance all corporations' interests (preferably without golden parachutes.) They would use information from around the world, as well as from within the public and private sectors of the United States, to establish and update their guidelines. The second-tier task forces would provide oversight for a narrower set of corporate core businesses and would periodically report to the overarching taskforce.

A small staff would be a part of CAMCO. They would provide task force support, collect needed data, and provide information analysis. They would also develop methods for communicating information (such as average core business CEO compensation) with stakeholders, thereby aiding the understanding and acceptance by stakeholders and building public trust without revealing individual or specific corporation compensations. Public knowledge that corporate compensation is reasonable would be valuable to all parties. It would reduce (if not eliminate) a favorite set of individuals many politicians like to blame.

Second, corporations should not perceive membership as being voluntary. Either through peer pressure, by stakeholder pressure, or both, every corporation of a certain size would be required to become a dues-paying member. The member companies' size and dues they pay should be based on the type of core businesses, sales, etc. The dues burden on corporations should be negligible, and likely would easily be recouped from reductions in compensation payouts.

Public Perceptions

A systemic issue also needs to be addressed. Many of us do not give corporations much respect. This is due, in part, to our aversion to large, complex, and uncontrollable entities such as large corporations, and, in part, due to our politicians using corporations to play their blame games and other tricks to drive wedges between Main Street and Wall Street.

Let's reset our perceptions. The average salary for a major league baseball player in 2009 was $3,240,000. Many earned more (about $ 25,000,000), while some earned less (down to $400,000). They did this by working only part of the year. Movie stars make tens of millions of dollars per movie. Some are not model citizens. All are entertainers. Corporate executives of large companies are responsible for businesses worth from hundreds of millions to tens of billions of dollars. They are responsible for millions of existing jobs, creating wealth for their shareholders and new jobs, paying taxes, aiding in lowering our national trade deficits, and hundreds of other things. Yes, a few of them are not model citizens, either.

Who are the most valuable to us citizens and our nation; the entertainers or the business and corporate leaders? Without good business and corporate leadership, we citizens would have no jobs and no money to spend on entertainment. The next time you hear a politician trying to put a wedge between Main and Wall Streets ask yourself why he or she is doing it. Why isn't he or she attacking highly paid entertainers, instead?

Deficient Corporate Compensation System Summary Bullets

✪ Establish a Corporate American Management Compensation Oversight (CAMCO) board similar to other professional societies to develop and monitor corporate senior management compensation criteria and guiding principles, as well as compile information and communicate it to the public.

✪ Require all major U.S. corporations to become CAMCO dues-paying members.

✪ Good business leadership is essential to our nation. These leaders are not our enemies but the politicians that try to exploit them are our enemies.

Fair News Media System

If you don't read the newspaper you are uninformed; if you do read the newspaper you are misinformed. — **Mark Twain**[2]

The Fundamental Right

Freedom of speech is an important right, as is freedom and protection of the press. Historically, current news and investigative journalism were considered adequate and informative. Early in our nation's history, the press was a dominant source of useful information for all citizens. Good journalism was respected and valued as being both informative and relatively unbiased. Newspapers were generally locally owned with, at most, limited competition. Early press journalism was a combination of current news, publisher opinion, and investigative reporting. It was generally clear when personal opinions were being presented, and investigative reporting was an important part of every major newspaper. Over time, the written press got competition from radio, and later TV, and now, the Internet. This has changed the written press and it may become extinct, as we have known it.

From News to Ratings

Radio's impact on the dissemination of news was significant, allowing citizens to hear directly from their leaders, but initially it did not significantly change the basics of the current news, publisher opinion, and investigative reporting of journalism. Now, political talk shows are a significant source of opinion reporting.

The biggest impact so far has been from TV and the Internet. Humans (and most animals) receive and process the vast majority of the information they receive from sight. As a means of obtaining information and knowledge, sight is generally acknowledged as hundreds of times greater than hearing, feeling, smelling, and tasting. Thus, both TV and the Internet are extremely powerful communication media since they couple sight and hearing.

But, there is a big problem. Whereas in the early years of our nation one could say journalists were relatively fair and unbiased, providing a balanced view, as we start the 21st century, that is not the case. Competition has driven all forms of visual media into a feeding frenzy to find the stories that make the best "sound bites" and, more importantly, will raise their ratings. Large corporations now own major TV organizations. The people with final power in these corporations rarely have experience as reporters or editors. They have no experience with journalistic ethics. They have a bottom-line mentality. Their primary allegiance is to their stockholders. If there is a conflict between responsible journalism and profit, profit usually wins. Journalists are smart and quickly learn that news sound bites, sad stories, and anything else that helps ratings is their ticket to success and promotions.

When journalistic success is measured in ratings, I believe it is no longer journalism as our Founding Fathers had intended. Amendment 1 to *The Constitution* says: *Congress shall make no law respecting an establishment of religion, or prohibiting the free exercise thereof; or abridging the freedom of speech, or of the press; or the right of the people peaceably to assemble, and to petition the Government for a redress of grievances.* *The Constitution* does protect the freedom of speech — but only from restriction by the Congress (and, by virtue of the 14th Amendment, by state legislatures, too). But none of these freedoms are all-inclusive, e.g., a religious belief does not allow you to kill someone, freedom of speech does not allow you to slander someone or yell "fire" in a crowded building. In addition, there are plenty of places where you could speak but where speech can be - and is - suppressed. For example, freedom of speech can be restricted in a work place (for instance, employers can restrict their employees' right to speak in the work place about politics, religion, legal issues, or even TV shows). Thus, even though the government cannot stifle speech about itself or its actions, freedom of speech does have its limits.

I believe our Founding Fathers, like many others since, regarded a free press as a "fourth branch" of government.[3] The Founding Fathers felt journalists would constantly keep tabs and report on the government's activities and actions and would expose any questionable activities or actions to "we the people" for possible action. This is why "the press" was included in the First Amendment. Tabloid-like television not withstanding, any news organization in the United States can report freely on the activities of the government. Similar organizations in other nations have to worry about toeing their leader's line or being shut down and in some nations a reporter can have his life ended because of a critical story.

Journalistic Ethics (News Manipulation)

The Founding Fathers' intent for free press is, I believe, reflected in the key phrase, "keep tabs on the government's activities and actions." This phrase suggests the news media should not be advocates for a person or party (unless it is stated as an opinion) and that the press should be fair, unbiased and balanced in their reporting. While this is not explicitly stated in the First Amendment this certainly would seem to be what our Founding Fathers expected.

Some of the news media understand the need for strong ethics and have developed policies to reflect these expectations. For example: the opening statements in *The New York Times* "Policy On Ethics In Journalism, Introduction and Purpose," are:

1. The Core Purpose of *The New York Times* Company is to "enhance society by creating, collecting and distributing high-quality news, information and entertainment." The central place of our news and editorial units in fulfilling that promise is underscored by the No. 1 statement in our Core Values: "Content of the highest quality and integrity: This is the basis for our reputation and the means by which we fulfill the public trust and our customers' expectations."

2. Companywide, our goal is to cover the news impartially and to treat readers, news sources, advertisers and all parts of our society fairly and openly, and to be seen as doing so. The reputation of our company rests upon that perception, and so do the professional reputations of its staff members. Thus the company, its separate business units and members of its newsrooms and editorial pages share an interest in avoiding conflicts of interest or any appearance of conflict. Conflicts of interest, real or apparent, may arise in many areas. They may involve tensions between journalists' professional obligations to our audience and their relationships with news sources, advocacy groups, advertisers, or competitors; with one another; or with the company or one of its units. And at a time when two-career families are the norm, the civic and professional activities of spouses, household members and other relatives can create conflicts or the appearance of them.

3. In keeping with its solemn responsibilities under the First Amendment, our company strives to maintain the highest standard of journalistic ethics It is confident that its staff members share that goal. The company and its units also recognize that staff members should be free to do creative, civic and personal work and to earn extra income in ways separate from their work in our organization. Before engaging in such outside activities, though, staff members should exercise mature professional judgment and consider the stake we all have in the irreplaceable good name of our company and its newsrooms.[4]

Unfortunately, instead of a strict adherence to ethics like these, my observations over the past few decades indicate there has been a trend by many in the news media outlets to extend ethical boundaries to include high proportions of sensationalism, privacy invasion, deception, and unfair reporting, particularly in the medium with the highest impact: television. While there are a lot of documented ethics statements for news corporations, television news does not seem to follow many of them. Hot stories of any kind that will boost ratings are what count in today's news. Perhaps stories that are primarily about movie stars and other tabloid materials should be carried only by "tabloid TV stations" similar to the present-day tabloid press rags.

News can manipulate and be manipulated. Governments and corporations may attempt to manipulate news media, such as through a government's selective release of news, in the same way that corporations buy advertisements, share ownership, or other means. The methods of manipulation are subtle and many. Manipulation may be voluntary or involuntary. The final result from manipulation is an uninformed (or misinformed) public who are unaware it is happening.

News as Propaganda

"News" can also be used as propaganda. In this case, it is generally covert propaganda packaged as credible news without transparency as to its source, balance, or motivation. The lack of transparency is critical to distinguishing news propaganda from traditional press releases and video news releases. As with any propaganda, news propaganda may be spread for purposes, which include political or ideological reasons, partisan agendas, and commercial motivations (such as ratings).

A good example of questionable reporting is how the TV press treated President Obama. As a candidate, his lack of private sector experience, or of running a large organization, etc., was not a broadly covered TV news issue, but the age of Senator McCain and lack of experience of Governor Palin were often mentioned. Both omission and imbalance were evident. President Obama has had unrestricted airtime via television without challenges or penetrating questions. He simply refuses to be interviewed on the one TV network that does challenge some of his policies and rhetoric. While some of this is expected, President Obama has essentially daily TV airtime for his agenda. If you have not already noticed, I suggest you use a stopwatch to monitor the airtime afforded each political party's agendas on the three major news networks. It is not uncommon for one-third or more of their news time to be devoted to support of President Obama's agenda or personal life without any analysis or counterpoints by others.

Our Founding Fathers saw the press as being critical but reasonably fair, balanced, and unbiased rather than being focused on sound bites and ratings. If the present lack of critical fairness and balance, and obvious bias it is not propaganda then it is bordering on it. There is seldom "equal time" and rarely are the issues covered in this book mentioned. Are these issues unimportant or are they simply issues the generally liberal press does not wish to cover?

It appears to me that many members of the press today in our country are hypocrites when they claim they provide critical, fair, and balanced reporting. Most of them present information based on ratings to maximize profits and stay in business and they do so with very strong biases. Often the press - like our career politicians - tell us what they think we want to hear since this helps ratings; critical investigative reports are few. This was not what our Founding Fathers expected of the press. They saw the free press as a "check and balance" through honest investigative reporting on our federal, state, and local governments. This honest and balanced investigative reporting has now mostly disappeared.

Fixing the Problems

The ethics for most professions are enforced through professional societies that establish a code of ethics, or by state or federal law— usually through regulatory bodies created by statute. Many people who deal with the news media believe there should be similar supervision of the news media. Who regulates the media? The answer is "no one," and the First Amendment is used to prevent regulation. So we have no one to serve as a "check" or "balance" to the news media that are now driven by ratings, profits, and strong biases rather than a code of ethics for journalism.

Fixing these problems will be difficult because of the lack of media ethical constraints in *The Constitution*. Since one political party or another is the primary beneficiary of the unfairness, imbalance, and biases at any given time, political pressure is unlikely to change it. Only "we the people," can change this trend. We must demand that a nationwide entity establish a code of ethics for all news media to follow. The media must establish processes to oversee and "enforce" these ethics using any reasonable means.

One way to work this problem is to charter a group of fair and unbiased journalists to investigate news media journalists' compliance to a set of ethics. If this does not happen, then we need to establish citizen groups or non-governmental organizations (NGOs) - "news media fairness checking" web sites similar to the "political fact checking" web sites that exist. They would need to expand from their present information and issue fact checking to include determining if the amount of airtime is fair and if reporting shows a strong bias. Then "free press" may regain the status its name implies.

Deficient New Media System Summary Bullets

✪ News reporting and journalism has drifted away from the Founding Fathers' intent.
  ★ It is no longer the fourth branch of government that "keeps tabs on the government's activities and actions" through investigative reporting.
  ★ The current media presentations focus is on sound bites and ratings, and what they feel their audience wants to hear and see. They portray whatever they present with strong personal biases.
✪ Introduction of radio, television, and the Internet have changed news media reporting and journalism.
  ★ Large corporations now own the news media.
  ★ Media focus is on ratings, with an aim to improve profits.
  ★ Effectiveness of reporting for the nation has diminished; due to less fair, more biased, and less informative reporting.
✪ At minimum, news media checking and reporting by journalists and NGOs is needed.

PART IV: THE CURRENT AGENTS OF DYSFUNCTION

We have looked at many of the tactical tricks politicians use to scare, mislead, and seduce us into fighting in their wars— the same wars that have caused many of our failing and seriously deficient policies and systems. To win *our* war and reclaim America we must examine the actions of our career politicians, the president, the political parties, and the political systems in which they operate. If our career politicians were doing their jobs, we likely would not have as many serious problems we face today.

Chapter 13: President Obama as a Charismatic Political Leader

Chapter 14: Indicators and Expectation for President Obama

Chapter 15: Political Parties and Extremists

Chapter 16: Overview of Our Dysfunctional Political System

Chapter 17: The Root Causes That Led Us Here

Chapter 18: The Solutions For Reclaiming Our Liberties

Chapter 13:
President Obama as a Charismatic Political Leader

E ffective leadership is vital to successfully addressing our nation's problems. In this chapter I present the quintessential characteristics of a charismatic political leader and provide my insights on President Obama.

Charismatic Political Leaders

A charismatic person is one who exercises compelling charm, attractiveness, or magnetism to inspire others. Charismatic political leaders may be more likeable and intelligent than others, but their beliefs and values may not be consistent with yours. Their political leadership can result in outcomes ranging from appalling (such as Hitler's legacy) to inspiring (such as Gandhi's). A charismatic leader is successful because he or she simply has more "tools" to convince you and others that he or she has the "correct answers."

Charisma has different sources and any attempt to pin it down to a specific set of human qualities or personality traits would be futile. I define charisma based on "what people *see* their leader as" rather than what their leader *is*. Generally, charismatic political leaders are seen as successful but that success is perceived as good or bad depending upon your beliefs and values.

Recent charismatic political leaders in the United States include: former presidents Bill Clinton, John F. Kennedy, Ronald Reagan, Franklin D. Roosevelt, and current president Barack Obama. Charismatic political leaders from other countries include: Fidel Castro, Winston Churchill, Charles de Gaulle, Mahatma Gandhi, Adolf Hitler, Ho Chi Minh, Vladimir Lenin, Golda Meir, Joseph Stalin, Margaret Thatcher, Mao Tse-Tung, and many others. These were national (or international) leaders who had a mesmerizing effect on their constituents and appeared to enjoy a degree of power and influence far beyond what was vested in their formal political status. While they all were charismatic and powerful, their differences were their beliefs, values, and most importantly, the policies they pursued.

As human beings our heredity (genes or "nature") and experiences (environment or "nurture") contribute to the development of our personalities, our value systems, and our own personal identities. These shape how we think, what we think, and how we act. So what makes it possible for a person to become a charismatic political leader? There are many books and articles on various leadership types and their corresponding characteristics. This is not an attempt to summarize or define all of these leadership types. Instead, we will observe and compare individuals generally considered as charismatic political leaders. While most leaders have a handful of these charismatic characteristics, a truly charismatic political leader exhibits a large number of them and possesses a unique ability to exploit them.

Common Characteristics and Environments

There are at least eight things that are common to all charismatic political leaders:

Characteristic One: The ability to understand and tell them (the audience) what they want to hear

An important characteristic of a charismatic political leader is an ability to determine exactly what his or her audience wants to hear. He then uses his other characteristics to convince the audience that his point-of-view is correct and congruent with theirs. While he may tell them what they want to hear, he may not do (or even intend to do) what he says.

Frequently he does not need a lot of words to satisfactorily make his point. The number of words is carefully controlled to allow wiggle room. A short story that was passed along on the Internet illustrates this point. It is called "The Cow and the Ice Cream." The story is provided below, narrated by a third grade teacher in 2008.

> The most eye-opening civics lesson I ever had was while teaching third grade this year. The presidential election was heating up and some of the children showed an interest. I decided we would have an election for a class president. We would choose our nominees. They would make a campaign speech and the class would vote. To simplify the process, candidates were nominated by other class members. We discussed what kinds of characteristics these students should have. We got many nominations and from those, Jamie and Olivia were picked to run for the top spot. The class had done a great job in their selections. Both candidates were good kids.
>
> I thought Jamie might have an advantage because he got lots of parental support. I had never seen Olivia's mother. The day arrived when they were to make their speeches. Jamie went first. He had specific ideas about how to make our class a better place. He ended by promising to do his very best. Everyone applauded and he sat down.
>
> Now it was Olivia's turn to speak. Her speech was concise. She said, "If you will vote for me, I will give you ice

cream." She sat down. The class went wild. "Yes! Yes! We want ice cream." She surely would say more. She did not have to. A discussion followed. How did she plan to pay for the ice cream? She wasn't sure. Would her parents buy it or would the class pay for it? She didn't know. The class really didn't care. All they were thinking about was ice cream. Jamie was forgotten. Olivia won by a landslide.

We can use this example to point out some of the drawbacks of a politician running solely on charisma.

✪ Why worry about "the cow" when it is all about the "ice cream?"
✪ Every time a charismatic political leader speaks, he offers ice cream and many of us react like those nine year-olds: We want ice cream.
✪ The rest of us know we're going to have to feed the cow and clean up the mess, but we are shouted down or ignored.
✪ Few consider the fact that the government cannot give anything to anyone that they have not first taken away from someone else. Who is going to care for the cow? No cow, no ice cream!

Characteristic Two: The ability to clearly and effectively communicate (a "Great Communicator")

Charisma requires great verbal and written language skills, and considerable self-confidence. Verbal skills include great oral delivery, frequently using "I," commanding phrases (e.g., "let me be clear"), and a range of moods while weaving in statements the charismatic speakers know their audiences want to hear. Supporting the verbal presentation are unspoken body language skills such as gestures and facial expressions. Early in their careers these leaders commonly write a book about themselves and/or their ideology (a "self-defining" book). President Reagan was called "the great communicator," but certainly Presidents Clinton and Obama also have these skills.

Characteristic Three: Creates "believers"

Many followers become "true believers" early, few true believers admit or realize the potential problems of being captivated by a person's words and personality rather than their likely policies. Therefore, believers tend to defend their leader's positions - good or bad. As a result of the first two characteristics, charismatic political leaders quickly attract these believers who perceive that the leaders are transformers, superhuman heroes (even god-like), and individuals whose personalities set them apart from ordinary people. Their charismatic leadership may overlap with so-called "transactional" leaders who control through bureaucratic mechanisms and knowledge, and "traditional" leaders who control through loyalty, favoritism, and policies, but the results are the same. True believers become so devoted that they no longer listen to or question what is said, which makes some of these leaders potentially very dangerous, as history has shown. To believers, experience is not an issue; it's all about what the charismatic leader - the preacher or savior - says. This relationship between the leader and his followers gives considerable, some might say unearned, power to the leader.

Politics is perhaps the only profession for which no preparation is thought necessary. – **Robert Louis Stevenson**[1]

Characteristic Four: Exploits crises and past poor leadership

Adverse environments (political, economic, and natural stresses, or wars) are opportunities through which many types of leaders can evolve and flourish. Charismatic political leaders have the skills best able to take full advantage of following perceived, or actual, poor leadership in countries under stress or turmoil. The Bush-to-Obama, Carter-to-Reagan, and Hoover-to-Roosevelt transitions fit this model in the United States.

Characteristic Five: The ability to develop or exercise propaganda machines

These leaders have the support of one or more powerful communications mechanisms that may be used as propaganda or "educational" machines. There are many examples of the influence of propaganda machines in history. An obvious one was when Joseph Goebbels became Adolf Hitler's propaganda minister in 1933, giving him power over all German radio, press, cinema, and theater. Other propaganda machines are subtler. Any extremely biased communications source can become a propaganda machine. Some of these machines already existed and were just exploited by potential leaders while others (such as Hitler's), were created later specifically for the leader. All of these machines use words, pictures, icons, cartoons, the tricks described within this book, and other means to make their points. Examples of potential propaganda machines include news media, the entertainment industry, corporate and union lobbyists, and professional and non-governmental organizations.

Characteristic Six: Capable of gaining access to large resources

As a result of one or more of the first five characteristics we have discussed, these charismatic leaders quickly gain access to large resources, money, labor, and sometimes even a whole government. These resources are essential to all aspects of political life. Resources can be used to buy votes, inform or hide a failure, confuse citizens (voters), and improve public relations.

Characteristic Seven: Quickly consolidates power and sets new policies

With the winds of "believers" and one or more crises caused by (or able to be blamed on) previous poor leadership before them, these leaders seek to rapidly solidify power and change policies and practices before their swell of "true believers" and any other advantages decline. Actual implementation of policies may be delayed to avoid unforeseen consequences. All actions focus on increasing the charismatic person's power. All new leaders have some advantages, but again a charismatic political leader has an early advantage and can often hold this power advantage throughout his or her reign.

Characteristic Eight: Knows and uses all described psychological and financial tricks

Many psychological and numerical tricks are used to convince followers and potential followers that the leader is correct. Most experienced politicians are aware of these and many other tricks. New politicians learn them quickly, since these tricks are their pathway to being career politicians. Charismatic political leaders have honed these tactical and manipulative skills.

Charismatic Political Leader President Obama

The press tells us that President Barack Obama has "charisma," the special power of a person to inspire fascination and loyalty. In the near term, his followers will judge President Obama's charisma. Recognizing a leader as charismatic tells us voters something about a candidate, but even more about ourselves, the mood of the country, and our desire for change. Becoming too involved in what the leader (or candidate) says without considering our mood and desire for change can lead to undesired results.

A vast majority of U.S. citizens want to see every president succeed in a way ultimately beneficial to both our country and our people. President Obama is no exception, indeed as our first non-Caucasian president, it may be even more important for him to succeed. Below, President Obama is assessed in terms of being a charismatic political leader. This information might help us to better understand him and where he might want to take our nation in the future. Our responsibility is to help direct President Obama and our other political leaders down paths we believe are best for our country.

The ability to understand and tell them what they want to hear.

Candidate Obama was outstanding in his ability to read what citizens wanted to hear and to communicate this information back to them. In fact, his message of change was strong enough to recruit and solidify "believers" well before the election. His message was powerful enough to break the backs of the strongest political machine in the country run by the Clintons. It is interesting that his message was strong enough that few of his followers questioned how it would be achieved or noted that he did not have particularly relevant personal experience to draw upon.

The ability to clearly and effectively communicate (a "Great Communicator").

As president, Obama's communications skills have continued to be a strong point in his favor. He frequently uses the word "I." He often uses powerful phrases such as "let me be clear" which implies he has analyzed and clearly understands whatever he is talking about, as well as "make no mistake" which implies that you are making a mistake if you disagree with him. He changes moods as appropriate to the topic. Before the presidency, Senator Obama wrote a book about himself and a book on his ideology.

Creates "believers."

President Obama established a big pool of "believers" before being elected. It is not clear whether this pool has increased over time, but it is hard for a believer to lose faith or to admit a mistake. Thus, only time will tell if President Obama can hold on to this pool of believers.

Exploits crises and past poor leadership.

The financial crisis, coupled with an increasingly unpopular war and a Republican in the White House, was timed perfectly for candidate Obama. He could tell people what they wanted to hear, and there was someone to blame for both the crisis and the war.

President Bush was also an easy target due to some of his policies and personal traits.

The ability to develop or utilize propaganda machines.

There are two propaganda machines that overwhelmingly supported Candidate and now President Obama: the news media and the entertainment industry. Earlier, I indicated why the news media system has been serving us poorly. The vast majority of the media favored and did not question candidate Obama. The entertainment industry and TV entertainers flooded the public media with movies and TV satire favoring Obama, while often demonizing republicans Bush, McCain, and Palin. Another clever thing Obama's campaign did was to create a memorable icon: a circle with a red and white field that originally contained his picture. Icons are used to remind people of something familiar. Obama's logos have been stamped on his website as well as other democratic websites long after he became president. Historically, after an election, the Presidential seal is used for the President, but Obama's marketing team continued using his icon.

Capable of gaining access to large resources.

Besides the typical Democratic political supporters (trial lawyers, entertainment industry, labor unions, etc.), Candidate Obama was successful in obtaining funds from early "believers." He first stated he would take federal funds that would have limited his total campaign funds, then he switched when it became clear he could collect a larger amount on his own.

Quickly consolidates power and sets new policies.

President Obama quickly named over thirty "czars" to advise him on a wide variety of policies. President Obama started his presidency by pushing several major policies crafted by some of these czars. These czars bypassed the usual congressional approval processes. This is the first time any president has done this. If George W. Bush or Bill Clinton had created dozens of "czar" positions that reported directly to them, bypassing House and Senate approval, would they have been able to do it? President Obama could do it because the Democrats controlled both the House and Senate and because his charisma makes challenging him more difficult for his opponents. Mrs. Obama added to the Obama power base by hiring over 20 personal staffers. The largest staff by earlier first ladies was three for Hilary Clinton. With the efforts of this staff she, too, has gotten unprecedented TV coverage to help her husband and his political party.

Knows and uses all described tricks.
    This list is extensive. No examples are included here since several examples were presented earlier. President Obama has used all of the tricks discussed in Chapters 4., 5., and 6. The tricks he seems to use most often are the blame game, wedges, "Isn't it awful?," tell them what they want to hear, and number manipulation.

President Obama as a Charismatic Political Leader Summary Bullets

✪ A charismatic person is one who exercises compelling charm, attractiveness, and/or magnetism that can rightly or wrongly inspire others.
✪ Charismatic political leaders can be defined by eight characteristics.
✪ President Obama is a charismatic political leader based on general public opinion and these characteristics.

Chapter 14:
Indicators and Expectations for President Obama

As I stated earlier, we are all shaped by our experiences and our genetics. So where and how we grew up, what we have done and been exposed to throughout life, and how we have acted and reacted to our experiences, are all good indicators of the future. In this process, we have had some control over aspects of our experiences (by choosing our friends, careers, education, etc.), while other aspects have been outside of our control (such as our childhood economic status). Let's first look at President Obama's experiences since these are the indicators for the future, and then estimate what we might expect from him based on both the characteristics in Chapter 13 and his indicators.

Indicators of President Obama's Beliefs

Early Years

Our early life experiences strongly shape our personality and beliefs. As a young boy, President Obama grew up in several countries with different cultures. These experiences greatly influenced his views and abilities to sense what individuals from different cultures in these countries want to hear about America. He has used these experiences, and his excellent rhetorical skills, to give speeches to people in these countries. These countries span Europe and the Muslim world. The speeches given by President Obama early in his presidency likely led to his receiving the Nobel Peace Prize. His early speeches likely helped him continue the wars against terrorism without much foreign criticism, thus allowing him to move forward with his war strategy.

What is not clear is whether or not his early rhetoric will continue to work in the future. Let's hope it does. What he said might have sounded good at the time to those to whom he was speaking, but whether he can meet their expectations is uncertain. Also, in being apologetic about our nation's past in his speeches, he may be seen as weak by some foreigners and may have upset many citizens who have contributed greatly to our nation. His charisma and what he learned as a child will be tested as time passes.

His Book

In his second book, *Audacity of Hope,* then-Senator Obama gave a clearer picture of his experiences and values. Not surprisingly, since he is a good politician, the book is laced with virtually every trick described in this book. For example, he starts in Chapter One ("Republicans and Democrats"), by heavily playing the adversarial truths and blame games. He selectively blames the previous administration for a lot of mistakes, blames the Democrats for some mistakes but implies he played no part in them. He then blames conservatives for Tom Daschle's defeat based on negative ads, but fails to mention Daschle's breaking the law, or that both parties commonly use negative ads. He talks about how bad the Republicans were and are, and talks a lot about right wing faults and failures (using the "Isn't it awful?" trick). He faults, and then praises, former-President Reagan.

In Chapter Two ("Values"), we get some insight into his values. The first seven and last eleven pages are political rhetoric. He quotes *The Declaration of Independence*: *"We hold these truths to* be self-evident, that all men are created equal, that they are endowed by their Creator with certain unalienable Rights, that among these are Life, Liberty and the pursuit of Happiness." The words that follow show he puts a strong value on equality for all people. He also mentions (Benjamin Franklin's) values of "drive, discipline, temperance, and hard work" and he states: "Our system of self-government and our free-market economy depend on the majority of individual Americans adhering to these values." I believe this is the only time economics in the context of hard work and self-sufficiency is discussed in his books. Senator Obama also takes aim at corporations in this chapter: "In 1980 the average CEO made forty-two times what an hourly worker took home. By 2005 the ratio was 262 to 1." He goes on to take on those who he feels are conservatives, stating: "Conservative outlets like The Wall Street Journal try to justify…"

In Chapter Three ("Our Constitution"), Senator Obama writes a nice short summary on parts of The Constitution, with many personal comments, almost all of which deal with human rights and politics. The traits of our Constitution's Founding Fathers: generosity, service, courage, resilience, hard work and personal responsibility; are not part of this discussion. It appears this chapter is intended primarily to show Obama is familiar with The Constitution and has strong human rights views.

Chapters four and five ("Politics" and "Opportunity," respectively), are more enlightening. In these chapters, Obama's relationships with the unions are discussed, and he states: "So I owe those unions. When their leaders call I do my best to call them back right away." Again, he talks about FDR, welfare, and safety nets, all of which seem to be his passion. He also includes a nice summary of his positions or suggested improvements for a variety of topics, including education, energy, and science. I was left with the feeling these would be governmentally funded programs. Not much is said about how to get our economic engine going to generate the capital needed to achieve these. There is nothing nice said about businesses or business leaders.

Chapters Six through Nine are interesting, but add little to this discussion. Thus, no comments are provided here.[1] My summary of this book is this: Senator Obama shows he has no love for business or its leaders, and feels both are out of control. He likes unions and fully supports them. He is passionate about equality (including in economics) and is comfortable having governments redistribute wealth to achieve it.

We should expect his future policies to focus on what he has written.

The Presidency

Since Senator Obama became President Obama, I have not been surprised by what he has done based on his experiences and values. He inherited a financial mess, which he attributes to the Republicans, even though both parties failed to provide adequate oversight of or controls on the financial system. He made sure the government funds (TARP funds, the automobile bailout funds, and stimulus funds) were used to support his constituency (including the auto unions) and, not surprisingly, to support his longer-term agendas such as green technologies. He did this while continuing to blame and demonize businesses, even though not all were at fault. While some of this may have been reasonable, was he fair?

He has moved fast to solidify his early support, but not without some problems. Using the automobile industry as an example, the conditions for the government monies loaned was such that the federal government would own sixty-one percent of General Motors, and ten percent of Chrysler. This leaves the autoworker union owning 17.5 percent of GM and fifty-five percent of Chrysler, and the previous owners (mainly bond holders) would get from five percent to twenty percent back on their dollars invested. This was really a union bailout at bondholder expense, even though labor union costs caused part of the bankruptcy problem. Of course, many Corporate Executives had contracts with "golden parachutes." Those of us who favor capitalism over socialism noticed business investor's money went to cover unions and a few senior managers.[2]

The Health Care Bill exemplifies the point that what President Obama says and what he does are completely different and, like most politicians, he uses tricks to redirect or justify the differences. For example, what happened to full transparency, stopping pork barrel spending, bipartisanship, no tricks, and no new debt campaign promises? As covered earlier, none of them happened on the Health Care Bill.

The Gulf Coast oil spill disaster will be an interesting long-term test of President Obama's skills. I wish him and his administration success.

As we see more of President Obama, he has become more combative and accusatory than most recent presidents. This stirs anger and division among many of our citizens, rather than having a calming and unifying effect. This may be good politics, but it is bad for the nation and, as its leader, this is not good for Obama. Thanks to the media's interest in their ratings, he is able to be on a wide variety of media anytime that he wants, without challenge from the journalists or equal time provided for others. This is a bully pulpit that no other president in recent history has had!

President Obama finished his first year by giving his first State of the Union speech. As expected, his great oratory skills resulted in a great presentation. Also, as usual in these speeches, he credited his administration with great accomplishments and introduced his solutions to the nation's problems.

Unfortunately, the content was aimed more at driving wedges between politicians and groups of citizens, rather than uniting them. In his speech, he blamed everyone except common citizens and the military for everything. He blamed the previous administration for all the problems he inherited, and he blamed Republicans, the Supreme Court, the financial industry, and even corporate lobbyists. Then he discussed how people are discouraged by all of the "finger pointing" being done by politicians, and called for us all to working together. Obviously, there is a fat chance that this will happen after he just beat up everyone. This hypocritical speech indicates why charisma is so powerful. There was little, if any, mention of these conflicting messages by any public media. A more skeptical and vigilant media would have pointed out the conflicting messages and tricks in the speech.

What To Expect From President Obama

The November 2010 elections were just completed as this book was being finalized. Many Republicans and Tea Party supported candidates were elected. The resulting shift of power from the Democrats to the Republicans in the House of Representatives will cause President Obama to develop new operational strategies. It will be interesting to see if he can really cooperate and change or will simply continue to exploit his pleasant personality and use of political tricks to drive his policy agendas.

The Bad News

Looking at what President Obama has done in the past, I predict that we can expect a lot of excellently delivered speeches that: (1) are what we want to hear, at least at the time they are delivered, (2) are almost like sermons from the pulpit thanks to his frequent use of a teleprompter, (3) use a lot of interwoven political tricks, and (4) contain promises he cannot deliver. He will continue policies favorable to his (liberal) constituencies and give lip service to other ideas. He will occasionally throw an old bone to his opposition just so he can say he tried to be inclusive, but he really does not want their cooperation, he wants total control. He likes to play the blame game and drive wedges between groups of us. He will continue to play all of the political games because he honestly believes he knows best and needs two terms to make it happen. He will do what it takes to be re-elected and, thanks to the media's love of him, he will get away with his actions.

How will he get people on his side? He will promise jobs to the jobless and money to the money-less. He will likely advocate better wages and better jobs, while continuing to demonize the capitalists and capitalistic system that provides them. He will do all of this with a compliant media that no longer is capable of honest investigative reporting on the government. He will do all of this all in the name of justice and change.

So far, his policies have translated into more divisiveness, more debt, more taxes, more welfare, more regulations, more government, more wasteful spending, and fewer actual jobs. Hopefully one of his changes will be a significant change in direction from where he has started.

The Good News

Despite all of these somewhat negative observations, I believe President Obama is very intelligent. President Obama is also a very likeable person— someone who would make a great friend. His past is driving his policies that many of us question. His intelligence suggests he can be redirected and may change course when and if the voices of the people are loud enough. So, let's start shouting, since we all want him to be successful in leading the nation for a few more years without damage to future generations.

I believe that if President Obama were to understand and believe in the issues and solutions discussed here, he would have the capability to be our leader rather than the leader of just his party and his more liberal special interests. It will be hard for him to make this transition, since it may cost him some of his "believers." But we need to convince him that it is truly *the right thing to do*. If he stands up to both party extremes and calls for actions as described in the next chapters, he may become our greatest president in history to date.

We need to convince him we are ready for the "tough love" that is needed. We must convince him we will not tolerate less personal responsibility and more entitlements or a shift from capitalism to socialism or more debt placed on our future generations. We need his help to fight our really important war: the war to reclaim our national liberties. This means he, too, must make the status quo go!

Indicators and Expectations for President Obama Summary Bullets

✪ We are all shaped by our experiences and our genetics. In the case of President Obama and other political leaders, it is worthwhile to study "who, what, and where" helped shape them into the people and leaders they are today.

✪ Policies determine if "success" is good or bad for constituents and the world.

✪ Based on his charismatic characteristics, and what he has said and written, President Obama's policy passion is focused on economic and social equality; he dislikes or distrusts the principles and individuals associated with capitalism.

✪ President Obama's innate intelligence may result in his being a great leader if he changes directions (as described herein).

Chapter 15:
Political Parties and Extremists

Here I summarize my observations about our two major political parties before moving on to a discussion of our dysfunctional and failing political system. Presidents George Washington, John Adams, Thomas Jefferson, and many other contributing Founding Fathers had fears about political parties that, as indicated by their quotes, now have come to pass.

Political Party Principles and Power

Talking about political parties, President Washington stated in his farewell speech: *"However combinations or associations of the above description* [i.e., political parties] *may now and then answer popular ends, they are likely, in the course of time and things, to become potent engines, by which cunning, ambitious, and unprincipled men will be enabled to subvert the power of the people, and to usurp for themselves the reins of government; destroying afterwards the very engines, which have lifted them to unjust dominion."*[1]

Two major parties have ruled for decades. As time has progressed, the divisive nature of their interactions has nearly torn our nation apart. Despite President Obama's rhetoric, it is still continuing and he has even added to its divisive nature. The two parties have quite different agendas and, while the moderates of both parties seem amenable to working together, the party extremes further polarize the two parties. Here are my summary thoughts on the two parties.

Republicans

Republicans have tended to be the party wanting modest-to-small government, focusing on business as a means of generating jobs and wealth, and seeking strong national security. Their right-wing constituencies want to include moral issues like abortion, gay marriage, and religion in their party platform. Their interest in generating jobs and wealth generates a constituency from those in the business sector, both managers and workers, who have some understanding of the business cycle, capitalism, and the changing world economic environment. Republican fiscal philosophy for stabilizing the economy and generating jobs is to reduce taxes and government spending, allowing jobs and wealth formation in the private sector. They believe in a "let the chips fall wherever they may - sink or swim" philosophy. They argue that as the economy grows, tax revenues more than offset the earlier reductions in taxes. They have most of the "Under 50 Percent Club" (the voters paying most of the taxes) on their side. Their party politicians have more diverse work experiences— meaning fewer lawyers, and a larger variety of professionals and businesspeople.

It seems to me the Republicans have several self-generated issues working against them. First, they cannot meet their own principles and give away free money except through tax reductions, which then puts a target on their backs for the Democrats. The Democrats can say the Republicans are indifferent to the poor and needy, or that entitlements (free money) will be cut if the Republicans are in power. The Republicans also have been on a spending spree. Perhaps this is an attempt to catch up with the Democrats in handing out free money (e.g., the Medicare Drug Bill passed with Republican approval is very costly). I feel their

POLITICAL PARTIES AND EXTREMISTS

spending spree has damaged an important Republican principle, which citizens have resonated with in the past.

Second, claiming religious moral stands is a "no win" situation and should be left to the states or individuals as indicated in *The Constitution* and by our Founding Fathers. No one is without "sin" so every time a "morally right" Republican "sins," the media make the issue a big negative news item for Republicans. If a state, or even a municipality, has a vast majority of its citizens that favor some religious or moral issue, let them pass a constitutionally approved law favoring the issue.

Third, many members of the right wing would rather have candidates that are "right" than "electable." In California, where the right dominates and gerrymandering prevails, this right ultraconservative Republican position has helped the Democrats attain a near-supermajority (two-thirds) in the state legislature.

Democrats

Democrats have tended to be the party liking big government and believing big government is the answer to all social ills; thus, they focus on equal opportunity, spreading money around, and championing the "little guy" over "business." Their left-wing constituencies are willing to spend, tax, borrow, and expand government to achieve what they believe are injustices and to provide significant financial aid to those in the bottom half of the economic chain. The Democratic fiscal philosophy to stabilize the economy and to generate jobs is to increase taxes and increase government spending directing new monies to government-paid jobs, which as discussed earlier, only temporarily increases wealth. Political debate is centered on what happens when the government-funded tasks are done, how long the government must pay for these jobs, and the impact of government-funded jobs on the private sector. They have most of the "Over 50 Percent Free Money Club" votes that benefit most from the taxes paid by others. The Democratic Party has more lawyers with little or no business experience.

It seems to me that the Democrats also have several self-generated issues starting to work against them. First, they have just about killed the goose that lays the golden eggs: the "Under Fifty Percent Club" citizens who pay taxes are about "tapped out." Taxing business slows the economy, costing jobs and tax revenues. Borrowing by increasing debt is "tapped out," too.

Second, the entitlements - and other social payouts that they have promised are driving the debt, so they will need to back off on entitlements or continue to raise taxes to avoid another financial system instability. Either action slows the economy, costing jobs and lowering tax revenues.

Third, the liberal wing is unhappy their agendas were not higher on President Obama's and the party's lists. Some of the "believers'" enthusiasm may wane. Republicans had a similar problem when they were in charge of both Congress and the executive branch.

Moderates

Both parties are so polarized (to the right and left) that there is no balance between "wealth and capitalism," and "generosity and socialism." This is one of the critical balances our nation must get right. Moderates in both parties frequently anger their party leaders by voting their consciences for the good of the nation. They are in "party trouble" whenever they vote their own values and consciences. Their parties threaten them with replacement during primaries, give them little power, and sometimes even give them bad office locations while in Washington. It seems that party loyalty is significantly more important to many extremists than doing what a member of Congress believes is the right thing to do. How despicable is that?

So long as wars continue between the two parties, there is little that moderates can do. Fortunately, the few that do exist sometimes work together to sponsor bills. Some, like Senator Evan

Bayh of Indiana, have given up hope for any significant bipartisanship and are not seeking re-election.

Left, Right, and Extremist

First TV, and now the web have helped the left and right to make their points to the masses. These topics range from economic policies to moral issues. Unfortunately, the result of the TV and web media intrusion is more divisiveness between and within the parties: a "no win" for the nation. Here, again, the separation of powers in *The Constitution* would allow the individual rights and freedoms needed to address the differences between the left and right, if only the extremists could quit playing tricks and trying to "win" for their parties.

For example, *The Constitution* indicates most moral issues should be addressed at individual, local, or state levels, and not at the national level. Our politicians fan the flames of moral issues because these issues outrage some citizens, who then become foot soldiers for that politician or political party. The battle over the one word "marriage" is an example. In my opinion, this argument is a waste of everyone's time and resources at the national level. How many hungry people could we have fed if we had used the money and energy spent on this "no win" fight to feed them? It is time to move on, without any winners or losers, on this and many issues that should not be part of our national debate. I doubt this will happen, however, and likely "winners and losers" will evolve. I hope the winners are happy knowing that they will have alienated a large group of citizens for a long time over one word. This is only one of many examples of our loss of focus on what is really important.

I do not believe the left and right wings of our political parties are necessarily radicals or extremists, but their polarizing effects have dominated both parties. This has the same effect as that sought by extremists. "Extremism" is a term used to describe the actions or ideologies of individuals or groups outside the perceived political center of a society, or otherwise claimed to violate common moral standards. Under this definition, our politicians must be mostly extremists since we have a right and a left, but almost no political center!

There are all kinds of extremists in the world. Governments, political parties, religious groups, environmental groups, cultural groups and other entities all have fringe elements that can be called extremist. There is often a fine line between extremism and terrorism. Unfortunately, in the United States, we have a potentially explosive situation. The explosive fuel includes:

- ✪ The anger and outrage politicians intentionally initiate using their tricks
- ✪ The anger and outrage the news media amplifies
- ✪ A nation divided by the wedges used by politicians to make us become adversarial groups

✪ An Internet-based communication system that allows sharing of that anger and outrage without fact checking
✪ A less optimistic future as a result of our many self-generated financial and social problems

This is a gathering storm that has been (and could become even more) destructive unless significant changes occur quickly.

I believe a third national party that is somewhere in the middle of the right-left extremes would make a big difference. This party would need to be one that takes a *Constitution*-oriented position on all issues, is fiscally responsible, capitalist leaning, and without strong desires to legislate moral extremes (allowing states or localities to address the moral extremes). This party would return the federal government to the prime purposes of providing for our protection, focusing on job and wealth creation, and the balancing of generosity against what we can afford as a nation.

The timing of the formation of such a party is critical. I believe this new party's strategy should be to announce they would form their official party *after* the 2012 elections, develop draft party principles in platforms before the 2012 and 2014 elections and seek (new) party candidates to run for the 2014 election after the 2012 elections. The new party, if it is not the Tea Party, should provide Tea Party-like rallies to listen to and support the traditional candidates before the 2012 elections. The potential new party members should be encouraged to vote for the candidates that come closest to supporting the new party's draft platforms.

There are several advantages of this strategic approach. First, establishing a new party before the 2012 election would be difficult and would likely simply result in victory for the democrats. The proposed new party principles would be closer to past Republican Party platforms thus drawing more votes away from the republicans than democrats. Second, the new party draft platforms should add pressure on the existing parties to change and for their candidates to lean more toward the new party principles. Third, individuals interested in becoming new party candidates will have time to establish their strategies and start developing a support base by participating in the rallies.

The existing parties will most likely fight the formation of a third party with all the money and resources they can generate. Historically, we have had dozens of political parties with a wide range of ideologies. Consequently, even coming up with a new descriptive name could be a problem. The "Free America" Party or "Freedom" Party or "Citizens" Party might work.

Political Parties and Extremists Summary Bullets

✪ Our Founding Fathers recognized that political parties' needs for power could become the nation's downfall.
✪ The two major parties have become polarized, left and right, with no middle.
✪ Both major political parties ability to effectively govern in the future may be impacted by their use of political tricks to win party power (wars) and self-generated issues.
✪ A strong new party that takes Constitutional-oriented and moderate positions on issues is needed to provide balance.

Chapter 16:
Overview of Our Dysfunctional Political System

The agents of dysfunction have evolved over time. Some were out of necessity caused by changing times, technology, and a changing world. Unfortunately, many others evolved or were driven by ambitious career politicians primarily interested in their own power and their ability to be re-elected. In this chapter we will look at our political system's evolution from the perspective of what our Founding Fathers wrote.

Government is not reason; it is not eloquence. It is force. And force, like fire, is a dangerous servant and a fearful master.[1] — **George Washington**

The Constitution is not an instrument for the government to restrain the people, it is an instrument for the people to restrain the government.[2] — **Patrick Henry**

Debates Verses Wars

There is a great difference between a "debate" and a "war" between two (or more) entities. Debate topics may range from solutions to a problem to ideological, economic, religious, or even racial differences. A formal debate involves the discussion of each party's positions and thoughts about a topic. There are formats and rules that are followed. Each side puts forth its best arguments for the topic at hand. Words are the tools used to execute the debate. Those watching and listening to a debate draw their own conclusions. Those participating in the debate, at worst, may feel they failed to make their points.

A war is an armed conflict executed by whatever means necessary. (For instance, two completely different means were used for the "Cold War" and World War II, but both had the purpose of compelling the defeated side to do what the victors wanted.) Those involved in wars seek out and use tools such as psychological, military, and financial weapons for fighting, as well as for recruiting supporters. Successful combatants are generally aggressive and effective in developing and using these tools to divide and conquer their opponents. Any trick that provides an advantage is fair game in a war.

Debate is what our Founding Fathers envisioned as the base for the processes for governing our nation. Unfortunately, our career politicians now engage in political party wars. Some fighters in these wars are true believers in their causes, but most of us need to be recruited or convinced to join them through scare tactics, misinformation and/or seduction tactics. Political tricks are the mechanisms used to get us to join sides in these divisive wars, which often leave both winners and losers with lasting scars. We need to stop the political wars and start debating again. Unfortunately, our two political parties and career politicians find these political wars to be in their best interest.

We have heard a lot about the need for "change" lately. We *do* need change, but what needs to change? I feel our political system is what needs to be changed, and then all of the other necessary changes will naturally evolve. Our political system devolved from a good set of principles and processes developed by our Founding Fathers into a dysfunctional system that is on the verge of total failure. What we need is a " back to the future" change— a return to what our Founding Fathers envisioned for our political system.

The bad news is that this will require a major overhaul of our present system. The good news is that a few changes will make a gigantic difference and "we the people" can force these changes to happen. We must do what our politician "representatives" have not done: collectively work for the betterment of our nation in the long-term rather than just looking out for ourselves in the short-term.

Career politicians do not work on long-term issues because they are difficult, and do not add to or contribute to their next re-election bids. They do not need to work on them because they know they can use political tricks to get off the hook if a problem arises. This is how career politicians survive. Most of us know "in our gut" that something is not right with this system. Let's change the political system to make it right for "we the people."

Recent History vs. The Founding Fathers

Let's review our Founding Fathers' vision for government and the individuals they believed would fill positions in government. Specifically, what did they envision as the roles and responsibilities for our three branches of government? What would their views be of our twentieth- and twenty-first-century politicians? How did political changes occur, and what caused them? When did these changes start to evolve? Answers to these questions will help us assess what has happened that negatively impacted our whole political system.

Government

The federal government of the United States is the central government entity established by *The U.S. Constitution*, which shares responsibilities with the government of the individual states. Through a system of separation of powers and the system of "checks and balances," each of the three federal government branches has some authority to act on its own, some authority to regulate the other two branches, and some of its own authority (which is, in turn, regulated by the other branches). *The Constitution* limits the powers of the federal government. The Tenth Amendment states that all powers not expressly assigned to the federal government are reserved to the states or to the people.

Briefly stated, powers and duties of the executive branch are in Article II of *The Constitution:* the president has the authority to be commander-in-chief of the armed forces; to grant pardons; to make treaties; and to appoint ambassadors, Supreme Court justices, and other government officers. More generally, the president is responsible for making sure that the laws be faithfully executed, though the Founding Fathers did not specify how the president was to accomplish this goal.

In Article I, Section 8, of *The Constitution,* Congress's powers are enumerated, requiring the execution of two primary functions:

1. Provide processes and laws as needed to meet national needs. They are empowered to levy and collect taxes, coin and regulate money, establish post offices and roads, issue patents, create federal courts, declare war, raise and support armies and a navy, regulate land, and make laws necessary to properly execute these powers.

2. Provide oversight of the laws as executed through the executive branch. This oversight is intended to prevent waste and fraud, protect civil liberties and individual rights, ensure executive compliance with the law, gather information for making laws and educating the public, and evaluate executive performance. This oversight also applies to cabinet departments, executive agencies, regulatory commissions, and the presidency.

The Supreme Court is the highest court in the federal court system followed by the Courts of Appeals, and then District Courts. The Supreme Court deals with matters pertaining to the federal government, disputes between states, and interpretation of *The U.S. Constitution*. It can declare legislation made or executive actions taken at any level of the government as unconstitutional, nullifying the law or action in question and creating precedent for future laws and decisions.[3]

Politicians

What would our founders think of career politicians?

Our Founding Fathers felt politicians were to be the servants, while the citizens were to be the royalty, not the inverse. Career politicians were something none of the Founding Fathers would ever have thought about or thought could happen. Their idea was that a person would serve his country for a short time and then go home to his business or farm. They would be upset to see what has happened. The Founding Fathers saw government as a means to serve the common good, not to serve the individual good. There is little doubt that most of them would be strongly opposed to career politicians. Let's look at some of the Founding Fathers in more detail, then discuss what has happened to our present day politics.

Political parties did not exist in 1789. Many of the Founding Fathers had quite different views from each other, but worked together to develop the world's most outstanding governmental system to date.

President George Washington despised the idea of political associations (or parties), formed in such a way as to pit one group of citizens against another. In his farewell speech stepping down as president in 1796 he said:

"They [political parties] serve to organize faction to give it an artificial and extraordinary force; to put, in the place of the delegated will of the nation, the will of a party, often a small but artful and enterprising minority of the community; and, according to the alternate triumphs of different parties, to make the public administration the mirror of the ill-concerted and incongruous projects of faction, rather than the organ of consistent and wholesome plans digested by common counsels, and modified by mutual interests."[4]

He further warned in his farewell address, discussing factions between people, between North and South, between states and between nations, *"...it is seen in its greatest rankness, and is truly their worst enemy."* Washington went on to say,

"The alternate domination of one faction over another, sharpened by the spirit of revenge, natural to party dissension, which in different ages and countries has perpetrated the most horrid enormities, is itself a frightful despotism. But this leads at length to a more formal and permanent despotism. The disorders and miseries, which result, gradually incline the minds of men to seek security and repose in the absolute power of an individual; and sooner or later the chief of some prevailing faction, more able or more fortunate than his competitors, turns this disposition to the purposes of his own elevation, on the ruins of Public Liberty."[5]

In summary, President Washington was fearful that political parties would use wedges, blame, and other tricks to gain power over the masses. He wanted to honor voters as the masters, with politicians the servants. He did not believe politicians should be in service for a lifetime, and he is not the only Founder who understood this problem. Others had similar concerns:

As long as we have career politicians, political expediency will always trump rational long-term thinking and problem solving.

In my many years I have come to a conclusion that one useless man is a shame, two is a law firm and three or more is a congress.[6]— **John Adams**

I predict future happiness for Americans if they can prevent the government from wasting the labors of the people under the pretense of taking care of them.

My reading of history convinces me that most bad government results from too much government.[7]— **Thomas Jefferson**

Others had quite different views from Washington. For example, Alexander Hamilton was an extreme anti-federalist, inclined toward what is referred to as "the far left." His philosophical bent would fit comfortably within the modern political spectrum of the Democratic Party. He would be best described as "radical left."

Born in the West Indies, Hamilton came to New York City as a young man and studied politics "up close and personally," from the European perspective. He found no problem with the concept of a monarch, as long as the king was kind, had a good heart, and was interested only in the welfare of the nation. Hamilton thought his mentor, George Washington, was just right for the job of "King of America." He never grasped the reality of human nature that, unlike lower forms of life, humans often perform poorly when left without the pressures of personal accountability.

Toward the other end of the political spectrum, Thomas Jefferson and James Madison believed central power should be tightly restrained, restricted, and controlled. Yet, when Jefferson was president, he departed from those views by using the power of his office for the Louisiana Purchase without any "controlling legal authority."

Does the above indicate that Hamilton would have been a liberal Democrat and Jefferson and Madison conservative Republicans (in the terms of the popular public doctrines)? The answer is "no."

Jefferson or Madison would not embrace today's Republican Party stances on prayer in schools and abortion. The original notion to keep the federal government out of religion - and religion out of government - was Jefferson's, and he would be appalled to see the federal government interfering with local decisions on religion, gay marriage, or any similar subject. On abortion, or "a woman's right of choice," both Jefferson and Madison most likely would have taken the position to keep the federal government out of personal lives. Jefferson and Madison perceived the central government's role as strictly national defense, international and interstate commerce, treaties, a postal system, and similar functions. Everything else was a state or local matter.

Hamilton, on the other hand, the "ultra-liberal" thinker of the group, would have had the president decide all of the above, eliminate the state and local governments, let Congress raise the money, and shovel it over to the president with few strings attached. Hamilton would have expected his president to outlaw abortion, write a "middle of the road" prayer to be recited in all schools, and require every citizen to own a gun, whether they wanted a gun or not. In other words he was a "big government" guy.

Washington chose Hamilton as his right-hand man, and gave him almost total leeway in establishing a federal financial system, because Washington saw the necessity in a start-up situation of pushing the boundaries - not because he agreed with Hamilton. [8]

As for the other famous Founding Fathers, Patrick Henry, said *"...give me liberty or give me death"*[9] and meant just that. He had no patience with any form of governmental control over individual lives, which would place him to the right of Jefferson and Madison but, as with their beliefs, his views would cut across today's party lines, and he would be railing against the current governmental tyranny. In his day, Henry served as governor five times (each were one-year terms), but refused appointment to the U.S. Senate and later refused to serve as governor when he was, once more, elected to that office. Seems he did not like the idea of becoming a career politician.

Benjamin Franklin may have been the centrist (moderate) of his time. More of a philosopher than a politician, Franklin's perspective appeared to float above all the rest, ebbing and flowing with the consensus of the group so long as "the group" remained generally on track.

John Adams was a Federalist, believing in a strong central government, virtually ignoring the principle embodied by the Virginians (Jefferson, Madison, and Henry) of keeping government at bay where private lives are concerned. Adams' beliefs would fit neatly into the political atmosphere around the late Senator Ted Kennedy and the left wing of today's Democrats.

Samuel Adams, who never served in national elective office, could be placed somewhere in the spectrum with John Adams and Hamilton. A colleague described him, and he never denied the portrayal, as follows:

"Samuel Adams would have the state of Massachusetts govern the union; the town of Boston govern Massachusetts; and that he should govern the town of Boston; and then the whole would not be intentionally ill governed."[10]

John Hancock, the maverick of Massachusetts's politics, held views closer to those of Jefferson and Madison, but he did not have the "fire in the belly" for pushing a national agenda. Hancock was the wealthiest of the famous Founding Fathers. He could have gone far in national politics but chose to spend his time closer to home, serving eleven times (in one-year terms) as governor of his state.

How did political changes occur and what caused them?

Simply stated, we have career politicians who perhaps were well-intentioned when they ran for, and got elected, as politicians. Once in office, however, there are many temptations that offer opportunities for personal gain. The perks of being a politician now are great on every governmental level. For example, there are many financial perks such as great retirement benefits, and (if you move up the government chain) often you get funds from more than one retirement system. Other perks are the prestige of being a leader, many sources of free money for "business" travel, transportation, and housing expenses, and, if you play your cards right, you get lots of campaign money with great spending flexibility. At the federal level you even get money to send out propaganda (in the form of newsletters) to your citizens to inform them of how great you have been.

Once a politician, convincing yourself it is your duty to continue being one is not hard to do. As soon as this shift in mindset happens, the corruption begins. To continue as a politician, you must shift from being a servant to your constituency to being the master of your personal and professional destiny. To be a master of your destiny you must continue to be re-elected. To be re-elected continuously you need to start telling people what they want to hear rather than the hard, sometimes disappointing, facts. You need to learn the political mode of operation and the tricks mentioned in earlier chapters. By definition, you have to manipulate the thoughts of your constituency into believing you are representing them— even though you are spending most of your effort representing yourself. There is nothing that drives animals (and humans) more than self-preservation. Career politician, like animals, all work to preserve their jobs.

Of course, we all try to preserve our jobs. So, why is it bad for politicians to preserve theirs? Because, to do so, they do not make decisions based on root causes or address long-term issues critical to the nation's future, and this is how we have gotten into the present political, financial, environmental, and economic messes (to name just a few). Politicians have focused mostly on the next election, instead of the issues. They will wait until an issue becomes a crisis, a "hot button" issue, and then they will blame others and develop wedges. And the mode of operation starts all over again!

Politicians will argue they need time in office to learn the processes. This statement always makes me shudder when I hear it. The "processes" they are talking about are a combination of those described in this book and the actual processes used to govern under our *Constitution*. If we have selected smart people, scholars could provide them with a crash course of how the governmental system should work and how to make contributions to the governing processes.

Yet another perk of being in office for a long time is that the longer you are in one political entity (such as the U.S. House of Representatives or the U.S. Senate), the more "perks" and "pork" you can get. For example, the late Senator Robert Byrd, a defender of the republic and its *Constitution*, and the longest-serving U.S. senator diverted many billions of dollars from the rest of the states for the state of Virginia. Historically, between 1981 and 2005 (the latest year for which I could find the data), Virginia had gotten between $1.38 and $1.59 for each federal dollar the people of Virginia contributed. A few states have done better, but these are generally our poorer states or states that have many large federal facilities. New Mexico, with many military and energy facilities, tops the list at $2.03 in 2005. Mississippi, a poor state, is second at $2.02. I live in California. We have paid in more taxes than have come back to us since 1986. Only five states receive less than California: Delaware, Illinois, Minnesota, New Hampshire and Connecticut. In 2005, California got back $0.78 for every dollar sent to Washington - or one half of what Virginia got.[11] Given the fact that California generates thirteen percent of the United States Gross Domestic Product and has approximately twelve percent of the U.S. population, I am one Californian who is not happy about these differences.

When did the changes start to evolve?

Many of the career politician perks, political party power struggles, and lack of fiscal responsibility seem to have started during the administration of President Johnson when our national leaders started rapidly expanding social programs while fighting a war. A mere one to two decades before that time, things were certainly different. For example, "give 'em hell" President Harry Truman, a Democrat, probably made as many important decisions regarding our nation's history as any of the other thirty-two presidents preceding him and perhaps any who have followed him. However, a measure of his greatness may rest on what he did *after* he left the White House.

The only asset he had when he died was the house he lived in, which was in Independence, Missouri. His wife had inherited the house from her mother and father and, other than their years in the White House, they lived their entire lives there. His income was a U.S. Army pension reported to have been $13,507.72 a year. Congress, noting that he was paying for his stamps and personally licking them, granted him an "allowance" and, later, a retroactive pension of $25,000 per year.

After President Eisenhower was inaugurated, Harry and his wife, Bess, drove home to Missouri by themselves. There were no Secret Service protectors following them.

When offered corporate positions at large salaries, he declined, stating, *"You don't want me. You want the office of the president, and that doesn't belong to me. It belongs to the American people and it's not for sale."*

Even later, on May 6, 1971, when Congress was preparing to award him the Medal of Honor on his 87th birthday, he refused to accept it, writing, *"I don't consider that I have done anything which should be the reason for any award, congressional or otherwise."*

As president, Truman paid for all of his own travel expenses and food. Good old Harry Truman was correct when he observed, *"My choices in life were either to be a piano player in a whore house or a politician. And to tell the truth, there's hardly any difference!"*[12]

Modern politicians, including presidents, have found a new level of success by cashing in on their positions, which has resulted in untold wealth. Political offices are now for sale. Vote buying is commonplace through primarily two means. Promising and promoting free money entitlements and other goodies to blocks of voters. These are essentially bribes by politicians given to selected citizens. Political contributions and other perks provided by lobbyists and other special interest groups are also essentially bribes given to politicians. Both are given to garner votes without regard to short or long-term impacts on the nation as a whole.

We are hypocrites when we accuse other countries of being corrupt because their politicians and government employees take bribes. After all, we have allowed our politicians to pass laws that allow public unions, corporations, and special interest lobbyists to pay-off politicians on a daily basis through "political contributions" and other means. We are hypocrites when we accuse other countries' politicians of buying votes. We allow our politicians to pass laws that take money from a minority of the citizens and give it to others - sometimes without preconditions - knowing full well that robbing Peter to pay Paul assures Paul will vote for them. Just because politicians can pass laws saying that it is legal for them to do these things does not change the fact these are bribes!

Overview of Our Dysfunctional Political System Summary

Bullets

✪ The political parties conduct party wars rather than the peoples' business.

✪ Based on written statements from our Founding Fathers their vision for our political system was different than what is practiced today.

✪ Examples of these differences that our Founding Fathers would not have expected include:

★ Today's career politicians' primary focus on being re-elected
★ Perks career politicians provide themselves
★ Laws and rules that allow "legal" bribes of voters and Congress members for their personal gain

Chapter 17:
The Root Causes That Led Us Here

Politicians own our political system in the sense that they control the processes and make their own rules. We have little to say about what they do and most of the time we are not even aware of their actions. If politicians do something too blatant, it may be challenged in the courts. We do sometimes find out the consequences of their actions but it is usually too late to change the outcome. In this chapter we will explore questions about Congressional actions then look at root causes for the system failures.

Political System Failure Causes

Is Congress doing its job?

There are numerous examples indicating the answer to this question is a resounding *"NO!"* Congress has two key constitutional functions: provide processes (systems) and laws as needed to meet national needs, and provide oversight of the laws as executed through the executive branch. I believe they are failing miserably at both.

The financial crisis in 2009 was a failure of both political parties. Both Republicans and Democrats failed to establish appropriate bounds, performance standards, and regulations that would prevent a catastrophic failure. They also failed to oversee the performance of existing regulations, and to see, assess, and address the problem as it was developing. What they did do was initiate their standard mode of operation. They quickly determined whom they could blame and developed wedges between Main and Wall Streets. Of course, they then quickly stuck existing (and future) citizens with more national debts to fix the problems they created. They continue to kick the "cost can" down the road for future generations to pay. Action was needed, but rather than assess what would give the most "bang for the buck" in the shortest time, they funded their pet political dreams and paid off their special interest groups.

The Health Care Bill points out other failures of Congress. The facts were known for many years that not all citizens were covered by health insurance, preexisting conditions were problematical, coverage was not portable from job to job, and costs were rising. Congress could have fixed all of these problems years ago. They did not fix them because the political heat might have made their next elections more difficult. They did not need to address it earlier since it was not yet a crisis. When it became a crisis of costs, they simply blamed the insurance industry (whom they had not adequately regulated or overseen), developed wedges between groups of citizens and businesses, and started the usual cycle. They also did not properly assess causes for the high health care costs or what might be the best solutions. They instead focused on more government control, resulting in more power to career politicians.

The patterns that emerge from these examples are the same for almost every other major issue our present politicians pursue. White House Chief of Staff, Rahm Emanuel, said: *"You don't ever want to let a crisis go to waste: it's an opportunity to do impor-*

tant things that you would otherwise avoid."[1] What he meant is not clear but one possibility is that he wants to use crisis as a pretense for engineering a permanent increase in the size and scope of the government.

Crises are easier to deal with politically than correcting problems as they arise, particularly in a political party war setting. But crises are very costly and seldom provide the best (or even *good*) solutions. We are, and will be, paying for past errors developed through political crisis management for many years to come unless we demand change.

It is not any wonder that we have seen wild political swings in Washington. First, one party has majority control, then the voters get disappointed and the power shifts. A Congress that truly represents us, one that uses a debate process to expose the whole truth both good and bad, is needed.

Why does Congress keep spending money we do not have?

One of the biggest problems with Washington is that politicians seem not to know the difference between $1 million and $1 trillion. So, when Congress starts counting our tax dollars in the trillions of dollars all citizens need to remember that one trillion dollars is a million million dollars, or a thousand billion dollars, or about $3,250 per citizen. A trillion dollars is a lot of money, no matter how you stack it.

Both the Republicans and Democrats have claimed fiscal responsibility, but the truth is that in recent decades neither political party has been a particularly good steward of taxpayer resources. Government spent four-to-five times more of America's national output (GDP) in 2009, than in 1900. The government's share of all the money from what we produce and earn has doubled since the end of World War II.

The 1994 Contract with America[2] that Newt Gingrich and others proposed was not sufficient to stop the federal career politicians from their excessive spending and borrowing. The "Bush 2" Administration lowered taxes while increased spending for the wars on terrorism that added costs and debt. The Democrats, particularly the liberal ones, continued to push for more and more expensive social programs. Almost all of the growth of government in the past fifty years has been a result of increased civilian social-program spending.

Federal spending increases are only part of the burden on our nation. State and local politicians also have jumped on the spending bandwagon. In 2009, the total for federal, state, and local spending was $6,600 billion.[3] Specifically, federal spending was $3,518 billion, state spending was $1,343 billion, and local spending was $1,739 billion. The total divided by our population indicates over $21,000 per person was spent in 2009!

Many of you might think that a lot of your $21,000 went to protect us and to fund the wars on terrorism. Ironically, the one area of the budget where Congress has a clear constitutional authority to spend money (national defense and homeland security) has historically been about one-third to one-half of all federal expenditures. In 2008 with two ongoing wars, that percentage is down to about one-fifth (See **Figure 9-1).** The percentage of the total federal, state, and local revenues going to defense is about twelve percent. So, about $2,500 of your $21,000 goes toward defense, leaving about $18,500 for direct benefit to you. Ask yourself: Did you get $18,500 per person - or $74,000 for a family of four - worth of benefits from your government in 2009? If you did not, why not? The bad news is this number is continuing to go up.

In addition to direct spending, the government regulations add to the overall burden. In 1938, a year before I was born, there were approximately 3,194 pages of federal regulations in the Federal Register. In 2008, there were 80,700 pages and more were being added, over a twenty-five-fold increase in seventy years.[4]

We work almost half our lives now complying with government rules, edicts, levies, paperwork, taxes, and fees. Regulations are needed, but there should be renewal clauses in all of them so that they could be periodically reviewed for efficiency and effectiveness. According to *The Constitution*, oversight of regulations and regulators are part of Congress's job and they are failing miserably.

Unless there are some major changes, at least in the short-term, government will continue to rapidly expand. After all, the ink is not even dry on Medicare Drugs Bill passed under President Bush when Health Care under President Obama will add more costs. The costs just keep increasing. There is nothing to bound the debt or spending.

What this country needs are more unemployed politicians.[5] — **Edward Langley**

Root Causes

There are four root causes, and several associated lower level causes for most of our political system problems. The four key root causes that need top priority attention are:

Root Cause #1: A politician's primary goal is re-election

Career politicians:

- Need to be re-elected, which requires:
  - ★ Continuously seeking money, more frequently for two-year-term House members than for six-year-term Senate members or the four-year-term Presidency
  - ★ Continuously using tricks to scare, mislead, and seduce constituents to convince voters to support their positions and re-election
  - ★ Continuously seeking votes including buying them with free money
  - ★ Gerrymandered voting blocks to improve each politician's re-election chances
- Have no re-election term limits
- Receive a great set of benefits even for serving only one term
- Receive many perks not provided to most citizens
- Have big egos, and think they know what the masses need

Root Cause # 2: No hard fiscal bounds to require fiscal accountability of Congress

Congress has no:

- Limits on debt accumulation; can raise the debt limit as they please
- Hard fiscal bounds on spending

✪ Bounds on campaign funding, so money - a proven winner of votes - controls election outcomes
✪ Bounds on funding, services and other similar perks provided by lobbyists
✪ Significant worry about investigations by news media

Root Cause #3: Short-term perspective on issues due to short time between re-elections

Career politicians:

✪ Only work on short-term issues without worrying about the costs or impacts on future generations and the nation's long-term health
✪ Allow festering problems to becoming crises rather than conducting timely reviews of laws and regulation for long-term efficiency and effectiveness
✪ Use financial tricks when a longer-term problem does become a crisis, then re-engineer the system, rather than seeking long-term, cost-efficient, and effective solutions

Root Cause #4: Lack of civility between politicians is driven by party wars that make voters take sides and invoke strong voter emotions

Political parties and politicians:

✪ Use wars to gain party power; debating the real causes or the most costs effective solution is less effective in gaining power
✪ Use sound bites and political wars to draw media coverage; debates are too boring to attract media attention

While these root causes are not all of the causes for our dysfunctional and failing political system, they do represent four key causes, which, if addressed, would significantly change the present course of our nation. Presidents and congresses in the recent past have failed to address these causes. Only we can drive solutions, and politicians will only act if we make them. The status quo has got to go if we are going to reclaim our nation.

The Root Causes That Led Us Here Summary Bullets

- ✪ Politicians' first priority is being re-elected.
- ✪ Congress is not doing its constitutional oversight job.
- ✪ Politicians are fiscally irresponsible.
- ✪ Politicians and their parties have a very short-term perspective.
- ✪ Continuing party wars interfere with possible favorable compromises.

Chapter 18:
The Solutions For Reclaiming Our Liberties

O ur Founding Fathers felt politicians were to be the servants, and the citizens the royalty, not the inverse. This chapter explores my personal view of what our Founding Fathers might have envisioned for us in a 21st-century world, and provides possible system solutions for attaining this vision. The solutions are aimed at addressing the root causes provided in Chapter 17.

The Ideal vs. the Possible

Some of the solutions offered may not be possible in the near future, but some can, and all the root cause problems need solutions. In a few cases, I describe my view of the ideal solution followed by a more practical one. My suggested fixes are aimed at the root cause's problems, but the first sentence of this chapter - politicians are servants and citizens are royalty - is the underlying theme, driving the solutions.

Career Politicians

1. Number of Political Parties
    I believe, ideally, a minimum of three political parties is needed. Perhaps they might be Democrat, Moderate, and Republican, moving from left to right. We should offer our support to any party that comes close to being moderate and constitutionally based. Wars are waged between two entities or ideologies (for instance the Cold War was between the Communist East and the Capitalist West). It is much harder to conduct a war when there are three or more ideologies or interests involved. We need a political system that has difficulty waging war and must seek compromises, but both the Republican and Democratic parties will fight with all the resources at their disposal to keep this from happening. Attacks on the Tea Party, which does not even claim to be a political party *per se*, have already started.

2. Balance of Congressional Power
    If there are only two principle parties, ideally a split of approximately fifty-one percent to forty-nine percent advantage in the House for one party (say Party A) should be balanced by approximately a similar advantage in the Senate for the other party (say Party B). The president could be from either party. This would result in a balanced approach to both legislation and oversight. A three-party system would be even better, since wider percent ranges (for example, forty percent, twenty-five percent and thirty-five percent) would still assure balance. If we, as voters, seek balance we can get it with our votes by simply not re-electing incumbent politicians.

3. Single-Term and Multi-Term Durations
    When *The Constitution* was written, even a two-year term for House members was considered a long time for them to be away from their livelihood, their families, and their busi-

nesses. Congressmen did not get large wages or benefits. Since Washington, D.C., was reasonably close to the politicians' homes, they could go home from time to time, as needed, to tend to their businesses. Serving in Congress was considered an honor, not a career, so the Founding Fathers envisioned citizen legislators would serve one or two terms, then go home and go back to work. The Founding Fathers did not envision the state of affairs we have now. If so, they certainly would have put limits on congressional service in *The Constitution*.

Ideally, federal political careers should range from two years (one house term) to twenty years (a maximum of twelve years total of any combination of House and Senate terms, plus two terms as president). This would allow an outstanding public servant, working as a politician, to rise to the top as president, while most politicians would be off the federal payroll in no more than twelve years. Unfortunately, some of them may also have served at the state and local levels, essentially still making them career politicians. Nevertheless, I believe this ideal situation may be possible and should be implemented as soon as possible, but it will take great effort by us citizens to make it happen.

Some argue that term limits do not allow time for politicians to learn the processes of governing. As mentioned earlier, learning what one needs to do to make a contribution could be easily taught as a political crash course. What politicians do not need to know are all of the tricks covered in the earlier chapters. Another argument against term limits says that they do not allow a group of voters to again re-elect the "termed-out" congressmen they really like. One solution to this problem might be to allow an exception, provided the termed-out congressman obtains a two-thirds majority of the votes cast. If he does not, then there would be a second election wherein presumably the party primary runner-up to the termed-out person would participate.

4. District Allocations Process

Gerrymandering is a form of boundary redistricting in which constituency boundaries are deliberately modified for electoral purposes, thereby producing a contorted or unusual shape. Gerrymandering is used to achieve desired electoral results for a particular party, or may be used to help or hinder a particular group of voters that may have similar interests such as political, racial, linguistic, religious, or class-connected group. With the advent of the computer, gerrymandering has become an art form when done by politicians and is simply another disgrace to the political process. It needs to stop.

Any state using gerrymandering should, as soon as possible, redistrict itself by developing an independent process wherein a group of people with minimal political bias is chosen to conduct the redistricting. The selected group should establish non-political objectives and set criteria to be used to meet these objectives. Politicians still in office should be listened to for their observations, but not be a part of the actual redistricting process. A panel of judges, not politicians, should select the group's members. Various groups would be encouraged to submit names of candidates to this panel of judges.

Again, balance is key. First, representation on this independent process should include an equal balance from all parties - making it one-third Republican, one-third Democrat, and one-third a third party or independents - and not be based on voter registration percentages. This would allow equal party representation independent of political leanings, and no one party could dictate results as they can now. Second, racial and mixed racial groups should be represented based on the percentage of them in the state. This would assure a voice for everyone. Third, all "classes" of citizens from the private sectors should be represented (service and craft workers, managers, small businesses owners, and corporate leaders). Actual percentages of each may vary depending upon the state so that farm states would have more small business representation, etc. The first task for the independent group would to establish goals and criteria for redistricting which would be shared with the public. The state would also have to provide resource assistance for redistricting, such as source data and computer support.

A process similar to the one described above is currently being implemented now in California. But even before a panel could be selected, special interest groups have challenged the process and, of course, few politicians support it. But California's approach may be a good model for other states with politicized gerrymandering processes.

5. Perks and Benefits for Congress

In this fast-moving age, we do not want our congressmen worrying about their personal finances while in office. Ideally, they should put their businesses and other interests into trusts held and managed by independent firms. As our servants, they should *not* get special privileges. They should be held accountable through our votes and also through their pocketbooks, as we are each day. They should get:

a. A generous salary. In 2010, $129, 517 is the highest salary for a rank and file federal government (Grade 15, Step 10) employee. Higher-level managers can receive up to approximately $200,000, I propose starting in 2010 with a House and Senate member salary of $200,000, which is about $26,000 more than it is right now.[1] The House and Senate leadership should get ten percent to fifteen percent more. Frankly, if I thought Congress would really do things described herein for the nation rather than for their party and for themselves, I would be happy to see them get a much higher salary. Another possible wage and benefits solution is to have "we the people" vote on their wages and benefits package every four years. The ballot would provide selection options for wages, benefits, and perks. If the following principles were implemented, there might not be a reason to include Congress's wages and benefits package on the ballot.

b. A retirement IRA with matching funds allowance, but no other retirement benefits. Congressmen can buy what they need, as do their constituents. They are not to be part of the Federal Employees Retirement System (FERS). They should continue to pay into Social Security and any other entitlements.

c. A health care insurance allowance sufficient for a minimum family policy based on the size of their family. They would need to buy their policy just like the rest of us.

d. A modest travel allowance based on the distance they must travel to their districts. The air travel allowance would be for coach class. They would have to pay for upgrades.

e. A modest living allowance, since they may need two places to reside while in office. This should be no more than the average rental price for a three-bedroom apartment in Washington, D.C.

f. Raises tied to inflation, just like Social Security and other things. However, a non-refundable *negative raise* equivalent to the percentage of budget over-run should result whenever expenditures exceed the Hard Fiscal Bounds defined below.

Hard Fiscal Bounds

The national debt and spending that need hard bounds to avoid a catastrophe were covered in **Chapter 8**. For completeness, these are summarized here in items 1. and 2.

1. National Debt Bound
   a. Impose a hard upper national debt bound of sixty percent as a fraction of the Gross National Product *as a starting point*. This is about the ratio it was in the year 2000.

b. In less than ten years, by 2020, lower the sixty percent debt bound to fifty percent as a fraction of the GNP. This value is still above the historical average before and after WWII.

c. For significant wars, these bounds might need to be raised, but following a war we must return to these bounds within fifteen years as we did after WWII.

    i. For a congressionally approved regional or non-conventional war, the maximum hard bound is not to exceed seventy-five percent of the GNP.

    ii. For a major world war, the maximum hard bound is not to exceed one hundred percent of the GNP. This is slightly lower than during WWII. NOTE: We are already over the sixty percent limit, and will soon be past the seventy-five percent limit, but we have no ongoing congressionally approved regional or non-conventional wars. Given the present world economies, at no time (including during a major war) should we exceed one hundred percent of the GNP.

d. Immediately stop selling national debt paper to foreigners.

2. Spending Bounds

a. Impose a hard bound that does not allow mandatory spending to exceed sixty percent as a fraction of total annual spending. NOTE: No additional hard bound is needed for annual spending since when our government spends more than it collects in revenues, the difference comes from borrowing and, in turn, raises the national debt. The debt bounds therefore control annual spending.

3. Campaign and Lobbyist Bounds

Campaign financing is a travesty that begs to be changed. A 2010 Supreme Court ruling allows every special interest group to use their funds for campaign ads. Even without this new ruling, lobbyists have filled politicians' campaign election or re-election coffers. Campaign ads are filled with political tricks, if not with outright lies. Ideally, all sources of campaign funds should be curtailed to assure that vote-buying stops. Given the Supreme Court ruling, this does not seem possible. Lobbyists and others will continue to provide gifts and other perks to members of Congress unless significant changes occur.

The Bipartisan Campaign Reform Act (BCRA), also called the McCain-Feingold bill, was signed into law by President Bush in March 2002. It was an attempt to add reason and bounds to the process. Others have tried public financing approaches. So far, the politicians' satisfaction with the status quo has stopped any attempt for a reasoned, fair, and balanced approach that allows candidates to present their views to voters and to limit special interest involvement. Here are two changes that could address this present problem:

a. The first change involves the media. Recent history shows that the media will air anything for which they get paid without questioning either the ads or political claims that they air. The citizens of the nation own the airwaves that radio and TV news media use. They can only broadcast on the frequencies allocated to them by the government. Since "we the people" own the airwaves, we should demand prime time for political discussions. Here is how free prime time for political discussions might work.

Each party's federal candidates would get time on na-tionally syndicated stations, and state and local candidates would get time on regional and local stations. All national stations would air the same candidates at the same time similar to a presidential address. Regional and local stations would follow similar requirements for state and local can-didates. Significant time would generally only be needed every two years.

Candidates would be given appropriate formats to fol-low. For example, the first event might allocate an hour per candidate (including questions and closing arguments) to discuss the top five to ten issues the candidate feels are most important and what he or she would do to address them. If there were costs for a proposed action, they would be required to state how they would pay them. Station reporters would ask five to ten questions of each candidate at the end of the each candidate's briefing. Simply attacking the opposing candidate would be discouraged. Five-minute closing statements would be allowed at the end. Finally, all candidates would be encouraged to develop and provide position statements on a web page for viewers to get additional information about them and their views. Note that this proposed solution is not a set of narrowly focused debates; rather it is a focus on policy substance. Any debates, if warranted, could follow these individual candidate discussions. This change offers a way for voters to listen to each candidate in a fair and unbiased way.

Many details would need to be worked out, but this format could be very useful to a public being bombarded with negative ads. It might start to restore one of the media's national roles as envisioned by the Founding Fathers. The paper media (newspapers and selected magazines) could also be asked to participate. Also, both audio and newspaper media should be encouraged to investigate each politician's advertisement claims for accuracy.

Some agencies or groups are doing political fact-checking now. For example some fact checking is done by the Annenberg Public Policy Center and many other checking websites have sprung up. They all are trying to determine how to provide the best results. Perhaps some of the not-for-profit entities should consider building unbiased web sites for fact checking. The Bill and Melissa Gates Foundation could do us a great service by taking on this important issue. If good fact checking were available, it would make most of the negative ads moot. This should change the focus to the real issues and might reduce the amount and influence of monies spent for political ads.

b. The second change is to assure absolute transparency of all forms and amounts of monies, services, and physical objects from any and all sources, and assure that they are reported and recorded in a database for viewing by citizens. The money, service, or objects must be listed with an actual cost (or an estimate of its cost), the date it was received, and who (by name or entity) provided it to the politician. All data base entries must be reported within a week of when the money, service or object is received.

Reporting categories could be defined and a government-owned database that is easily available to all of us must be kept current and easy to use. *There must be no exceptions.* Our representatives should not be accepting a free cup of coffee without us knowing it. Any exceptions to this are simply opportunities for politicians to find ways to misuse them. Who gives us free coffee? Other federal employees cannot accept gifts from citizens, so why should members of Congress? Only total transparency will be credible to citizens. True full transparency will allow voters access to information needed to make politicians accountable.

I feel these solutions are something we citizens can demand our leaders implement. The media will not proceed on their own, even though this was likely the intent of our Founding Fathers when "freedom of the press" was added to *The Constitution*. Certainly politicians will not act without great pressure. So far, they have talked but have taken no serious actions. Instead they have thumbed their noses at us while raking in the bucks!

Short-Term Perspective

The solutions proposed under "Hard Fiscal Bounds" and "Career Politicians (above) will help solve this short-term perspective problem as well. The Senate tends to take a longer-term view of our nation's needs than does the House. This is partly a result of their longer time between elections. Presently, re-election forces politicians' thinking to be focused on today's issues and raising money. Getting no perks, and free campaign radio and TV time, should encourage politicians to think about and vote with a more futuristic focus. Finally, a paradigm shift away from two parties waging war and back to rational debate is needed. Debate would allow discussion of long-term issues and costs.

Lack of Civility

Early in our history, there was a tacit understanding that political debate should be civil. While strong disagreements might have occurred, the debate would not be made personal or nasty. While there has always been some nastiness, this seems to gradually have gotten worse in the late 1980s. A few decades ago I can recall Senators Mitchell and Dole on TV news shows having disagreements, but always being polite and respectful of each other. This civility was fascinating to watch. I felt both sides did really want to do the right things, might disagree on how to do them, but were willing to work toward a compromise that, while not perfect, was a reasonably good solution.

Lately this civility seems to have disappeared. Now, even President Obama seems to feel the need to demonize his rivals. Both political parties seem to prefer wars to debates. What caused this change is hard to know for sure, but it may have been the increased access to visual media and the personalities of the newer leaders. I believe the corruption caused by politicians' needs to be powerful, be the winners, and get re-elected, add to the problem. The present lack of civility is further dividing the people of our nation. Instituting the suggestions mentioned above should restore some civility. With civility, politicians can begin doing their jobs using modes of operation that foster civil debate on causes of problems, consider the cost-benefits of solutions to the nation, and address how the costs will be paid for in the short and long-terms.

Thoughts For Career Politicians

At this point, you might conclude that I do not believe any politician is a good one. On the contrary, history is full of what I consider great politicians. I have provided quotes from many of our early politicians. As a more recent example, Winston Churchill was willing to "tell it like it was" in his public discussions when he stated he could only offer England "blood, toil, tears and sweat" during World War II. I admire all of today's politicians who mean what they say, have a strong set of values, and attempt to do the right things for the short and long-term success of our nation - even if some of these things are not popular at the time with the majority of their constituents. We have many brave soldiers willing to give up their lives and many other volunteers willing to provide some of their time and money to serve and benefit our nation. It is disappointing to me that our career politicians are not willing to do the right things for our nation simply because it might threaten their jobs. I believe we do not have many brave politicians serving us.

If you are a career politician reading this, you probably keep saying that none of what has been stated in this book is true. You find yourself saying, "I *do* represent the interests of the nation. I am right, this author is dead wrong." Such thoughts would not surprise me, as this is what you have been telling us for years: that you are right and we are wrong. But rising national spending and debts are facts as are many other topics discussed herein. You are the politicians whom "we the people" need to vote out of office.

Career politicians who are truly interested in change to sustain our nation have some work to do. My observation is that almost all career politicians who have been re-elected one or more times believe they are like our well-known athletes, entertainers, and some business leaders— many of whom feel they are superior intellectually, physically, and morally to the rest of us. Therefore, they feel they are entitled to have affairs, break laws, receive perks, take illegal drugs, disregard facts, tell us only what we want to hear, and do anything else they want.

There seems to be an unending list of famous people who have been caught exploiting their fame. These include sports personality Tiger Woods, entertainer David Letterman, politician John Edwards, and a long list of others. "Caught" famous people, who have obtained some level of forgiveness by a generally forgiving nation, have publicly confessed their mistakes and have avoided repeating them. This is where sincere career politicians should start. Next, you should be prepared to act accordingly. If you continue with the status quo, we will know once again that you are simply telling us what you think we want to hear. We will make it clear that this is not acceptable by throwing you out of your political office.

The Solutions For Reclaiming Our Liberties Summary Bullets

✪ Support any new political party, or any existing political party that is moderate and has the most constitutionally based philosophies.

✪ Vote to minimize political wars by balancing the power between parties in both the House and Senate, thereby forcing more debate and compromise.

✪ Establish your own personal practice of not voting to re-elect your Senator members for more than two terms or House members for more than four terms thereby encouraging new ideas and longer term thinking in Congress.

✪ Eliminate gerrymandering. Determine a candidate's view on redistricting and do not vote for a candidate that does not fully support fair independently established redistricting.

✪ Make politicians' wages attractive but do not provide special benefits. Seek to force elimination of *all* politicians' perks and special benefits that "we the people" are not afforded. Consider including wage and benefit options for congress members on the ballot every four years.

✪ Support hard fiscal bounds as a percent of the GDP on the national debt, and annual discretionary and mandatory spending.

✪ Insist on stopping the sale of national debt paper to foreigners.

✪ Require radio and TV stations, as a part of their licensing processes, to provide free prime time to political candidates to present what they view as the top issues, their position on those issues, and how they would cover any costs.

✪ Demand web-based transparency for all congressmen's activities. Require absolute transparency of all forms and amounts of monies, services, and physical objects (from any and all sources) that each politician receives.

✪ Vote to replace politicians who insist on conducting wars rather than debating the issues. Demand political candidates discuss issues including long and short-term impacts and costs.

PART V: STRATEGIES AND TACTICS FOR WINNING OUR WAR

Now that you are equipped with knowledge of politicians' tactical tricks, our many failing and deficient systems, and the current agents of dysfunction, it is time to develop our war's strategic framework— our path forward. In this Part, you will be called upon to join the movement, or suffer the consequences.

Chapter 19: You Must Join The Fight

Chapter 20: Our Winning Strategies

Chapter 21: Closing Remarks

Chapter 19:
You Must Join The Fight

Career politicians have caused most of our problems. The moment politicians decide to make politics a career, their set of values change to increase their chances of being re-elected. They do the right things for *their* re-elections, including collecting as much money as possible and using tricks to hide their mistakes. As we move forward, if a politician is playing one or more psychological or financial tricks and in your gut you feel they are not to be trusted, turn them off. Career politicians are the enemy in our war— perhaps not all of them, but certainly the vast majority. Look at each one closely and "if in doubt, vote them out."

A few news media "talking heads" or other "political elitist" may claim to be balanced and neutral voices of reason, but then do not hesitate to provide one-sided views supporting select politicians or political positions. If we are going to listen to their "reports", we must always remain cautious and aware. They, too, can be our enemy by being an effective propaganda machine for political parties.

We citizens are also partly responsible for our problems. We citizens have allowed career politicians to get away with what they have done. I have often heard people say "it's just politics" when politicians or political parties sling mud, lay blame, or promise what they cannot deliver, etc. The next time you hear someone say that, correct the speaker by telling him or her: "No, it is a career politician who believes it is his way to be re-elected and gain power." We all have a lot to lose if we do and say nothing.

You may be asking yourself why you, personally, should become involved. The answer depends upon your age and your abilities. Groups of individuals will be affected differently if the status quo continues. Let's look first at history and then how you personally will be impacted.

A History Lesson

Few Germans were true Nazis, few Russians and Chinese were true Communist and a similar statement can be made about many nations dominated by a particular religion. So how did these smaller groups end up ruling their nations and instituting policies that included new socio-economic systems, killing millions of people, and other radical changes? How did the radicals and extremists win?

Many of these nations' people liked the radicals' promises to return national pride, provide "free (money) entitlements," and institute changes to address some present national problems, but many more were just too busy to care. So, the *majority* of the nation's people just sat back and let it all happen. Then, before they knew it, they were owned by a *minority* of the population, and had lost control of their nation. Their nation, as they had known it, had come to an end. It was then too late and too dangerous for them to speak or act.

The hard, quantifiable fact is that the less radical majority, the 'silent majority,' became cowed by the radicals and extraneous in these nations. The radicals were "talking heads" repeatedly making their cases for change, peace, dominance, national pride, the promise of money and jobs, or whatever else that would gain recruits and citizen supporters. The radicals and their recruits are who marched in the streets and cowed those of the silent majority who dared to challenge the radicals' policies.

History repeats itself and we seem to be following this model. No one is suggesting we are headed toward a future where we will see massive killings of our citizens, but we are in the mist of radical changes and unless the 'silent majority' starts speaking and acting this is what we can expect:

- ✪ Freedom as envisioned by our Founding Fathers will be made irrelevant.
- ✪ Today's freedom-loving citizens will become our enemy since they will awaken one day and find that the radicals and ex-trenists own them, and the end of their world will have begun.
- ✪ The many freedom-loving Americans who have died to pro-tect the underlying principles that have made America great will have died in vain. The silent majority can watch it all un-fold or speak and act to counter the radicals who threaten our way of life.

Impacts By Age Group

The impacts of our political leaders actions by age groups, under age twenty-five, twenty-five to fifty, and over fifty (including retirees), are briefly summarized, below, using the findings from earlier chapters. These impacts set the stage for our war strate-gies and for the tactical actions of individuals. Our war is a call to action for all age groups. Each person has good reason to be out-raged by what has happened and the future impacts these actions will have on you, personally.

- ✪ Each individual in each age group owns at least $43,000 of the national debt. In addition, each individual owns at least $128,000 of the "mandated program debt" for programs, such as Social Security and Medicare that were also under-funded. These two debts total more than $171,00 per citizen with some high end estimates more than doubling this amount. State and local governments debts add thousands of dollars more to these totals. Current and past politicians accumulated these debts to pay for various social programs, wars, and numerous other programs for which there were insufficient funds. Both national debts are increasing faster than either inflation or population growth. The same is true for state and local governments. The national political plan was to pass the debt on to future generations of citizens.

★ If you are younger than twenty-five, you have a bigger problem than your parents and grandparents have. Since the "baby boom" population precedes you, you will either add to the debt or will be force to pay more while you get less. You will pay for one half of one retired person's Social Security, and you will pay even more for other mandates. You likely will get significantly less (or nothing) from these programs when you retire. Yet, you will be paying on these debts for the rest of your life.

★ If you are twenty-five to fifty, you will also get less from retirement and mandated programs than your parents got. You will be paying on these debts for the rest of your life.

★ If you are older than fifty, a lot of this debt occurred on your watch, but you will likely not pay off much of your portion. You may, however, be significantly impacted. For example, a failure of the financial markets, leading to high inflation, would result in a lower standard of living for you in your retirement.

✪ Starting in 2014, you will be required to have health care insurance, unless you can get an exception by claiming to be of a certain exempted faith-based group (e.g., Amish or Muslim). You will pay taxes on health insurance payments paid by your employer and on any medical equipment you may need. Low-wage earners' insurance costs will be subsidized.

★ If you are younger than twenty-five, health insurance will cost at least twice what it would have cost without passage of the new health care program. You will pay this for at least one half of your life, after which other younger persons may pick up the slack.

★ If you are twenty-five to fifty, you, too, will likely pay more through a variety of taxes included in the bill.

★ If you are older than fifty, starting in 2014 your insurance premiums may decline slightly and some of you may receive supplemental money for continuing your insurance coverage. Other costs will rise because you will pay taxes on any employer payments you receive and on any medical equipment you may need.

✪ If you are reasonably successful over time, you will be considered "wealthy" by our leaders and will pay significantly more in taxes. The reason for this is that, since 1940, incomes have on average gone up about fifty percent per decade due to inflation and related factors. Assuming this trend continues, your taxes, as a percentage of your income will go up.

★ If you are younger than twenty-five and are reasonably successful, you will likely reach the "wealthy" category by mid-career and certainly before you reach retirement age. You will pay more taxes as you fall into higher tax brackets.

★ If you are twenty-five to fifty and successful, before you reach retirement age you will be considered "wealthy" and will pay extra taxes since you will be in higher tax brackets.

★ If you are older than fifty and successful, you are likely already wealthy enough to receive fewer benefits and pay more taxes on both benefits and investments.

✪ Jobs will continue to be scarce as world competition continues. Government actions such as selling debt to foreign countries, adding more costs to be carried by U.S. businesses, and excessive wages and benefit funding for public employees, will ensure even fewer jobs are available for other citizens.

★ If you are younger than twenty-five, and management and labor fail to work as a team, even more jobs will be outsourced. Job creation policies are extremely important to your future.

★ If you are twenty-five to fifty, outsourcing may put your job at risk and many present policies drive businesses to outsource.

★ If you are older than fifty, you may not be worrying about jobs, but without near-full employment, there will be fewer funding sources for your retirement whether you are living on a pension, investments, and/or mandated programs.

✪ Local, state, and federal governments are growing faster than inflation or population increases. This means higher taxes or debt, and less money for the private sector to spend creating jobs and wealth. This will affect all age groups.

✪ If you have voted, chances are high you have been tricked by one or more career politicians into voting for something that was not clear to you at the time, but which has had an unexpected impact on you and the nation. You, as well as people in all age groups, heard what you wanted to hear and not the whole story at the time.

★ If you are under the age of twenty-five, you should be outraged because you and your children will be the ones who will pay for what we (the older generations) have left for you.

★ If you are between the ages of twenty-five and fifty, you should be outraged because your visions of retirement will not likely become reality.

★ If you are over age fifty, you should be outraged that our career politicians have been so cavalier with our hard-earned money. Our rights, as provided in our *Constitution*, have been lost and you may not retire as you had planned. If you are retired, you should be outraged that your economic quality of life may well diminish in your "golden years."

What should you do? Become educated about the facts and the tricks that career politicians play. Do not be suckered by politicians or members of the news media who say only what you want to hear to garner your vote or improve ratings. They are not telling you the whole story. Then, register and vote in every election. Vote out those who promise something for nothing and fail to take actions to truly make changes that stop (or at least reduce) the burden placed upon you, your children, your grandchildren, and other not-yet-born citizens. Vote to reduce debts, and to increase private sector job opportunities for yourself and others. Last but not least, join in *our* war.

You Must Join The Fight Summary Bullets

- History shows that when the "silent majority" fails to speak up and act, undesirable consequences for the nation are the result.
- All age groups are affected by our leaders' past mismanagement and failures.
- Every age group should be outraged that our leaders' self interests have resulted in numerous difficult national problems.
- Increasing jobs and wealth are not a sure thing for our nation's future. Our many problems must be quickly addressed to assure future job and wealth growth.

Chapter 20:
Our Winning Strategies

All wars require strategies and the tactics to maximize an army's chances of winning the big battles. In this chapter I provide framework and implementation strategies to help us fight our war against career politicians. It is time we stop being recruited for their party wars, and we start defending our liberties, and protecting our future. Battling as a collective group, we can win!

Strategic Framework

We need a strategic framework for our war and we need to recruit our own foot soldiers. In earlier chapters, I provided strategies and tactics for specific problems. Here, I will expand upon those strategies and tactics and suggest more. Several sources of information were used in helping me develop this plan of action. Most of the information referenced is listed in this book.

I followed this sequence to develop our strategic framework:

First, I tried to listen to what my friends - and you, the general public - seemed to be saying you wanted and needed from our government. My sources include private conversations, letters to newspapers, social networking sites, and the printed, audio and visual medias. Obviously each person who tries to determine needs and wants will likely develop slightly different lists. I believe I have captured most of our prevalent needs and wants for our nation.

Second, I used part of this book's theme, "reclaim our liberties," as our mission. This mission sums up most of the needs and wants into a single action for us.

Third, I believe we can all agree that our nation has had a magnificent and great past. Our Founding Fathers were brilliant in crafting *The Constitution* and other important documents. I believe we would all be delighted to return to that past with, of course, some modifications to account for a new national and world environment. Thus, the vision became "return our nation to its great past."

Fourth, strategic goals were developed based on the concepts, issues, problems, and root causes discussed in earlier chapters, combined with my understanding of the average citizen's needs and wants. These are the high-level goals, which, if achieved, would take us several steps closer to our vision.

Fifth, strategies to achieve our goals are needed. These are the actions we need to take to achieve the strategic goals. Generally there is a one-to-one relationship between the goals and strategies.

Finally, I listed the quintessential American values that serve as the underpinning of our country's beliefs. I used the traits of our Founding Fathers and added "freedom" to the list. Freedom was added to reflect the fact that many of our most current, pressing issues evolve from the lack or deviance from this core American value.

My results are shown in **Figure 20-1: Strategic Framework: American People's War (2010-2016).** This figure provides a one-page graphic summary of how to achieve our vision, and win our war. Not coincidentally, it also serves as a one-page summary of much of this book. The Vision, Mission and Values are shown in column one and Citizen Needs and Wants are listed in column two. Strategic Goals are listed in column three and Strategies for each Strategic Goal are listed in column four.

Figure 20-1: Strategic Framework: American People's War (2010-2016)

3. **Vision**	1. **Citizens' Needs/Wants**	4. **Strategic Goals**	5. **Strategies**
Return Nation to its Past Greatness	Status quo goes Return to our roots Politicians serve us, not themselves	Political system and politicians meet Founding Fathers' intent	Educate & train citizens • For example, this Book • H.S. courses on daily living & political operations Limit politicians • Total transparency of gifts, lobbying, and contributions • Limit Perks • Fair district allocation • Finite terms • No public union contributions • Short and long perspective • Restore civility, stop wars
2. **Mission** Reclaim our Liberties (from career politicians)	Control Nation's debt and spending Maintain a safety net for needy		
6. **Values** Service	Minimize free money — No new taxes	Stable, bounded systems	Fix critical systems • Rational health care • Fair, growth-oriented taxes • Bound National debt • Bound annual spending • Bound mandatory spending
Courage Resilience Hard work	Ensure that hard work and taking risks pays off Require jobs for all able to work	Maximize capitalism and minimize socialism	Individual ownership and responsibility • Individuals/ families buy health insurance • Work if and when can • Everyone pays General Fund taxes
Personal responsibility Generosity Freedom	Strive for teamwork and reasonable wages for labor and management Promote a fair, investigative, balanced, vigilant, Press Citizens regain control of Nation	Maximize jobs and job formation	Government actions • Jobs needs predictions • System to link jobs to workers and transportation Private actions • Corporate/Labor Teams • Standards for Corporate compensation
		Ensure the Press does its job per the Constitution and Founding Fathers' intent	Standards required for license • Free prime time for candidates • Standards for journalism

Implementation Strategy

The strategies in **Figure 20-1** are actions to take, but the figure does not indicate *when* or *how* to take the actions. A strategic plan for their implementation is also needed. For example, term limits may be a constitutional issue; however, the perks Congress has granted itself are not. Nowhere in *The Constitution* does it say or imply that congressmen can dictate their wages and benefit programs, thereby providing themselves lifetime retirement pay. Nowhere does it define gifts, free transportation, or any other perks that Congress has allowed itself to have. So, a good implementation strategy would be to focus first on eliminating all congressional perks. Indeed the argument for elimination of these perks is imbedded in the early days of our history, where most politicians did not serve long terms and did not have any of the perks afforded to 21st century congressmen. Without all of their perks, I doubt that many of the career politicians we have "serving" us would want to spend their whole lives as politicians. Also, several of the other strategies may fall into place once the career politician issue is resolved. Below, I have developed a rough implementation strategy using this kind of logic.

You will note there are five strategic goals, each with several strategies that are not in the same order presented in the book. Doing a time-ordered listing of all of these is neither practical nor optimum since many strategies should be done simultaneously. Thus, I have instead chronologically ordered the strategies within each goal and briefly presented the rationale for this ordering. At the end of each strategic goal, I provide a bullet summary that brings together key information from earlier chapters.

Goal 1: Political System and Politicians Meet our Founding Fathers' Intent

Without information and comprehension of how career politicians and effective governmental systems work, there will be as many frustrated citizens as we have now. Through education, we can train many foot soldiers to be ready for our fight. The proposed education curricula could be a start toward educating the general population. Other sources include grassroots organizations such as the Tea Party, enlightened journalists, business leaders, and some truly concerned political leaders - to name a few. Certainly President Obama, if he can be persuaded to do so, would be a great spokesperson. The education curricula proposed would ensure that younger people become available to sustain the base of new soldiers.

A relatively straightforward beginning along the road to regain control of Congress is to demand transparency of the monetary value of all items members receive. There can be no exceptions. With this information available, anyone, including journalists and fact check groups, will be able to see and expose inappropriate or questionable actions, blatant misconduct, and abuses of power. A second congressional control mechanism would be to make the wages, benefits, and perks politicians receive mirror what we have as citizens. This step should be easier to do following the total transparency actions.

Fair district allocations are essentially a decision for each state to make. Some states have developed reasonable approaches to this, but it must become commonplace for district boundaries to be set by non-political criteria and by non-politicians. This item needs to be addressed when a state does its next redistricting, if not before.

Since finite congressional terms are a constitutional issue, this is low on our list. But if transparency, appropriate wages and benefits, and fair districting are in place, term limits may not be needed.

Eliminating public union contributions is a straightforward "fairness and conflict of interest" issue that should get wide support once the public understands it.

Taking both a short and long-term perspective and restoring civility to debates should be substantially improved once all of the above items are in place.

Goal 1: Summary Bullets for Political System and Politicians Meet our Founding Fathers' Intent

- ✪ Educate "we the people"
    - ★ Require high school courses in
        - ❖ Daily living efficiency
        - ❖ Politics in the United States
    - ★ Demand fair and balanced investigations of issues by the press and media
- ✪ Limit career politicians
    - ★ Politicians' income and expenditures must be controlled, transparent, and available to public scrutiny, this includes
        - ❖ Accounting for all gifts (what, when, who, and how much)
        - ❖ Accounting for all contributions (what, when, who, and how much)
        - ❖ Accounting for all "business expenses" (what, *why*, when, who and how much)
        - ❖ Allowing no exceptions, not even for something as small as a cup of coffee
    - ★ Make politicians' wages, benefits, and perks similar to those of other citizens
        - ❖ Fixed substantial salaries commensurate with positions
        - ❖ Salaries ten percent to fifteen percent more for leaders
        - ❖ Raises increased with inflation, and reduced if spending exceeds limits
        - ❖ Wages and benefits become a ballot issue every four years
        - ❖ Modest living allowance for family rental in D.C.
        - ❖ Retirement IRA with matching contributions

- ❖ Minimum health insurance coverage, requiring personal contributions for upgrades
- ❖ One trip per month to/from his or her home district
- ❖ All political "pork" must be fully transparent or eliminated
- ❖ No more propaganda (newsletters) can be sent to voters at taxpayers' expense
- ❖ No lifetime benefits or special treatment for politicians
- ★ Establish districts without political influences (no gerrymandering)
- ★ Establish new laws to forbid public unions from using taxpayer resources to support politicians and political parties
- ★ Stop using political tricks to manipulate and divide "we the people," instead unite "we the people" through open and fully truthful civil debate

Goal 2: Stable, Bounded Government Systems

All strategies for this goal should be implemented at once. If not, then this is the order I would suggest.

Rational health care requires a "do over" to replace political warring with a rational debate that focuses on what should be the health care goal: to improve the health of the nation's citizens. Health care reform is high on this list because it is timely and is a good opportunity for Congress to enact a new, more effective, and more honest mode of operation.

Higher taxes that reduce job and wealth-growth cannot be relied upon to fix all of our problems, but a tax policy that increases individual responsibility (as well as jobs and wealth) is highly desirable. If you do not own a piece of something, you are not likely to feel responsible for it. When everyone feels some pain from spending, then most citizens will want to influence how the government spends their money. Working the tax issues at the same time as the health care issue provides a foundation for the possible government income needed to address debts and spending.

The national debt, annual spending, and mandatory (so-called "entitlement") spending are all intertwined, but should be worked separately. Due to accumulating debts, the nation's financial system is at its tipping point and may fail catastrophically if not addressed soon. It also is the starting point in addressing annual and mandatory spending.

Goal 2: Summary Bullets for a Stable, Bounded Government Systems

- ✪ Redo the health care system debate, focusing on improving health as the primary way to cut costs
- ✪ Establish a fair tax policy based on its ability to creating wealth and jobs (see, also, Goal 4)
  - ★ Create job opportunities to allow for the achievement of the American dream for our expanding population
  - ★ Develop standard tax rate formulas that minimize political manipulation
  - ★ Increase rates for progressive capital gains taxes on the truly super-wealthy
  - ★ Ensure that all progressive tax rates are inflation-adjusted
- ✪ Control spending and debt
  - ★ Limit national debt to percent of GNP
    - ❖ Initial limit would not be allowed to exceed sixty percent
    - ❖ Steady state limit (within ten years) would not be allowed to exceed fifty percent
    - ❖ During wars:
      - Congressionally approved regional war: could not exceed seventy-five percent;
      - Congressionally approved worldwide war: could not exceed one hundred percent.
    - ❖ Foreign countries are not be allowed to purchase debt paper
  - ★ Limit mandatory spending so that it does not exceed sixty percent of annual spending

★ Limit annual spending so that it is controlled by debt limits and mandatory spending limits

★ Define and explain spending criteria and priorities for every bill

Goal 3: Maximize Capitalism, Minimize Socialism

Increasing individual responsibility through ownership is a constitutional "basic values" concept. Therefore, as individuals earn money they should pay for what they need from food, housing, and clothing, to insurance (auto, health, property). For individuals, working hard and prudent risk-taking is part of our American values. All individuals should pay (progressive) taxes on earnings so that they own part of what our government spends for everything from entitlements to wars. Limits on mandatory spending should help control the shift from capitalism to socialism.

Goal 3: Summary Bullets to Maximize Capitalism, Minimize Socialism

✪ Renew our focus on individual responsibility versus "entitlements"

★ Each individual (or family) should be responsible and accountable for his or her (or their) own choices (to the extent possible)

❖ Balancing personal and family needs versus wants

❖ Accepting any risks taken and facing any consequences (no more bailouts)

❖ Protecting your self, your family, and the general public, e.g.:

• Paying for at least minimum-coverage insurance (for automobile, health, residence, etc.)

• Providing for emergencies and retirement

★ Each able-bodied individual must

- ❖ Work hard and take some risks to get ahead
- ❖ Not rely on entitlements or other handouts
- ★ All individuals with income from wages, benefits, entitlements, etc., must pay income and other progressive taxes.
  - ❖ Responsibility only comes with (partial) ownership by (voting) citizens
  - ❖ A progressive tax policy that starts with lowest wage earners paying some taxes assures a level of ownership by all citizens
  - ❖ All progressive tax rates from the lowest to the highest must be moved up (or down) together to ensure the pain of higher taxes is felt by all citizens, and to minimize political game-playing

Goal 4: Maximizing Jobs and Job Formation

Maximizing jobs and job formation needs to be done in parallel with everything else. Jobs, particularly for the unskilled, are disappearing in the nation. Politicians' may attempt to develop policies that penalize business who outsource, but such policies will only decrease jobs over the long term since this would have the same effect as increasing business taxes.

Our government, the private sector, and labor force must start facing these facts and become teams with common goals to stop (or even reverse) these trends. Teamwork, instead of adversarial divisions, is the key. Our government should stop being an employer and free money provider and, instead, become an employment agency that helps people find and fill jobs. Politicians and political parties need to bring together labor and management, rather than dividing them for their political gain.

Goal 4: Summary Bullets for Maximizing Jobs and Job Formation

✪ Maximizing jobs by management-labor-political teamwork is a needed paradigm shift
✪ Private sector business and labor leaders aided by government policies must work together to create jobs by
  ★ Management more effectively using labor brainpower to improve efficiency and profits
  ★ Labor recognizing that businesses need to make a profit, and that labor-management teamwork is needed to create and save jobs
  ★ Government becoming an employment agency, instead of being an employer – should provide
    ❖ Present and future needs information
    ❖ Resources to help the jobless find jobs
  ★ The two political parties working to unite management and labor to create jobs, and stop using wedges between management and labor for their political gain
✪ Larger corporations must re-gain public trust by
  ★ Establishing employee retention polices aimed at retaining U.S. jobs to the extent possible
  ★ Establishing and implementing nationwide compensation standards for senior executives in order to re-establish public credibility

Goal 5: Press Does Job Per *Constitution* and Founding Fathers' Intent

Journalism is changing rapidly due to advances in electronic communications. Unfortunately, to survive, the media has lost much of its utility to our nation. Since electronic media use radio frequencies[1] controlled by our government, we should require free prime time broadcasts prior to elections for use by all major candidates at all levels of government. Web-based video recordings of the candidate views should be made available for viewing by anyone. Political ad fact-checking sites need to become commonplace at all governmental levels as part of investigative journalism. A common, enforced code of ethics is needed to reinstate fair, balanced investigative reporting.

Goal 5: Summary Bullets for Press Does Job Per *Constitution* and Founding Fathers' Intent

✪ Require government-owned radio frequencies license grants to include the requirement of free prime time broadcasts for political candidates
  ★ National candidates should be given time on national TV/radio, with local candidates on local stations
  ★ Use set formats, where each major candidate is allotted time to
    ❖ Cover key issues
    ❖ Indicate how he/she would address the issues
    ❖ Indicate the projected costs and payment methods for each issue
  ★ Reporters would follow up with "challenge" questions
✪ Require the press and broadcast media to perform the tasks envisioned by the Founding Fathers, when it was considered a fourth branch of government that investigated our politicians and governments
  ★ Establish a common code of ethics and enforce it using techniques used by many other professions
  ★ Re-establish fair, balanced investigative journalism
  ★ Encourage web-based "truth investigations" of the news media by tax-exempt entities

Uncle Sam Needs You!

As in any war, various types of tactical tools are needed to aid in fighting the war. Guns, tanks, ammunition, and airplanes are tactical tools used in violent wars. In our nonviolent political war with career politicians, they are currently defeating us with their tactical tricks and strategic actions described earlier in this book.

For *our* war, I have defined the enemy, provided the issues, developed a strategic framework, provided a rough implementation strategy, and offered some solutions. These are all part of our tactical tools. Now I am asking you, the readers, to join our fight by helping to put these tactical tools to use.

We need an army ranging from generals to foot soldiers who:

✪ Communicate the various messages to recruit large numbers of the masses
  ★ By the web
  ★ By the radio and TV
  ★ By press articles
  ★ By word of mouth
✪ Carry out rallies either planned or as a result of citizen outrage
✪ Organize public and special interest groups
✪ Solicit funds for media blitzes and other organizational purposes
✪ Recruit new "generals" with leadership skills and public and financial clout
✪ Seek financial support for the war

Chapter 21:
Closing Remarks

At this point I feel sad that I have had to provide so much bad news. Sometimes bad, though true news helps us to view the world in a different light, no matter how much it hurts. A doctor can only treat a patient when the doctor understands the symptoms and their causes, and has the tools and abilities to treat them. Our nation needs immediate treatment actions to keep it alive and healthy.

The good news is that we can and we must win our war to reclaim America. We must make sure the status quo is replaced with honest responsible federal, state, and local governments. These governmental leaders and workers must not be allowed to be our elitist masters, but rather our servants. They should not be treated better than the vast majority of us whom they are supposed to serve. These governmental leaders and workers must be responsible for, and held accountable for, controlling spending and debt "urges." These urges may satisfy a "me," "now," and "feels nice" craze, but these urges have gotten us into deep trouble. Even though we might like to take on every problem, as socialist countries' histories have shown us, we cannot afford to do so. If we act *now* we can save our nation. We need to turn our outrage into action.

The following quotes are from Rev. William J. H. Boetcker's pamphlet entitled *The Ten Cannots*. Originally published in 1916, it is often misattributed to Abraham Lincoln who made some similar statements. These statements reflect the conclusions I hope I have made in this book.

> *You cannot bring about prosperity by discouraging thrift.*
> *You cannot strengthen the weak by weakening the strong.*
> *You cannot help little men by tearing down big men.*
> *You cannot lift the wage earner by pulling down the wage payer.*
> *You cannot help the poor by destroying the rich.*
> *You cannot establish sound security on borrowed money.*
> *You cannot further the brotherhood of man by inciting class hatred.*
> *You cannot keep out of trouble by spending more than you earn.*
> *You cannot build character and courage by destroying men's initiative and independence.*
> *And you cannot help men permanently by doing for them what they can and should do for themselves.*[1]

My final point is this: culture is shaped by circumstances. We need to change our circumstances in order to change the culture. The battle plan I have offered should change the circumstances to allow a more favorable future for our country. A future that is built on our great past and one that can continue for many generations to come. Let us all load and fire our word- and-action weapons toward the enemy, the "they" we often talk about as being a source of our problems and issues: the career politicians. We can save our nation if we act now with true changes, and not just political rhetoric.

I have asked myself what I would say if I were giving a speech to a large group of citizens from all age groups. I have used two speech styles – one from a great Democrat, Martin Luther King, Jr., and one from a great Republican, Abraham Lincoln - to write my speech. It is a speech I would like to share with all Americans.

I Have A Dream for a New America

I am happy to join with you today in what will go down in history as the second greatest movement for liberty in our nation.

Eleven score and fourteen years ago our brave Founding Fathers signed The Declaration of Independence and later developed The Constitution, *which is now envied by people throughout the world.*

Let me remind you that the origin of our government and the source of its power is "the people's Constitution, *the people's government; made for the people, made by the people, and answerable to the people."[2] That great beacon of hope has lighted the way for our nation to overcome many obstacles and thrive in the past.*

But now, more than two hundred years later, America's citizens have fewer liberties. Personal responsibility and accountability have been replaced with "I want it now and I want someone else to pay for it." Capitalism, which has been the magnet attracting foreigners to seek opportunity and freedom, is slowly being eroded by socialistic causes. Both present and future citizens are heavily indebted to their government, each adult and child citizen owing over $171,000 to pay his or her share of the national debt and unfunded entitlements. To make matters worse, many citizens have added personal debt and most states have high debts. Frequently, these debt burdens have been placed on citizens unfairly, or they rely on future generations to pay them. We have also become a highly regulated and highly taxed nation adding even more burdens to our "freedom."

Now, more than two hundred years later, our government "of, by, for and answerable to the people" is in question. "The people" have been overtaken by elitist career politicians who use psychological and financial tricks to get themselves re-elected and use these tricks and other political tricks to divide our nation's peoples into warring groups to support political party agendas rather than solving the people's problems.

"For the people" has been replaced by what career politicians whose re-election relies heavily upon handing out what is perceived as "free money" - the people's money - to garner some of our votes.

Now, more than two hundred years later, we do not have a government "answerable to the people." This is the bottom line. We are here today to reveal the negative impacts of these changes on the future of our nation and to reaffirm the vision of our Founding Fathers.

We are here, today, to demand a return of our nation to "we the people" and to make our government "answerable to the people." We will take whatever steps are necessary to peacefully accomplish this goal. The Declaration of Independence *and* The Constitution, *which have successfully guided us in the past, will only fail us if we fail to follow their principles. These principles reflect several balances - paramount among them is individual responsibility and accountability. The present positions of "me, "now" and "someone else pays" by some of our citizens was never part of that vision. This is clearly stated and implied throughout the Founding Fathers' documents.*

Other fundamental principles sought by our Founding Fathers include a nation that provided liberty: the freedom from oppressive restrictions imposed by authority on one's way of life, behavior, political views, or religious beliefs. A nation dedicated to the proposition that all men are created equal. A nation that weighs what is merely desirable against practical realities, our national interest, our own self-interest, and the importance of helping others. A nation that balances the powers between the federal, state, and local entities, and the powers of individuals. Our Founding Fathers developed documents, culminating in The Constitution *and its* Bill of Rights, *which they felt codified the nation they envisioned—including government systems responsible for implementing these principles.*

Today our America has deviated from these historic principles insofar as being a nation controlled by its people. "We the people" refuse to believe these principles are bankrupt. We refuse to believe there are better ways to provide opportunities and liberties for our citizens. We continue to believe we must recommit to these principles. We believe time is of the essence. We believe our political leaders - through the expenditures of "the people's" resources and trickery - are corrupting these principles to ensure their continued positions of control over "we the people." We believe, and are highly concerned, that some of our critical government systems are about to fail, and that many others are deficient. This is the eleventh hour and we have little time to save our nation. We must act now to retrieve our nation from the rock pile on which our politicians have thrown us before the desired state of our nation becomes irretrievable. Now is the time to resurrect our nation and reclaim our liberties .

But, first, we must understand what has caused the deviation from our Founding Fathers' enlightened path. Our Founding Fathers expressed their concerns that political parties' desire for power would serve to polarize groups. We have two polarizing parties considered to be "far left liberal" and "far right conservative." Any "moderates" who might have other values and perceptions of what is right for their constituents are kept "in line" by their own parties. Unfortunately, the Founding Fathers did not - or could not - explicitly address this issue in **The Constitution** *and this has come to pass, as they had feared.*

Our Founding Fathers did not foresee that career politicians would ever evolve. This is unfortunate for us because career politicians - together with their political parties - have been wreaking havoc with the Founding Fathers' vision. Over time, career politicians have developed policies allowing themselves many "perks," including the use of government funds to garner votes, and to receive funds from lobbyist and other special interests for their re-election coffers. These policies have provided incumbent politicians with significant power, personal wealth, and significant re-election advantages over any challengers.

The political corruption of our **Constitution's** *"of, by, for and answerable to" the people has created the need for a new great ideological war - our war - testing whether our nation, as conceived by our Founding Fathers, can continue to endure. We are met here on a battlefield of that war when the nations future is in great jeopardy. "We the people" have two options. The first is to continue the status quo, which will surely destroy our nation as we have known it. The second option is to unite as "change foot soldiers" in our ideological war until victory is in hand. This is a winnable war. It is a war we* **must** *win to protect and vindicate our generation. We must win for our children. We must win for grandchildren. We must win for all future generations.*

I say to you today, my fellow Americans, even though we face difficulties today and tomorrow that we have been dealt by our political leaders, I still have a dream. It is a dream deeply rooted in our American Founding Fathers' dream.

I have a dream that one day this nation will rise up and reconstitute the principle of individual responsibility and accountability for all citizens. Where individual hard work, and personal responsibility and accountability are again the norms that replace governmental "bailouts" of persons and businesses. We have many brave soldiers protecting our constitutionally-based republic that daily demonstrate the highest level of individual responsibility and accountability. I dream that all citizens will fully support what our soldiers, present and past, have fought for, and that all citizens will choose to participate in protecting our American dream by becoming soldiers in our ideological war to reclaim our nation.

I have a dream that one day soon liberty will reign and that all men and women will be treated equally. I dream a balance will be restored between what we would like to do and what we can afford to do, as well as between our individual liberties and national interest. I dream that "we the people" will regain control of our federal, state, and local governments and their roles and actions will more closely align with the intent of our Constitution. This dream can only become reality by taking power away from political parties and career politicians; returning politicians to serving "we the people."

I have a dream of a politically well-educated citizenry who will demand full transparency of all politicians' financial activities, a return to civil political debates that consider short and long-term consequences and costs, the elimination of policies that favor career politicians', and an end to perks that are not afforded to "we the people."

I have a dream in which capitalism is restored, allowing great job and wealth creation.

I have a dream in which debt and spending are under control and our children live in a nation where they will not be indebted beyond their capability to pay.

I have a dream in which our government's systems serving the people are rational, fair, balanced, cost effective, and stable.

In my final dream, our government's source of power is "the people's Constitution" where the people's government is made "for the people," "made by the people," and "answerable to the people."

This is my hope, my vision, and my dream. We can no longer ignore the facts. Many have died protecting our way of life. We must, here and now, highly resolve that those dead shall not have died in vain; that this nation shall have a new birth of freedom; and that this government of the people, by the people, and for the people, shall not perish from the earth. And when this dream comes true, when we regain control of our governments, when we resurrect the principles of our Founding Fathers for every individual from every state and every city, we will have attained our vision. Then we will have returned our nation to its past greatness. Then we will again have liberty.

Liberty again for our nation!
Liberty again for our states!
Liberty again for our cities!
Liberty again for all races and religions!
Liberty again for all the people!
Liberty forever!

Thank you,

Acknowledgements

I would like to acknowledge my wonderful wife of 49 years, Mary, for both putting up with me while I labored to write this book, and for being the first to read a very rough and final manuscript.

Special acknowledgement is due to my niece, Abbey Cleland, for her assistance in organizing the book to make it readable and more interesting. She worked long and hard to make my many rough book edges smoother. I also want to thank all of my family and friends who have listened to me and provided feedback on many topics over the years. Special thanks goes to my brother Edward Lee Cleland who provided insightful observations after reading the first edited draft.

Finally, I have had the good fortune of interacting and working with thousands of people in both my private and work lives. I have learned something from each of you. Without you, my thoughts would not have coalesced to the point of writing this book.

NOTES

Introduction
1.   Albert Einstein, *Treasury for the Free World* (1946), The Quotations Page http://www.quotationspage.com/quote/3214.html (accessed February 19, 2010).

Chapter 1
1.   We will show in the following chapter there is a common political mode of operation that leads to decisions like this one that are good politics but often are not the best solution for solving the problem at hand.
2.   Christina D. Romer & David H. Romer , "The Macroeconomic Effects of Tax Changes: Estimates Based on a New Measure of Fiscal Shocks," http://emlab.berkeley.edu/users/dromer/papers/RomerandRomer-AERJune2010.pdf (accessed July 20, 2010).
3.   Christopher J. Nekarda and Valerie A. Ramey, "Industry Evidence on the Effects of Government Spending," http://weber.ucsd.edu/~vramey/research.html (accessed July 20, 2010).
4.   Yuval P. Fel Yonary. *The Struggle Over the Soul of Economics*. (Princeton, New Jersey) Princeton University Press, 1998), 29. Now out of print but available as e-Book (2001), ISBN: 978-1-4008-2252-2.
5.   Arthur Sullivan and Steven M. Sheffrin. *Economics: Principles in action*. (Upper Saddle River: Pearson Prentice Hall, 2003).
6.   *QuotationsBook,* Voltaire, http://quotationsbook.com/quote/38307/ (accessed July 20, 2010).
7.   "Free money" refers to cash, goods, and/or services received that

have not (yet) been earned. Some free money is good, such as payments to those with disabilities who cannot earn it, but most is bad. Free money includes some borrowed money, unfunded entitlements, "legal" bribes, etc. Most free money is *our* money.

Chapter 2

1.   *Wikipedia*, "Popular Sovereignty" (by Benjamin Franklin), http://en.wikipedia.org/wiki/Popular_sovereignty (accessed July 15, 2010).

Chapter 3

1.   *Englishforums*, Franklin D. Roosevelt, http://www.englishforums.com/English/FranklinDelanoRooseveltPolitics-Nothing/lnqbj/post.htm (accessed July 20,2010).
2.   *The Quotations Page*, Ernest Benn, http://www.quotationspage.com/quote/1324.html (accessed July 20, 2010).
3.   *Wikipedia*, "James Bovard" http://en.wikipedia.org/wiki/James_Bovard (accessed July 20, 2010).
4.   Other methodologies include: Management Oversight and Risk Tree (MORT) Analysis, Change Analysis, Events and Causal Factor Analysis (ECFA), Fault Tree Analysis, Event Critique with Expert Judgment, Five Whys, and What-if? Analysis. These methods range from formal to informal processes for problem solving and may be used in combination with each other.
5.   Steven A Holmes, "Fannie Mae Eases Credit To Aid Mortgage Lending," *The New York Times*, September 30, 1999.
6.   Quotes taken from actual video clip of congressional hearings as summarized shown by Fox News and shown on You Tube, http://www.youtube.com/watch?v=LPSDnGMzIdo (accessed September 30, 2009).
7.   *The Quotation Page*, John Kenneth Galbraith, http://www.quotationspage.com/quotes/John_Kenneth_Galbraith/ (accessed July 20, 2010).
8.   *Publicquotes*, Ronald Reagan, http://publicquotes.com/quote/39134/the-government-is-like-a-baby-s-alimentary-canal-with-a-happy-appetite-at-one-end-and-no-responsibility.html (accessed july 20, 2010).

Chapter 4

1.   To help remember these politician's tricks, I have suggested a (mental) chant for each one. You may wish to develop your own.
2.   *American Rhetoric - Online Speech Bank*, Abraham Lincoln, A House

Divided, http://www.americanrhetoric.com/speeches/abrahamlincoln-housedivided.htm (accessed September 2, 2009).

3.   *Wikio Blogs your way,* Top Videos, <u>*Why Healthcare Costs Are Shooting Through the Stratosphere,*</u> http://www.wikio.com/video/testimony-illegal-alien-care-florida-hospital-259360 (accessed September 2, 2009).

4.   *Google,* Barack Obama speeches, Barack Obama, http://www.google.com/search?q=Candidate+Obama's+speech+%22I+will+make+our+government+open+and+transparent+..&hl=en&sa=G&prmd=v&source=univ&tbs=vid:1&tbo=u&ei=niJGTOq1CYO6sQOx1a38AQ&oi=video_result_group&ct=title&resnum=4&ved=0CCgQqwQwAw (accessed July 21, 2009).

5.   *Mediamatters for America,* By focusing on earmarks -- less than 2 percent of spending bill -- media allow bill's opponents to dictate debate, March 10, 2009, <u>http://mediamatters.org/research/200903100001</u> (accessed August 22, 2010). The two major political parties differ on the earmarks costs. The larger number estimate is 8,500 earmarks costing $7.7 billion.

6.   *Wikipedia,* Negative campaigning, <u>http://en.wikipedia.org/wiki/Negative_campaigning,</u> (accessed June 20, 2010).

Chapter 5

1.   *World Nuclear Association,* World Nuclear Power Reactors & Uranium Requirements, http://www.world-nuclear.org/info/reactors.html (accessed October 10, 2009).

2.   Peter M. Sandman, "Risk = Hazard + Outrage," *Twelve Principle Outrage Components and Seven Conclusions about Hazards and Outrage* (1991). (See also *The Peter M. Sandman Risk Communication Website*: www.psandman.com/).

3.   Peter M. Sandman, "Risk = Hazard + Outrage," *New Answers to an Old Problem* (1994). (See also *The Peter M. Sandman Risk Communication Website*: www.psandman.com/).

4.   Peter M. Sandman, "Risk = Hazard + Outrage," *Twelve Principle Outrage Components and Seven Conclusions about Hazards and Outrage* (1991). (See also *The Peter M. Sandman Risk Communication Website*: <u>www.psandman.com/</u>).

5.   Peter M. Sandman, "Risk = Hazard + Outrage," *Seven Conclusions about Hazard and Outrage* (1991). (See also *The Peter M. Sandman Risk Communication Website*: www.psandman.com/).

6.   27 *The Quotation Page,* Benjamin Franklin, http://www.quotationspage.com/quote/34185.html (accessed July 20, 2010).

7.   *The Quotation Page,* Jeremy Bentham, http://www.quotationspage.com/quote/20793.html (accessed July 20, 2010).

8.   *Plain Language*, Legal Quotes, http://www.plainlanguage.gov/resources/quotes/legal.cfm (accessed July 23, 2010).
9.   *Plain Language*, Legal Quotes, http://www.plainlanguage.gov/resources/quotes/legal.cfm (accessed July 23, 2010).
10.   Jerome Cramer, "Above Their Own Laws" *Time* (May 23, 1988), http://www.time.com/time/magazine/article/0,9171,967427,00.html (accessed June 20, 2010).
11.   "Application of Laws to Congress – Laws That Do Not Apply to Congress" (June 14, 2009), www.rules.house.gov/Archives/jcoc2ai.htm (accessed June 20, 2010).
12.   *Patient Power*, Brian Schwartz, Congress & gov't employees would be exempt from new insurance mandates, (June 22nd, 2009), www.patientpowernow.org/2009/06/22/congress-federal-employees-exempt-insurance-mandates/ (accessed June 20, 2010).
13.   U.S. Office of Personnel Management, *Federal Employees Health Benefits Program*, http://www.opm.gov/insure/health/ (accessed July 20, 2010).
14.   Jerome Cramer, "Above Their Own Laws" *Time* (May 23, 1988), http://www.time.com/time/magazine/article/0,9171,967427,00.html (accessed June 20, 2010).

Chapter 6

1.   *BrannyQuote*, **Frederic Bastiat,** http://www.brainyquote.com/quotes/quotes/f/fredericba405172.html (accessed June 20, 2010).
2.   *New York Times*, In $3.8 Trillion Budget, Obama Pivots to Trim Future Deficits by Jackie Clames, Published: February 1, 2010. This $3.8 trillion divided by 365 days in a year comes to $10.5 billion per day.
3.   *USA Today*, Obama team makes it official: Budget deficit hits record. By a lot., http://content.usatoday.com/communities/theoval/post/2009/10/620000005/1 (accessed September 1, 2010)
4.   *Wikipedia*, 2010 United States federal budget, http://en.wikipedia.org/wiki/2010_United_States_federal_budget (accessed September 1, 2010)
5.   *The Quotations Page*, George Bernard Shaw, http://www.quotationspage.com/quote/179.html (accessed July 20, 2010).
6.   Sea Level Rise and Subsidence: Implications for Flooding in New Orleans, by Virginia R. Burkett, David B. Zilkoski, and David A. Hart, www.nwrc.usgs.gov/hurricane/Sea-Level-Rise.pdf, (accessed August 28, 2010)
7.   *Housetracker.net*, Home Asking Price and Inventory, http://www.housingtracker.net/ (accessed September 2, 2010)

8.   *Hurricane Katrina Relief*, FAQ's, http://www.hurricanekatrinarelief.com/faqs.html (accessed September 2, 2010)

9.   David C. John and Robert Moffit, Ph.D., "Medicare and Social Security: The Challenge of Giant Entitlement Costs," *The Heritage Foundation*, (*March 25, 2008).*

10.   *U.S Treasury*, Federal Budget, National Debt, http://www.federalbudget.com/ (accessed September 1, 2010)

11.   *Social Security Online*, "Ratio of Social Security Covered Workers to Beneficiaries Calendar Years 1940-2000," http://www.ssa.gov/history/ratios.html (accessed July 20, 2010).

12.   *About.Com*, Senior Living, "How Does Social Security Work?" http://seniorliving.about.com/od/socialsecurity101/a/how-does-social-security-work.htm (accessed July 20, 2010).

13.   *U.S.Spending*, State & Local Guesstimated* Government Spending, Expenditure GDP—CHARTS–Deficit Debt, http://www.usgovernmentspending.com/California_state_spending.html (accesses August 20, 2010).

14.   *Los Angeles Times*, California's $500-billion pension time bomb, David Crane, April 06, 2010.

15.   *North Bay Bussiness Journal*, Commentary: California needs a business climate that supports everyone, By Jack M. Stewart, August 14th, 2010, http://www.northbaybusinessjournal.com/23936/commentary-california-needs-a-business-climate-that-supports-everyone/ (accessed August 22, 2010).

16.   *COST OF STATE REGULATIONS ON CALIFORNIA SMALL BUSINESSES STUDY* by Sanjay B. Varshney and Dennis H. Tootelian, Ph.D. California State University, Sacramento, September 2009, http://www.google.com/#hl=en&source=hp&q=Impact+of+regulations+in+California&btnG=Google+Search&aq=f&aqi=&aql=&oq=Impact+of+regulations+in+California&gs_rfai=CN89ZCnBxTPH-A5L4pATGwsADAAAAqgQFT9C1Zcc&pbx=1&fp=7db4f7af4a13aa89 (accessed August 22 , 2010).

17.   *Los Angeles Times*, How California's income tax and sales tax rates compare, Tom Petrun, February 19, 2009, http://latimesblogs.latimes.com/money_co/2009/02/california-tax.html (accessed August 22, 2010).

18.   *The Quotations Page*, Thomas Jefferson, http://www.quotationspage.com/quote/2729.html (accessed May 2, 2010).

19.   *John Petrie's Collection of Benjamin Franklin Quotes*, http://jpetrie.myweb.uga.edu/poor_richard.html (accesses May 2, 2010).

20.   See political calculations at http://politicalcalculations.blogspot.com/2005/04/average-wages-in-us.html for more detail. The model is wages = $2547.7 \, e^{\, 0.0523x}$ where "x" is the year of interest minus 1951.

21.   *Quote DB*, Winston Churchill, http://www.quotedb.com/quotes/3463 (accessed July 20, 2010).
22.   *The Quotations Page*, Eugene McCarthy, http://www.quotationspage.com/quote/1195.html   (accessed   July   20,   2010).
23.   Vitaliy Katsenelson, CFA, "The Profit Margin Paradigm," *The Motley Fool*, (March 1, 2006), http://www.fool.com/investing/value/2006/03/01/the-profit-margin-paradigm.aspx (accessed July 20, 2010).
24.   *Mark J. Perry, "Profit Margin: Health Insurance Industry Ranks #86"* CARPE DIEM - Professor Mark J. Perry's Blog for Economics and Finance (August 12, 2009), http://mjperry.blogspot.com/2009/08/health-insurance-industry-ranks-86-by.html (accessed July 20, 2010).
25.   *Brainy Quote*, John Kenneth Galbraith, http://www.brainyquote.com/quotes/quotes/j/johnkennet122465.html (accessed July 20, 2010).

Part III
1.   A system is a set of interacting or interdependent entities forming an integrated whole that work or network together to accomplish a process or function. "Entities" could include physical elements and methods or rules governing behavior.

Chapter 7
1.   *Science Daily*, Bad Sign For Global Warming: Thawing Permafrost Holds Vast Carbon Pool, http://www.sciencedaily.com/releases/2008/09/080903134309.htm (accesses August 10, 2010).
2.   *The Quotation Page*, Benjamin Franklin, http://www.quotationspage.com/quote/8225.html (accessed July 20, 2010).
3.   *Wikipedia,* ""Obesity Statistics: U.S. Obesity Trends,"" North American Association for the Study of Obesity, http://en.wikipedia.org/wiki/Obesity_in_the_United_States, (accessed   May 1, 2009).
4.   Refined sugars: Sugars are simple carbohydrates (Conversions: ~4.5 calories/gram & ~4.2 grams/teaspoon). They are sweet, crystalline, and soluble in water. They are classified chemically as monosaccharides and disaccharides. Common monosaccharides are glucose and fructose; common disaccharides are sucrose and lactose. The most common sugar is white table sugar consisting of sucrose. Highly refined white sugar and its products are often called 'empty calories' because, although they provide energy, they are low in nutrients such as vitamins and minerals. Unrefined brown sugar, and the sugar in honey, is reputed to have more nutritional value than white sugar, but the difference is insignificant. Here we consider sugars in raw foods such as fruits and vegetables as unrefined. If

these sugars are processes or concentrated they may act similarly to white table refined sugars. See also *The Free Dictionary by Farlex*, http://encyclopedia2.thefreedictionary.com/refined+sugar (accessed April 29, 2009).

5.   *Wikipedia*, "Cigarette taxes in the United States," http://en.wikipedia.org/wiki/Cigarette_taxes_in_the_United_States (accessed May 1, 2009).
6.   *Global Healing Center*, "Soft Drinks – America," Judith Valentine, PhD, CNA, CNC, http://www.globalhealingcenter.com/soft-drinks-america.html (accessed May 1, 2009)
7.   *Oste.eu: Soft drink*, "Controversy, Nutritional value," http://www.oste.eu/soft_drink_en.html (accessed June 2009).
8.   *FactCheck.org*, "Gimmicks in the Health Care Bill?" (November 20, 2009), http://www.factcheck.org/2009/11/gimmicks-in-the-health-care-bill/ (accessed July 20, 2010).
9.   The presently passed Health Care Bill exempts some religious groups such as the Amish and Muslims from penalties.

Chapter 8
1.   *U.S Treasury*, Federal Budget, National Debt, http://www.federalbudget.com/ (accessed September 1, 2010)
2.   *Congressional Budget Office*, CBO's Baseline and Estimate of the President's Budget, www.cbo.gov/ftpdocs/100xx/doc10014/03-20-PresidentBudget.pdf (accessed September 2, 2010)
3.   *The Quotation Page*, Everett Dirksen, http://www.quotationspage.com/quote/170.html (accessed July 20, 2010).
4.   *The Heritage Foundation*, 2010 Budget Chart Book, http://www.heritage.org/research/features/BudgetChartBook/ (accessed July 2, 2010).
5.   *Congressional Budget Office*, Long Term Budget Outlook, http://www.cbo.gov/ (accessed July 2, 2010).
6.   *CNN*, Q&A: Greece's financial crisis explained, March 26, 2010, http://www.cnn.com/2010/BUSINESS/02/10/greek.debt.qanda/index.html (accessed August 22, 2010).
7.   *USA Today*, Obama team makes it official: Budget deficit hits record. By a lot., http://content.usatoday.com/communities/theoval/post/2009/10/620000005/1 (accessed September 1, 2010)
8.   78. *National Priorities Project*, Cost of Wars, http://costofwar.com/ (accessed September 1, 2010)
9.   As used in this book a "hard bound" is either an upper or lower (or both) boundary or limit that is not to be crossed. A "hard upper bound" is a limit that is not to be exceeded from below. A "hard lower bound" is a limit that is not to be exceeded from above. For example, if 10 is an upper

bound and -10 is a lower bound, then any number greater than -10 and less than 10 is within the bounds.

10.   Kent Conrad, Senate Budget Committee Chairman, http://budget. senate.gov/democratic/ (July 18, 2010), (accessed July 21, 2010).

11.   Interest is shown as part of Discretionary. If Interest is included as Mandatory, then 2009, Mandatory is 65%. Source: Congressional Budget Office, "Historical Budget Data, Outlays for Major Categories of Spending, 1970 to 2009, in Billions of Dollars," http://www.cbo.gov/ftpdocs/108xx/doc10871/AppendixF.shtml   (accessed January 10, 2010).

12.   "e" is the base of natural logarithms. Its value is approximately 2.718281828459045.

Chapter 9

1.   *Brainy Quote*, Winston Churchill, http://www.brainyquote.com/quotes/authors/w/winston_churchill_7.html (accessed November 10, 2009).

2.   *Famous Quotes*, Norman Thomas, http://www.larrywillis.com/quotes.html (accessed July 21, 2010).

3.   *Congressional Budget Office*, Long Term Budget Outlook, http://www.cbo.gov/ (accessed July 2, 2009).

4.   *The Heritage Foundation*, 2010 Budget Chart Book, http://www.heritage.org/research/features/BudgetChartBook/ (accessed July 2, 2010).

5.   *The Heritage Foundation*, 2010 Budget Chart Book, http://www.heritage.org/research/features/BudgetChartBook/ (accessed July 2, 2010).

6.   *Tax Foundation*, Fiscal Facts (updated July 30, 2009), http://www.taxfoundation.org/news/show/250.html (accessed August 2010).

7.   *The Heritage Foundation*, 2010 Budget Chart Book, http://www.heritage.org/research/features/BudgetChartBook/ (accessed July 2, 2010).

8.   *Forbs.com*, The Richest People In America, http://www.forbes.com/2009/09/30/forbes-400-gates-buffett-wealth-rich-list-09_land.html   (accessed August 22, 2010).

9.   Scott A. Hodges, *Tax Foundation*, "Fiscal Facts No.214," (March 10, 2010),   http://www.taxfoundation.org/publications/show/25962.html (accessed August 7, 2010).

10.   Christi Parsons, "Geithner: Tax Cuts for the rich must end," *San Ramon Valley Times*, July 26, 2010.

11.   Julie Pace and Tom, Raum, "Obama: Wealthy will have to pay," San Ramon Valley Times, September 9, 2010.

12.   *The Washington Post*, Projected Deficit, March 21, 2009, http://www.washingtonpost.com/wp-dyn/content/graphic/2009/03/21/GR2009032100104.html (accessed August 22, 2010).

13.   *Gather*, http://www.gather.com/viewArticle.action?articleId=281474976887368 (accessed August 22, 2010)

14.   Scott A. Hodges, *Tax Foundation*, "Fiscal Facts No.214," (March 10, 2010), http://www.taxfoundation.org/publications/show/25962.html (accessed August 7, 2010).

15.   *U.S. Office of Personnel Management*, Salaries and Wages, http://www.opm.gov/oca/09tables/html/gs.asp (accessed July 21, 2010).

Chapter 10
1.   *Bureau of Labor Statistics*, Labor Force Statistics from the Current Population Survey, UNION AFFILIATION DATA, http://www.bls.gov/cps/tables.htm (accessed July 1, 2010).

2.   *Bureau of Labor Statistics*, Editor's Desk, "Union membership declines in 2009" http://www.bls.gov/opub/ted/2010/ted_20100201.htm (accessed July 1, 2010).

3.   James Sherk, "Majority of Union Members Now Work for the Government," *The Heritage Foundation*, http://www.heritage.org/research/reports/2010/01/majority%20of%20union%20members%20now%20work%20for%20the%20government (accessed January 22, 2010).
(January 22, 2010).

4.   *National Institute on Money in State Politics*, followthemoney, http://www.followthemoney.org/database/graphs/timeline/index.phtml?s=CA&y=2008&f=0&i[]=100&combine=0&c=0&t=0&pvscom=0 (accessed August 1, 2010).

5.   *Real Clear Politics*, Public Sector Unions Tarnish the Golden State By Carol Platt Liebau, March 9, 2010, http://www.realclearpolitics.com/articles/2010/03/09/public_sector_unions_tarnish_golden_state_104686.html (accessed July 30, 2010).

6.   *Table 17.5—Government* Employment and *Population, 1962–2006 - GPO ...*
Government employment, Population ... Federal Executive Branch civilian as a percent of all governmental units, www.gpoaccess.gov/usbudget/fy08/sheets/hist17z5.xls (accessed October 10, 2009).

7.   *Contra Costa Times*, Editorial: California Pension spiking bill needs to be stopped, 08/17/2010, http://www.contracostatimes.com/opinion/ci_15797417 (accessed August 22, 2010).

8.   'Mark J. Perry, *CARPE DIEM - Professor Mark J. Perry's Blog for Economics and Finance* (August 12, 2009), http://mjperry.blogspot.com/2009/08/manufacturing-employment-drops-to.html (accessed July 21, 2010).

9.   *Congressional Budget Office*, "What Accounts for the Decline in Manufacturing Employment?" http://www.cbo.gov/doc.cfm?index=5078&type=0 (accessed July 21, 2010).

10.   See *Lincoln Electric Company website — Careers —* "The Incentive Performance System in place in the U.S. Lincoln operations features," http://www.lincolnelectric.com/corporate/about/vision.asp (accessed July 18, 2010).

Chapter 11

1.   *Bureau of Labor Statistics*, Overview of the 2008-18 Projections, http://www.bls.gov/oco/oco2003.htm (accessed July 21, 2010).

2.   *WiseGeek*, What Percent of the US Population Do Lawyers Comprise? http://www.wisegeek.com/what-percent-of-the-us-population-do-lawyers-comprise.htm (accessed July 21, 2010).

3.   *Ask Answer*, What country in the world has most lawyers per capita? http://wiki.answers.com/Q/What_country_in_the_world_has_most_lawyers_per_capita (accessed July 21, 2010).

4.   *PRISONMOVEMENT'S WEBLOG*, California's prison-guards' union: Fading are the peacemakers, Feb. 26, 2010, http://prisonmovement.wordpress.com/ (accessed August 22, 2010).

5.   *Ed-Data*, Teachers in California, (January 2010), http://www.ed-data.k12.ca.us/articles/article.asp?title=teachers%20in%20california (accessed July 21, 2010).

6.   Thomas Frank, "Illegal immigrant population declines," *USA Today*, http://www.usatoday.com/news/nation/2009-02-23-immigration_N.htm (accessed July 21, 2010).

7.   *Bureau of Labor Statistics*, Civilian labor force, ftp://ftp.bls.gov/pub/special.requests/lf/aat1.txt (accessed July 21, 2010).

8.   *Wikipedia*, "Illegal immigration to the U.S. Wages and employment," (April 2, 2009), http://en.wikipedia.org/wiki/Illegal_immigration_to_the_United_States (accessed July 21, 2010).

9.   *Wikipedia*, "Personal Responsibility and Work Opportunity Act, Consequences," http://en.wikipedia.org/wiki/Personal_Responsibility_and_Work_Opportunity_Act (accessed July 21, 2010).

10.   *Department of Health and Human Services*, TANF, Eligibility, http://www.dhhs.state.nh.us/DHHS/TANF/ELIGIBILITY/default.htm (accessed July 21, 2010).

11.	Welfare payments, which are part of welfare benefits, are provided by state governments. Who can receive these welfare benefits is determined by a number of eligibility requirements which may include:
- If anyone in the household is pregnant.
- Household gross income for the month.
- If there are migrant or seasonal workers in the home.
- How much the rent or mortgage payments are for the household.
- How much the utility bills are for the household.
- Any other necessary and required living expenses.
- Individual gross incomes for each family member.
- Actual available cash on hand for the household including checking and savings accounts.
- Whether any other benefits are being received in the home.
- If there are any disabled or infirmed persons in the home.
- If any family members live outside the home.
- Any criminal convictions within the home.

Source: *US Welfare System*, Welfare Information, http://www.welfare-info.org/programs/ (accessed July 27, 2009)

Chapter 12
1.	*The Conference Board*, Executive Compensation Task Force, (September 23, 2009), www.conference-board.org/knowledge/govern/executiv-etask.cfm (accessed September 2009).
2.	*Goodreads*, Mark Twain, http://www.goodreads.com/quotes/show/10001 (accessed July 21, 2010).
3.	*Wikipedia*, "Fourth branch of government," http://en.wikipedia.org/wiki/Fourth_branch_of_government (accessed January 2, 2009).
4.	*The New York Times Company*, "Ethics in Journalism, Introduction and Purpose," http://www.nytco.com/press/ethics.html (accessed May 22, 2009).

Chapter 13
1.	*Famous Quotes About*, Robert Louis Stevenson http://www.famous-quotesabout.com/quotation/Politics-is-perhaps-the-only-profession-for-which-no-preparation-is-thought-necessary (accessed July 21, 2010).

Chapter 14
1.	Barack Obama, *The Audacity of Hope: Thoughts on Reclaiming the American Dream* (New York), Three Rivers Press (2006).

2.   *The New York Times*, G.M.'s New Owners, U.S. and Labor, Adjust to Roles, By Steven Greenhouse, June 1, 2009, <u>http://www.nytimes.com/2009/06/02/business/02uaw.html</u> (accessed August 22, 2010).

Chapter 15

1.   Alex Jones, "George Washington: '... *The Constitution* ... is sacredly obligatory upon all'" *Infowars*, (March 5, 2010), http://www.infowars.com/george-washington-%E2%80%A6-the-constitution-%E2%80%A6-is-sacredly-obligatory-upon-all/ (accessed May 20, 2009).

Chapter 16

1.   *Spirit of America Liberty Quotes*, George Washington,
http://www.dojgov.net/Liberty_Watch.htm (accessed July 24, 2010).
2.   *Spirit of America Liberty Quotes*, Patrick Henry,
http://www.dojgov.net/Liberty_Watch.htm (accessed July 24, 2010).
3.   *Wikipedia*, "Federal Government of the United States," http://en.wikipedia.org/wiki/Federal_government_of_the_United_States (accessed May 20, 2010).
4.   Alex Jones, "George Washington: '... the Constitution ... is sacredly obligatory upon all'" *Infowars*, (March 5, 2010), http://www.infowars.com/george-washington-%E2%80%A6-the-constitution-%E2%80%A6-is-sacredly-obligatory-upon-all/ (accessed May 20, 2009).
5.   Alex Jones, "George Washington: '... the Constitution ... is sacredly obligatory upon all'" *Infowars*, (March 5, 2010), http://www.infowars.com/george-washington-%E2%80%A6-the-constitution-%E2%80%A6-is-sacredly-obligatory-upon-all/ (accessed May 20, 2009).
6.   *The Quotations Page*, John Adams, http://www.quotationspage.com/quote/30219.html (accessed May 20, 2010).
7.   *Goodreads*, Thomas Jefferson, http://www.goodreads.com/quotes/show/31588 (accessed May 20, 2010).
8.   *Golden Nuggets of U.S. History*, The Blue Quill Series - Concord Learning Systems, http://www.laughtergenealogy.com/bin/history/politics.html (accessed May 20, 2010).
9.   *The History Place*, Patrick Henry, http://www.historyplace.com/speeches/henry.htm (accessed May 22, 2010).
10.   *The American Revolution*, Samuel Adams, "The Glorious Cause for American Independence," http://www.theamericanrevolution.org/peopledetail.aspx?people (accessed May 20, 2010).

11.   Tax Foundation, Federal Spending Received Per Dollar of Taxes Paid by State, 2005, http://www.taxfoundation.org/research/show/266.html (accessed May 3, 2010).

12.   *Snopes*, Harry S Truman, "Plain Speaking," http://www.snopes.com/quotes/truman/truman.asp (accessed May 21, 2010).

Chapter 17

1.   N. Gregory Mankiw, "Is Government Spending Too Easy an Answer?" *The New York Times*, (January 10, 2009), http://www.nytimes.com/2009/01/11/business/economy/11view.html (accessed May 20, 2009).

2.   *Wikipedia*, "Contract with America," http://en.wikipedia.org/wiki/Contract_with_America (accessed May 22, 2010).

3.   *US Spending*, "Charts," (March 10, 2010) www.usgovernmentspending.com/ (accessed July 21, 2010).

4.   Published by the Office of the Federal Register, National Archives and Records Administration (NARA), the Federal Register is the official daily publication for rules, proposed rules, and notices of Federal agencies and organizations, as well as executive orders and other presidential documents.

5.   *Think exist*, Edward Langley, http://thinkexist.com/quotation/what_this_country_needs_are_more_unemployed/197997.html (accessed May 20, 2010).

Chapter 18

1.   *US Government Info*, US Congress Members, http://usgovinfo.about.com/od/uscongress/a/congresspay.htm (accessed July 22, 2010)

Chapter 20

1.   *Wikipedia*, Radio Frequencies, http://en.wikipedia.org/wiki/Radio_frequency (accessed June 4, 2010). Radio frequency (RF) is a rate of oscillation in the range of about 30 kHz to 300 GHz, which corresponds to the frequency of electrical signals normally used to produce and detect radio waves. RF usually refers to electrical rather than mechanical oscillations. These RF's are regulated by the federal government.

Chapter 21

1.   *Wikepedia*, "William J. H. Boetcker," http://en.wikipedia.org/wiki/William_J._H._Boetcker (accessed July 22, 2010).

2.   *Google Books*, Daniel Webster 'http://books.google.com/books?id=_
ecvAAAAMAAJ&pg=PA601&lpg=PA601&dq=the+people's+constituti
on,+the+people's+government;+made+for+the+people,+made+by+the
+people,+and+answerable+to+the+people&source=bl&ots=hqNg-tkr-
2&sig=wNotp-WfmceaiKvbaEuXdLRoys4&hl=en&ei=shlJTOzcLIn2tgP
Mn8TFCw&sa=X&oi=book_result&ct=result&resnum=5&ved=0CCEQ6
AEwBA#v=onepage&q=the%20people's%20constitution%2C%20the%20
people's%20government%3B%20made%20for%20the%20people%2C%20
made%20by%20the%20people%2C%20and%20answerable%20to%20
the%20people&f=false (accessed July 22, 2010).